FL Studio Cookbook

Over 40 recipes to help you master the art of music production with FL Studio

Shaun Friedman

BIRMINGHAM - MUMBAI

FL Studio Cookbook

First published: June 2014

Production reference: 1180614

Published by Packt Publishing Ltd.
Livery Place
35 Livery Street
Birmingham B3 2PB, UK.

ISBN 978-1-84969-414-8

www.packtpub.com

Cover image by James Lyle (doodlelyle@aol.com)

Credits

Author
Shaun Friedman

Reviewers
Boštjan Cigan
Xavier Durand-Hollis Jr.
Rodney Hazard
Ansh Patel
Shant Rising
Jasper Staal

Commissioning Editor
Mary Jasmine Nadar

Acquisition Editor
Nikhil Karkal

Content Development Editor
Sruthi Kutty

Technical Editors
Pragnesh Bilimoria
Aparna Kumar

Copy Editors
Dipti Kapadia
Insiya Morbiwala
Aditya Nair

Project Coordinator
Mary Alex

Proofreaders
Simran Bhogal
Ameesha Green

Indexer
Mariammal Chettiyar

Production Coordinator
Nilesh Bambardekar

Cover Work
Nilesh Bambardekar

About the Author

Shaun Friedman is a music composer who has publishing contracts with FreePlay Music in New York City, Smashtrax Music in California, and Prolific Arts Music in Dallas, Texas in addition to working with music libraries in the United Kingdom and Italy. He has been composing music since the age of five and has a tremendous passion for creativity in the music realm.

Shaun's own production website is www.UnbelievableBeats.com, where you can find original music, lyrical covers, and remixes. The website that he provides music lessons on is called www.FLStudioTraining.com. He also offers WAV files for music production at www.GlobalHeatWave.com.

Thank you to Jacqueline Giliberti for her constant support and encouragement, along with Zak Edelman for his honesty and motivation. Thank you, Dad, for bestowing me the Casio SK-8 when I was just a young kid and inspiring me to make music. Thank you to Packt Publishing for believing in my valued insights. Thank you Grandma Bina and Grandpa Ralph, for encouraging my piano playing after family dinners. Thank you to those who believed in me when I was starting to seriously produce music in 8th grade and high school. A big thanks to James Creer for introducing me to Reason by Propellerheads and teaching me invaluable audio concepts. Thank you Mom, Brian, and Meghan, for cheering me on through the years.

About the Reviewers

Boštjan Cigan has studied at the Faculty of Computer and Information Science at the University of Ljubljana. After completing his BSc, he started pursuing his MSc at the same faculty. Encouraged by the course on Computer Sound Engineering, he started involving himself with FL Studio and Reason. Consequently, he began creating the piano and orchestra renditions of game compositions. He tries to find the best orchestra samples available and uses various masterizing techniques to make them sound as realistic as possible.

Currently, he works as a freelance web developer; he mainly develops WordPress plugins and themes.

> I would like to thank Tjaša for encouraging me to take on this project.

Xavier Durand-Hollis Jr. is an aspiring video game developer who happens to make his own music on the side. According to him, while he's not the best producer out there, he has spent time casually working with FL Studio, enough to be familiar with most of its tricks.

As this book review is in process, he is working towards his degree in Computer Science at Michigan State University. He hopes to be developing some awesome video games someday, with equally awesome soundtracks.

Rodney Hazard is a multifaceted artist with a focus on art direction and music. His lucid production styles and astute design solutions are unlike anything seen or heard of in hip hop, to date. Some of his production credits include the artists AZ, Heavy D, and Joe Budden. Drawing from a wide range of inspiration, he had expertise in creating an enhanced musical experience that is guaranteed to keep listeners intrigued. His ability to distort and recreate sounds is incomparable. Rodney's work is a direct reflection of his left-field way of thinking.

Born and raised in Worcester, Massachusetts, Rodney began his journey into music at an early age. Starting out as a DJ, he felt the need to express himself as an artist and began to experiment using the Virtual DJ program. The son of a Haitian mother and an American Indian/African American father, he fused the rhythms of these cultures with the futuristic sounds of bands such as Radiohead, Mount Kimbie, and As Tall As Lions. He is a founding member of OBSG (a group of musical and visual artists) and works at VICE Media as a designer. Rodney stepped out from behind the boards and showcased his talent as a gifted emcee. After graduating high school in Worcester, Rodney relocated to New York City and attended St. John's University. It was in New York City that Rodney would develop his signature sound and grow from an aspiring beatsmith to a full-fledged producer.

Over the past three years, Rodney has released multiple projects with OBSG Collective. His notable releases include: *HZRDS RSNS*, *State Of Mind*, *Crown(s)*, *Same Season*, and *Guns x Gold*. Rodney stepped out from behind the boards and showcased his talent as a more-than-capable emcee. He is currently preparing for his biggest release to date—Victim | Volunteer—which is due to come out in 2014.

I would like to thank my family for always pushing me to pursue my passion and develop my craft. I would also like to thank Blind Barber (Andrew Kelly and Halley Hiatt) for helping me touch the sky and spread my wings as a musician. Lastly, I would like to thank my rock—Lauren Espejo—and Packt Publishing for this opportunity!

Ansh Patel is an experimental game developer, writer, and occasional pop culture critic who works under the moniker of Narcissist Reality. Most of his works are highly influenced by real-world issues, and he hopes to make whatever positive changes he can through his work. He has a deep passion for music, and this often extends into him creating music for his works or just for the sake of it.

I would like to thank my parents for constantly supporting me through whatever creative and offbeat ventures I took up for my career and for believing in me and in my skills, even when I wasn't confident about them.

Shant Rising is a writer, futurist, minimalist, and artist from Los Angeles, California. He grew up playing live music with his friends while in high school only to later adopt the art of electronic music and producing as an activity to help balance the stress of his educational goals. Currently, he is studying medicine and working on his degrees in neuroscience and neurology. More information about him as well as his contact details can be found on his website at www.ShantRising.com.

Jasper Staal is a Dutch beatmaker from the city of Groningen. Born in 1986 as the sixth son of a musician, he started producing hip hop in 2004 to follow in his father's footsteps. His first tracks were produced on Fruity Loops 2, and his passion for Fruity Loops (now FL Studio) has always remained.

Post 2010, his musical focus shifted to EDM/Trap production, drawing inspiration from everything, whether it was Motown soul or video game music. His first official single Nippon Slip was released on Darker Than Wax (a record label from Singapore) in 2014.

Apart from making music, Jasper is also pursuing a career in graphic design and fine arts, and he occasionally dabbles in video editing and rhyme writing as well.

You can enjoy his music at www.soundcloud.com/jasperstaal and go through his art at www.cargocollective.com/jasperstaaldesign.

www.PacktPub.com

Support files, eBooks, discount offers, and more

You might want to visit www.PacktPub.com for support files and downloads related to your book.

Did you know that Packt offers eBook versions of every book published, with PDF and ePub files available? You can upgrade to the eBook version at www.PacktPub.com and as a print book customer, you are entitled to a discount on the eBook copy. Get in touch with us at service@packtpub.com for more details.

At www.PacktPub.com, you can also read a collection of free technical articles, sign up for a range of free newsletters and receive exclusive discounts and offers on Packt books and eBooks.

http://PacktLib.PacktPub.com

Do you need instant solutions to your IT questions? PacktLib is Packt's online digital book library. Here, you can access, read and search across Packt's entire library of books.

Why subscribe?

- ▶ Fully searchable across every book published by Packt
- ▶ Copy and paste, print and bookmark content
- ▶ On demand and accessible via web browser

Free access for Packt account holders

If you have an account with Packt at www.PacktPub.com, you can use this to access PacktLib today and view nine entirely free books. Simply use your login credentials for immediate access.

Table of Contents

Preface

FL Studio is directly related to composing and producing music from scratch. This is similar to a painter who creates a work of art with a mix of colors and a blank canvas or a writer who forms a novel or story with a pen and paper. FL Studio lets you create a music production in whatever genre you are comfortable with. You will be able to create a drumbeat, percussion, or rhythm track. You will be able to add virtual instruments and harmonies. You will have access to the mixer, where you can add well-known effects such as reverb and delay. You will also be able to use equalization, compression, limiting, and other effects such as flangers and filters. You will be able to manipulate and arrange your musical components to create a song. You can also include external audio and record into FL Studio.

This means that you will be able to record into FL Studio using a microphone for vocals, with an analog keyboard, with a bass guitar, with a drum machine, using a microphone to record the output of a guitar amplifier, and any other instrument that requires you to place a microphone close by (violin, banjo, keyboard, and so on). You can also record from a vinyl record player and then use that recording in FL Studio. You will also find ways to sample other music if desired. Edison, an audio editing tool within FL Studio, will teach you how to time-stretch any sample to fit the tempo of your project in FL Studio. You will be able to seamlessly use sampled material in your own music production. You will also learn how to master your project and make it sound good in multiple playback formats, including entertainment systems, CDs, online streaming such as YouTube and Vimeo, smartphones, and e-mail attachments.

FL Studio stands for Fruity Loops, but the name is a little bit confusing because you do not have to work with premade loops at all. The reason for calling it Fruity Loops was because it started as a powerful drum sequencer. As far as creating music quickly and intuitively goes, there is arguably no other software as powerful as FL Studio. There are many digital audio workstations (DAWs) in the market, but FL Studio has the most features and also offers free updates for a lifetime. This means that you will never get shut out of an upgrade, and you will always be able to update your version for free.

When FL Studio updates their software to FL Studio 8 to FL Studio 9, it will be free. Even when they update to FL Studio 10, it will be free, and so on. Music productions made with FL Studio are now all over the charts worldwide. It is used heavily by electronic and hip hop producers. It is also used for orchestral music, rock, pop, and jazz. There is no genre of music that it cannot create; there is no genre of music that gets shut out. The tools are present, and it is up to the creator/user to manipulate the sounds to form whatever feeling and song they want to communicate. You can use the WAV and MP3 formats inside of the software, so it is also user friendly across many file formats.

Since FL Studio has become the standard for music production, many people who learned other DAWs feel a little bit threatened by it and are upset. They may have learned a program such as Pro Tools only to discover a couple weeks, months, or years later that FL Studio has better capabilities. They may also shrug it off because it's not an industry standard, but that is quickly changing.

Though FL Studio is extremely intuitive, the driving force behind its output is the people who use the software. It's not so much the software, but how you use it. You should be creating music that inspires both you and hopefully the people who listen to it. Musicians should not be fighting with each other over DAWs. They may believe that certain DAWs are inferior, but that is simply not the case, and sometimes, based on marketing beliefs, they may use something such as Pro Tools because they have no real talent and it is a crutch for them. The DAW doesn't matter as much as how you use it. That being said, it certainly helps that FL Studio is extremely easy to use, allowing your creativity to flow quickly and naturally.

During the music-making stages, you need to get your ideas from inside your brain to inside the FL Studio software. This can happen very quickly when using FL Studio.

The FL Studio technology is invaluable. You can produce music simply using your laptop or computer. You can set up FL Studio as the hub of your music productions at the place where you live or the studio you work at. You can be sitting at a coffee shop and producing music wearing headphones. For some, it will be a creative outlet that they can enjoy. Others will use FL Studio to make radio-quality productions and sell their music across the globe. You can easily create many variations of the same song, which can help you if you are a live performer. Perhaps your song is completely finished with vocals on it. You can make an exact version of that song but remove the lead vocals because you know that you will be performing it at a live venue. The FL Studio software is continually being upgraded, and if there are any bugs in it, the administration staff are quick to fix them. Perhaps, the biggest reason for creating music is to share your own emotion with friends and family.

This book will enable you to make a full music production, starting from scratch. From the initial stages of creation to the end stages of mastering your project, you have all the tools you need. The many stages of music production are all intuitively harbored under one roof.

You should throw all conventions out the proverbial window. As far as creating music goes, there are no real rules for your workflow or creativity. That being said, FL Studio makes it very easy to create songs, and there are certain concepts that will enhance your audio productions.

What this book covers

Chapter 1, Configuring FL Studio, introduces you to using their factory soundcard, using audio interfaces, understanding what an ASIO driver means, and installing virtual instruments and effects. You will learn how audio flows in and out of your computer with a factory soundcard or an upgraded audio interface. You will also understand the basic setup of a DAW. This chapter is crucial to understanding what you can and cannot do using ASIO4ALL (free download online) and the possible reasons for an upgraded audio interface.

Chapter 2, Using Browser, helps you understand the file structure of FL Studio, where most sounds, files, and instruments can be found in the browser. You will learn how to manage the folders of MP3, WAV, and recorded audio files, and also how to use the browser correctly during music creation. The browser is a way to preview sounds that may be used in your project, and you will learn how to utilize it properly to get the most out of the creative process.

Chapter 3, Working with the Step Sequencer and Channels, explains the channels in the step sequencer and the many parameters inside of each one. The step sequencer is also important when recording harmonies, MIDI tracks, audio tracks, and contains every sound you are using in your project. You will also see the fundamental areas in the step sequencer, such as volume and panning, and find ways to manipulate sounds using the Keyboard and Graph editors on the step sequencer.

Chapter 4, Building Your Song, explains how to add rhythm, percussion, and virtual instrument sounds. You will also learn the various ways to program sounds into FL Studio, which can be done with a mouse, MIDI controller, piano roll, or your actual QWERTY keyboard. You will understand how to build patterns, which are later arranged in the FL Studio playlist in order to make a full production.

Chapter 5, Using the Playlist, helps you arrange your song. You can copy, edit, paste, change, or remove the many elements of your song in the playlist. This is where you will mix all of your patterns together.

Chapter 6, Using the FL Studio Mixer and Recording Audio, shows you how to gain more control over each sound after inserting your sounds into the mixer. The mixer is one of the most important functions of FL Studio. It allows you to add effects such as EQ, reverb, delay, compression, and the like. It is also crucial because in order to record external audio such as microphones, keyboards, and guitars, you will have to prepare the mixer. This is where you will really be able to put a creative spin on your music project based on your individual taste or genre.

Chapter 7, Sampling Using Edison, explains how you will be able to time-stretch any sample or acapella sample to their project tempo in FL Studio. There is a set recipe for this that must be understood for a seamless loop to be used inside of FL Studio. You will learn how to accomplish a seamless loop and find the tempo using the FL Studio tap tempo functionality.

Chapter 8, Exporting and Rendering Your Project, will help you come to understand the different methods to render your song. This is crucial because there are differences between MP3 files and WAV files. If you need to use your individual project stems/audio stems in a separate environment or different DAW, you will learn how to export and render your wave stems correctly. There are also many ways to save, share, and back up your project files. You will also understand the concepts of sample rate and bit depth.

Chapter 9, Humanizing Your Song, demonstrates how you can separate your production from a good song to a great song. It is the little nuances and the groove of your song and rhythm that can take your music to the next level. There are a couple of methods that you can use for this depending on your own workflow and preference.

Chapter 10, Recording Automation, shows you how to use automation in order to enhance, build suspense, and automate any parameter or function in FL Studio. This means that you can program certain functions to occur in specific areas of your production, and when you are satisfied with the result, you can keep it that way for the final product. Readers will find many ways to use automation, including mouse movements, physical knobs or sliders on physical MIDI controllers, and drawing on automation curves and points in a visual manner.

Chapter 11, Rewiring Reason to FL Studio, introduces Reason, which is a music software that has been developed by Propellerheads. Inside of the program, there are instruments, software synthesizers, samplers, and drum sounds. Rewiring reason into FL Studio allows your creative palate to expand, but you will still be using the functionality of the FL Studio step sequencer, mixer, and playlist. When rewiring Reason into FL Studio, you will use FL Studio as the host and Reason as the client.

Appendix, Your Rights as a Composer and Copyrights, helps the reader understand the ins and outs of the music industry and music publishing industry. When a song is created, there are certain rights and permissions needed for it. There is a master recording and also the music within the song. These are two separate entities and shouldn't be confused if you want to understand your rights or anyone's rights who is representing or composing your song. This chapter will review U.S. copyrights as well as discuss how you can publish your music into film, TV, video games, ad agencies, music libraries, and all new media outlets.

What you need for this book

You will need to have FL Studio installed on your computer. You don't necessarily need knowledge as much as a good pair of ears when you start with the book. Your ears are the main tool that you will be using. It may help if you have knowledge of topics such as equalization, music theory, percussion, instruments, and the like.

Who this book is for

If you are a musician, producer, engineer, or artist, you will make use of this book. You can also use FL Studio for any type of audio production such as voice-overs.

This is the right book for you because it focuses on how to make music based on creativity and inspiration. There are no rules in music production, but there are certain concepts that separate a good production from a great production. This book will walk you through that process, including providing quick shortcuts to operate the software.

Conventions

In this book, you will find a number of styles of text that distinguish between different kinds of information. Here are some examples of these styles and an explanation of their meaning.

Code words in text, database table names, folder names, filenames, file extensions, pathnames, dummy URLs, user input, and Twitter handles are shown as follows: "Use an Internet search engine and type `clock chime free.wav` or something of a similar context."

New terms and **important words** are shown in bold. Words that you see on the screen, in menus or dialog boxes for example, appear in the text like this: "In these cases, use the **Browse parameters** function."

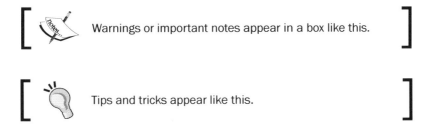

Warnings or important notes appear in a box like this.

Tips and tricks appear like this.

Reader feedback

Feedback from our readers is always welcome. Let us know what you think about this book—what you liked or may have disliked. Reader feedback is important for us to develop titles that you really get the most out of.

To send us general feedback, simply send an e-mail to `feedback@packtpub.com`, and mention the book title via the subject of your message.

If there is a topic that you have expertise in and you are interested in either writing or contributing to a book, see our author guide on `www.packtpub.com/authors`.

Customer support

Now that you are the proud owner of a Packt book, we have a number of things to help you to get the most from your purchase.

Downloading color versions of the images for this book

For your convenience we have also provided a PDF that contains higher resolution color versions of the images used in this book. These can be extremely useful as you work through various stages of the project when working with materials or examining small detail changes as we tweak individual parameters. You can download the PDF from `https://www.packtpub.com/sites/default/files/downloads/4148OT_ColoredImages.pdf`.

Errata

Although we have taken every care to ensure the accuracy of our content, mistakes do happen. If you find a mistake in one of our books—maybe a mistake in the text or the code—we would be grateful if you would report this to us. By doing so, you can save other readers from frustration and help us improve subsequent versions of this book. If you find any errata, please report them by visiting `http://www.packtpub.com/submit-errata`, selecting your book, clicking on the **errata submission form** link, and entering the details of your errata. Once your errata are verified, your submission will be accepted and the errata will be uploaded on our website, or added to any list of existing errata, under the Errata section of that title. Any existing errata can be viewed by selecting your title from `http://www.packtpub.com/support`.

Piracy

Piracy of copyright material on the Internet is an ongoing problem across all media. At Packt, we take the protection of our copyright and licenses very seriously. If you come across any illegal copies of our works, in any form, on the Internet, please provide us with the location address or website name immediately so that we can pursue a remedy.

Please contact us at copyright@packtpub.com with a link to the suspected pirated material.

We appreciate your help in protecting our authors, and our ability to bring you valuable content.

Questions

You can contact us at questions@packtpub.com if you are having a problem with any aspect of the book, and we will do our best to address it.

1
Configuring FL Studio

In this chapter, we will cover:

- ▶ Knowing your sound cards or audio interfaces
- ▶ Installing FL Studio
- ▶ Building your Digital Audio Workstation
- ▶ Installing virtual instruments and effects

Introduction

When configuring FL Studio, you should be familiar with the audio output on your factory sound card. After installing FL Studio and launching the program, you will not be able to hear any sounds from FL Studio if your sound card or audio interface is not selected in the audio settings.

Knowing your sound cards or audio interfaces

In this recipe, you will learn the differences between factory sound cards included on your computer and upgrades you can purchase. Upgrades are either in the form of a sound card or an audio interface. FL Studio works perfectly fine when using your factory sound card, but depending on your own individual needs, you may want to upgrade your sound card.

Getting ready

For this recipe, you should be familiar with your audio settings or sound properties on your actual computer system. It is beneficial to download a free software called ASIO4all instead of using your defaulted factory sound card. You actually need some sort of ASIO driver to record audio into the program. You can then record any source directly into FL Studio, including but not limited to microphones, **Music Production Centers** (**MPCs**), guitars, keyboards, and turntables. If you are purchasing an upgraded audio interface, it will give you low latency, driver stability, and multiple interface routing support. You should also be familiar with audio cables. Most of the time, you will be using 1/4-inch audio cables, XLR cables, RCA audio cables, SPDIF cables, and Y Cables that end up in a 1/8-inch jack.

How to do it...

In computers such as laptops and desktops, there is a place for you to connect your speakers, connect a headphone jack, and connect a microphone / line level cable from a mixer for recording. These will usually all be 1/8 inches in size.

Let's start with a laptop example. In this case, we will work with a Windows 7 Dell laptop, model N7010. This laptop has its own speakers that are physically imbedded in the computer, similar to a smartphone. When you listen to your own music, browse the web, and stream videos and other online content, you can hear the audio come through the speakers. This is something that happens automatically because it is a factory sound card, meaning that is the way your laptop was designed right out of the box. When you right-click on your volume icon, located on the taskbar of a Windows PC, you will see some options. You can also get here by navigating to **Control Panel | Hardware and Sound | Sound**. A click on **Playback devices** will show your factory sound card and any other options you have for audio playback, as shown in the following screenshot:

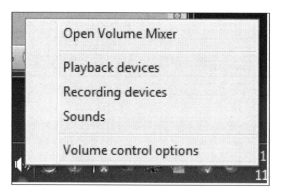

Fig 1.1

You will want to click on **Playback devices** to see how your audio is being outputted on your computer, as shown in *Fig 1.2*:

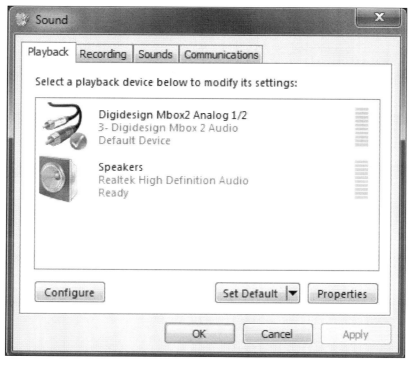

Fig 1.2

There are four tabs listed, which include **Playback**, **Recording**, **Sounds**, and **Communications**. In order to see how your audio is outputted on your computer, you want to focus on the **Playback** tab. The Mbox2 device listed above is our default device, and our Realtek factory sound card is also enabled, allowing us to choose it in the FL Studio settings (by pressing *F10*) if we need to. With an upgraded interface, all of your inputs and outputs will flow from it. With a factory sound card, you can use the 1/8-inch factory input and output included on your computer. We will review the factory Realtek sound card further in this chapter. You can also right-click on any blank white space on the **Sound** properties in order to show more devices. Although not directly correlated with FL Studio, this information about your sound card is crucial to know, because you can use the sound card during your music production and also while browsing the Web and streaming videos and music online. The sound card is not just exclusive to FL Studio. In general, all computer programs utilize the sound card for their audio needs. When you are watching YouTube videos, listening to your music library, or streaming audio online, the music will flow through the sound card that is selected.

Upgraded and/or purchased sound cards usually connect to a USB or FireWire port. They come with an installation disk or will be **Plug and Play** (**PnP**), where your computer will automatically install your new sound card very seamlessly. Your best bet is to consult the documentation of your equipment, because the steps involved to install the proper drivers will vary based on the manufacturer. Generally, this can be done online or through the manufacturers' CDs.

How it works...

We will now review the *poor man's* sound card setup to demonstrate what can be done without paying for expensive USB sound cards. This method can also come in handy when you are traveling, mobile, or not in your home studio. We will be working with our Realtek factory device, which is our computer's 1/8-inch in and out. A key part of the sound interface is the 1/8-inch headphone output jack, which also serves as a speaker/monitor output. You will be able to hear your music in three different ways by utilizing your factory sound card: through the small embedded speakers, headphones, or studio monitors. When plugging in headphones or studio monitors to the 1/8-inch jack, you will no longer hear the embedded computer speakers, as the 1/8-inch takes priority.

In order to record audio into your computer using the poor man's way, you simply have to download the software ASIO4all, available at `http://www.asio4all.com`. You will then be able to select it in the FL Studio settings by pressing *F10*, as well as select the input from your sources in the FL Studio mixer. An alternative way to install ASIO4all is to simply select its option during the FL studio installation process. Recording with the FL Studio Mixer will be reviewed in *Chapter 6, Using the FL Studio Mixer and Recording Audio*.

After ASIO4all is installed, you will be able to select it in your *F10* settings. You may find that the volume output is louder than the factory setting, especially when wearing headphones.

Once your ASIO4all driver is selected in the *F10* settings, you can record into the 1/8-inch input, which is usually a small microphone sign. The poor man's way allows us to realize that this 1/8-inch jack can also function as a line-level input. You can use a small external mixer (for example, a Behringer XENYX 802 mixer), and then the main outputs of the mixer will need to plug into the 1/8-inch jack with the microphone sign. One example of this is using a high-quality microphone. You can have a condenser microphone plugged into a mixer (Behringer, for example) and then the main outputs of the mixer need to reach your computer. This is done with a Y cable, which is a left (L) and right (R) output (usually 1/4-inch or RCA cables) that merges into a small 1/8-inch jack. The 1/8-inch jack is the end you want to plug into your microphone sign. Please note that you can record any type of audio in this fashion, based on your own individual needs. For example, you may have a keyboard or guitar connected to your mixer. Once the mixer's main output is connected to your computer's microphone mini input jack (1/8-inch microphone sign being treated as a line-level signal), you can record using ASIO4all. This will be reviewed in *Chapter 6, Using the FL Studio Mixer and Recording Audio*.

A key point in all of this is that the microphone small input jack on your factory sound card is only one input. You can record multiple parts at one time (if you have a separate mixer with various inputs), but it will only be one main recorded track in FL Studio. This is because the main outputs of your mixer will result in the Y cable. If you have a live band where you need to "mic up" and record multiple guitars, bass guitar, vocals, and a drum set, you want to record at the same time (to have chemistry between all of the players) and you want each recorded part to be completely separate in FL Studio, then that would be a reason to upgrade your sound card because each input can be separated. You can have many inputs on a mixer, but when you use the Y cable for your factory sound card, it will only be recorded on one track in FL Studio.

If you have an upgraded audio interface, you can then record everything at the same time and also separate each recording into different tracks in FL Studio. In that fashion, you can then add effects and mix each part as a separate track, instead of one lump sum of all of the audio. If you are recording live bands and many instruments at a time, professionally, you would obviously want a sound card with multiple inputs. This really just depends on the type of music you create. If you are a hip hop producer who is making beats in FL Studio, you may be able to get by using ASIO4all. If you are comfortable recording one single part at a time, you may not need to upgrade your sound card. At the very least, you can experiment with ASIO4all and see if it can handle your needs because it is free.

So far, we have reviewed using your factory sound card and hearing the audio come through the physical speakers, just like a smartphone. It certainly is not the highest quality output but it works fine. We have also reviewed plugging in a headphone jack and using headphones to hear the audio output. There is one more option when using your factory sound card and the headphone output jack. Your headphone output jack can be connected to studio monitors or any type of upgraded speakers! The headphone jack, although labeled with a headphone icon, is also the output to any speakers you want to connect to. You will use the same size jack as before, which is called a stereo mini jack or a 1/8-inch jack. This will then plug into your studio monitors or studio speakers. There are many configurations and many different speaker manufacturers, but as long as you have the speakers plugging into your headphone jack, your speakers will now work with FL Studio and any audio coming out of your computer.

In most cases, you will need a Y cable, which is a left and right chord for each speaker that merges into a stereo mini or 1/8-inch jack. You will plug in the stereo mini or 1/8 inches jack into your headphone icon on your laptop.

There's more...

In regards to purchasing an upgraded sound card or audio interface, there are many options depending on your needs. There are USB and FireWire audio interfaces that will connect to the USB or FireWire port on your laptop. Once this is done and the drivers are installed, all of the inputs and outputs will now be flowing through your interface, and it will take precedent over your factory sound card.

There are many reasons to have an upgraded sound card/audio interface. Remember to get a sound card that works with ASIO so you can record external audio in FL Studio.

An upgraded sound card will have greater audio quality and a greater volume range, which may allow you to mix better. You can also connect multiple external sources based on how many inputs the interface has, and then you are able to record these in a simultaneous performance while keeping them on separate recorded tracks in FL Studio. An audio interface will also sometimes have **Musical Instrument Digital Interface** (**MIDI**) inputs and outputs if you need that capability. Additionally, there is usually a dedicated headphone jack in addition to a dedicated monitor volume knob. This makes things easier while you are producing and you don't have to constantly plug devices in and out and switch things around. Your speakers will now connect directly into your interface. When you have an upgraded interface, your factory sound card no longer serves a purpose. All of the inputs and outputs on your computer will now flow through your audio interface. You can also record with less latency (delay from when you speak into a microphone and when you actually hear it come through your headphones) and have better audio recording.

A rule of thumb is to set your buffer size as low as possible while recording external audio, but while you are mixing your song and using virtual instruments, you may set it higher for better performance. When recording external audio, such as a microphone for vocals or guitar, you want to set the buffer size as low as possible without hearing a crackling sound. This crackling is referred to as dropout and occurs when your computer can't process the audio buffers fast enough. When you lower the buffer size, you will have less latency, but your computer system will be working harder. An analogy of this is a person filling and emptying small buckets of water again and again. A lower buffer setting means that the system is working quickly with little chunks at a time. A higher buffer setting is moving a very large bucket of water slowly. You want to bump down your buffer setting for vocal tracking and live instruments early in your production, and then bring it up when you are mixing and working with plugins. If you are serious about your productions, an upgraded interface is usually the way to go. An upgraded interface will also include extra outputs that can be used for extra speakers and to connect outboard gear like effect processors.

Another type of third-party interface is a PCI connector that connects internally to your computer and functions in the same way an external interface does. External interfaces are USB or FireWire devices, while PCI and PCIe are internal connections. These are popular with gamers who want high audio fidelity as well.

Installing FL Studio

This recipe will walk you through the basic functions of installing your software just like any other program you have installed. Be sure to install `FLRegKey` on your computer, because that will allow your installation to work properly and your computer will recognize that you did indeed pay for your license/copy of FL Studio.

Getting ready

You will need the FL Studio software and the FL Studio registration key. The easiest way is to be connected to the Internet, but there is also a way to install offline if you do not have Internet access. You will want to close any open programs on your computer so it is not fighting for resources as you install FL Studio. Yes, FL Studio is a DAW, or Digital Audio Workstation, but it will install like any other software you have installed on your computer before. The standard settings for installation are usually the easiest, and FL Studio will also install its own sounds, settings, plugins, effects, and template file folders during the installation process. This is very streamlined and intuitive.

How to do it...

FL Studio allows you to build a complete music production from scratch, while only using your computer. Sure, you can tweak it out and add additional components, MIDI keyboards, interfaces, control surfaces, and so on, but the heart of the program is being able to complete a full song under one roof. There is a very powerful sequencer to get started making percussion, an intuitive process to help you add synthesized sounds and harmonies, a full mixer to add effects such as reverb and delay, a playlist to help you arrange your song, and a mixer to blend all of the elements together. You can also add lyrics by recording into the program with a microphone and master your track. From the beginning phases to the finished product of listening to your song in your car or online, FL Studio has everything you need.

FL Studio can be comparable to any type of word processing program. You can copy, edit, move, arrange, and manipulate the content you are writing with words in a word processor. With a DAW, you can move, edit, copy, paste, and manipulate different sounds in order to create a full music production.

The instructions for installing FL studio on a Mac or PC are given at the following links:

- http://support.image-line.com/knowledgebase/base.php?id=35&ans=119
- http://support.image-line.com/knowledgebase/base.php?id=35&ans=119

 Both of these links have additional links within.

Building your digital audio workstation

In this recipe, you will learn the importance of a DAW in the field of music production. You will also learn to create your very own DAW for recording, playing back music tracks / digital audio, and audio editing.

Getting ready

The main part of your DAW is your computer. You want to have a computer system with the most powerful processor and most powerful memory for speed. Be sure to close other programs so they won't interfere with FL Studio's performance. You should try to get a screen with high resolution and make sure it doesn't have too much glare when near sunlight. The following image depicts the setup of Digidesign MBox2:

Fig 1.3

How to do it...

The basic setup of a DAW will include the following elements:

- **Computer**: Dell laptop, model N7010. Dell Windows 7.

- **Audio interface**: This will be selected in **Audio Settings** inside FL Studio and all of the inputs and outputs will flow through the interface (Digidesign MBox2, shown in *Fig 1.3*).

- **External hard drive**: This is what the MBox2 is sitting on. You can stay organized by saving your projects and keeping recorded vocals on this drive. For transfer and access speeds, external drives are slower than internal, and you will not see the same performance with files stored on external drives. A drive with 500 GB of storage is a good size to get started with.

- **Headphones**: The headphones are connected to a dedicated headphone jack on the MBox2 interface. There is also a dedicated volume control knob for the headphones.

- **Monitors/Speakers**: The speakers are connected to the monitor outputs of the MBox2. There is also a monitor knob to control the volume of the speakers.

- **MIDI keyboard**: The MIDI keyboard will control the sounds and parameters inside the software program. If you don't have a MIDI keyboard, your computer's QWERTY keyboard can also control the sounds and functions inside of FL Studio. In the **OPTIONS** menu in FL Studio, you will want to make sure you have a checkbox selected for **Typing keyboard to piano in order to use the QWERTY functionality**.

 There are also many devices that are related to MIDI controllers, including control surfaces and other devices with physical pads and knobs.

If you like having physical control and using your hands instead of clicking with a mouse, this may be good for you. Instead of clicking-and-dragging with a mouse, you can actually use your hands to turn knobs that control the functions of FL Studio. Some MIDI keyboards actually have knobs and pads on them and other type of control surfaces have knobs, faders, sliders, pads, and touchscreens. When using a MIDI device or MIDI controller, they will connect with five-pin old-style MIDI cables or simply a USB cord. This depends on the manufacturer. Newer MIDI controllers are generally USB based, though you can still utilize old-style devices with a five-pin MIDI plug. They both work the same way. The following screenshot shows the **Settings** window of the FL Studio:

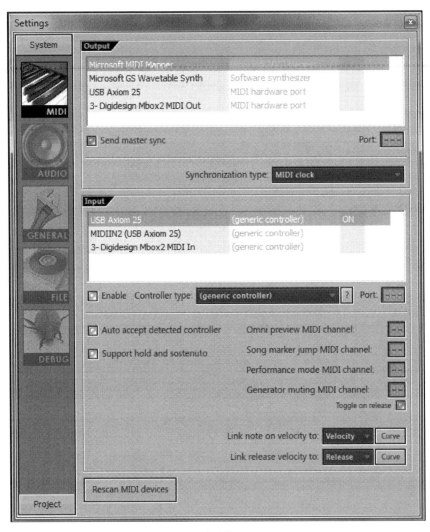

Fig 1.4

Most controllers must be connected and powered on prior to booting FL Studio. In order to make sure your MIDI controller or MIDI keyboard is working correctly, you can press the *F10* key and click on the MIDI tab. You can also go into the **OPTIONS** menu and select **MIDI** settings. You want to make sure the orange box is selected where it says **Enable,** in order for FL Studio to recognize your given MIDI device. You can see this on the upper left area of the FL Studio software, and the part that lights up orange looks like a small five-pin cable, which is FL Studio's symbol for MIDI. Furthermore, if you do not see any activity, you can also click on **Rescan devices** in **MIDI Settings**. Initially, your MIDI device will install to your computer using MIDI drivers it finds online, in a similar manner to installing an audio interface, or it may come with an installation disk to install the MIDI drivers and software. You will also want to select your controller and it will be selected in the blue color. In *Fig 1.4*, **USB Axiom 25** is selected and enabled. You will also see the **MIDI input activity** button light up in orange when you are triggering your MIDI device, as shown in the following screenshot:

Fig 1.5

The half-moon symbol, also known as the MIDI symbol (lower right-hand side of the preceding screenshot), will light up in orange when you trigger your MIDI device. When it lights up orange, that means everything is communicating properly and your MIDI device is able to control the sounds and parameters in FL Studio. This particular screenshot also shows the hint bar, which displays the useful clues that FL Studio provides while you hover your mouse on any function of the program. Depending on where you hover your mouse, this hint bar will provide you with certain insights. A history of MIDI and its capabilities are listed at `http://en.wikipedia.org/wiki/MIDI`.

- **USB hub**: You may need to purchase a USB hub, which will turn a one-port USB hub into a four-port hub or greater. This will help with connecting devices and having room for all of your devices. You may need to connect an iLOK key, USB MIDI keyboard, external hard drive, your printer, and any other USB accessories. Since USB hubs share bandwidth with all devices on the hub, having an external hard drive and a MIDI keyboard on the same hub can cause performance issues.

- **Secondary screen (Dual monitors)**: This is an optional setup. If you connect a separate screen to your computer, it can make it easier to organize your project and increase screen "real estate." With many main subwindows in FL Studio, an alternate screen can be taken advantage of by clicking on the triangle in the top-left-hand-side and checking the **Detached** option.

If you do not have an upgraded audio interface, you can still use the factory sound card with ASIO4all as previously discussed. You can use the stereo mini jack (1/8 inch) with the headphone label for headphones or connecting speakers and you can use the stereo mini jack (1/8 inch) with the microphone label for recording any type of audio.

Your speakers and your ears should be an equal distance apart from each other. This means everything should be in a nice equilateral triangle shape. They should also be at ear level. Please remember to turn on your speakers after your computer has booted up; otherwise, your speakers will make a popping sound when your computer boots up and it may damage them. You can turn your speakers on after your computer has booted. Similarly, due to voltage fluctuation, you want to turn your speakers off before you shut down your computer, because it may make a cracking and popping noise that can damage your speakers if they are on during the shutdown process.

Installing virtual instruments and effects

Installing virtual instruments and effects is how you tweak and enhance the production capabilities of FL Studio. We will review adding virtual instruments in *Chapter 4, Building Your Song*. A graphical interface consisting of many different sound patches will appear, in which you can scroll through the sound presets and play them on an FL Studio channel, MIDI keyboard, or piano roll. You will usually have the ability to shape new sounds or adjust presets to your liking with the various parameters on each virtual instrument plugin. These virtual instruments are also referred to as software synthesizers. With regards to virtual effects, the same principles apply; the only difference is that you will be utilizing effects on the FL Studio mixer effect chain, which is reviewed in *Chapter 6, Using the FL Studio Mixer and Recording Audio*. Generally speaking, virtual effects consist of compressors, limiters, equalizers, delays, and reverbs, as well as enhancing tools for vocals and instruments.

Both virtual instruments and virtual effects will generally have a dynamic link library extension, which is abbreviated as .dll. The .dll file must be placed in a specific path on your computer, and when enabled in FL Studio, it will turn into a beautiful graphical plugin. The .dll file can be thought of as caterpillar; once enabled in FL Studio, it becomes a beautiful butterfly. If downloaded from free Internet sources, you will generally have to place them in the correct file path on your computer. Virtual instruments and effects are referred to as **Virtual Studio Technology** (**VST**). These are made and coded by many third-party software designers and will usually work in various DAWs. During music production inside FL Studio, virtual instruments will come from the **CHANNELS** menu of the main FL Studio window. Virtual effects will come from a slot in your FL Studio mixer chain. Installing virtual instruments and effects is a great way to take your music production to the next level.

Getting ready

In order to install a virtual instrument, you will want to follow the installation instructions from your third-party manufacturer. We will now review how to handle the process when working with a `.dll` file.

How to do it...

Let us review how to install virtual instruments and effects inside of FL Studio with the following steps:

1. Download a virtual instrument `.dll` file and save it to your computer. In this example, we are working with a virtual instrument called `Pulsation.dll` from a free website, `www.vstplanet.com`.

2. Add your `.dll` file to your `VST` folder inside of your `Image-Line` folder. In this example, the total path is `C:\Program Files\Image-Line\FL Studio 11\ Plugins\VST`.

3. From the main FL Studio window, select **CHANNELS | Add one | More...**.

4. This will bring up the **Select generator plugin** box as per *Fig 1.6*. Click on **Refresh** followed by **Fast scan** to see your recently installed plugin, as shown in the following screenshot:

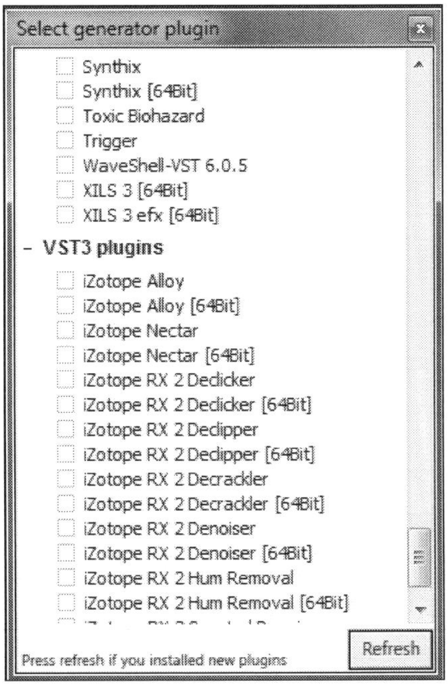

Fig 1.6

5. Your recently installed plugin will now show up in red. Click within the small box beside your plugin name as per the following screenshot (the **F** stands for favorite switch):

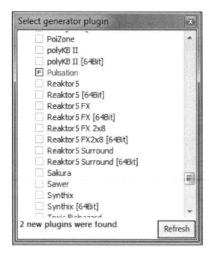

Fig 1.7

6. Your plugin will now be available in your list (listed in alphabetical order) when you click on **CHANNELS** followed by **Add one**. In this particular example, our graphical plugin looks like the one shown in following screenshot, and we have scrolled to the **Trance Pulse** preset:

Fig 1.8

How it works...

We will review how virtual instruments work in the *Adding virtual instruments* recipe in *Chapter 4, Building Your Song*. Using VSTs simply allows us to improve our sound palette! We can use the sounds in this VST like any other channel in the step sequencer, in addition to using automation.

There's more...

When using effect plugins, we will generally follow the same procedure with one big difference. We will open up the FL Studio mixer, click on the small triangle dropdown in the mixer effect chain slot (listed 1 through 8 on any mixer track), choose **Select/Replace**, and then **More...**. From that point, we will follow the same guidelines with regards to refreshing, using **Fast scan**, and clicking on the **F** button next to our new plugin shown in red to activate it. Our effect will then be available on any mixer effect slot when clicking on the small triangle dropdown and hovering on choose **Select/Replace**.

You may find some really great plugins as freeware online. True, it is wise to purchase high-quality third-party plugins, but sometimes the geeky coders working for these companies were the same people posting freeware online! Be mindful of downloading freeware as you do not want to induce a virus on your computer.

See also

- ▸ The *Adding virtual instruments* recipe in *Chapter 4, Building Your Song*
- ▸ The *Working with MIDI Controllers and MIDI Pads* recipe in *Chapter 4, Building Your Song*
- ▸ The *Adding effects and your effect chain* recipe in *Chapter 6, Using the FL Studio Mixer and Recording Audio*
- ▸ The *Recording with or without effects* recipe in *Chapter 6, Using the FL Studio Mixer and Recording Audio*
- ▸ The *Using automation for virtual instruments and effects* recipe in *Chapter 10, Recording Automation*

2
Using Browser

In this chapter, we will cover:

- ▸ Working with Browser
- ▸ Getting new sounds in Browser

Introduction

FL Studio Browser is a file listing of all of the WAV and MP3 sounds that you are able to add to your project. Bear in mind that we are not referring to an Internet browser of any sort; this is where we can browse our collection of sounds. The Browser is very important because it provides quick access to your library of WAV and MP3 sounds in an intuitive manner. You want to keep your Browser organized and labeled correctly to keep your workflow at an optimum level. It also holds all of your current project data and presets, and is a quick way to find older projects. The FL Studio Browser automatically synchronizes with your file path on your computer, and we will review exactly what that means in this chapter.

Working with Browser

In this recipe, you will come to understand the files and parameters within the FL Studio Browser. You can accumulate a wide range of sounds and build your own sound library. FL Studio also comes with its own factory sounds to get you started (25 folders in total in the factory Browser list, which also includes a plethora of presets and functions). This is also the area where FL Studio automatically keeps presets, projects, SoundFonts, automation curves, WAV files, the **undo history** button, the speech synthesizer, and the like. This is also where you can preview sounds while your mix is playing, so it is crucial to understand the Browser while building your track and adding additional sounds to it. When you add sounds from the Browser into the step sequencer, it automatically becomes a channel in the step sequencer, which is the building block of all the sounds in your given project.

Getting ready

In order to get started with using the Browser, you need to open up FL Studio and then push the *F8* key to toggle the Browser. Additionally, you may go to the **VIEW** menu and then select **Browser**. When **Browser** is selected, you will see a small checkbox next to it. A third way is to simply click on the Browser symbol. Browser is the fourth button from the left, as shown in the following screenshot:

Fig 2.1

How to do it...

Find a folder in the FL Studio Browser that contains WAV or MP3 sounds. Click with your mouse to trigger the sound samples or scroll using your arrow keys on your computer keyboard. Adjust your volume or effect in your preview mixer track on the FL Studio Mixer; we will discuss this in the next lines.

When you left-click on the folders in the **Browser** section, it will automatically open up the files inside of it, which you can then left-click to preview the sound. Keep in mind that you will be previewing all types of sounds, including drum kicks, snares, hi hats, and all types of percussion, but when a sound in the Browser is longer than 5 seconds, clicking on it will only preview the first 5 seconds of it. There will be a small symbol that helps identify what each file means. A small orange box with a small .wav audio symbol means that the file is, indeed, a WAV file. There is also a label that says MP3 when it recognizes an MP3 file. When you click on a file with your mouse, it will be previewed through your sound card, headphones, or speakers. Once you have engaged a file, you may also use your arrow keys (the up and down arrows) that are part of your QWERTY keyboard.

When working on the FL Studio Browser and triggering with percussion, rhythm, hi hats, cymbals, kicks, snares, claps, and the like, you can actually use your mouse to play musical patterns. This means treating your mouse button like a drum pad, and with practice, it can inspire you to get better. For example, if you have a drum kit called **APRIL Kit** full of WAV samples in the **Browser** section (as shown in the following screenshot) and the kick, snare, and hi hat or shaker are close by in the list, you can play a decent riff with only your mouse button on the fly:

Fig 2.2

In this example, you can left-click on **808kick** and then **beep1** in order to form a percussion riff with your finger and mouse. Sure, this is not recorded anywhere and is only a preview, but you can certainly get a good rhythm groove going no matter your type of WAV samples or musical genre. As discussed earlier, the wave symbol is the orange icon on the left of each sample in the Browser section, and it also says MP3 for the MP3 file titled **beep2,** as shown in the preceding screenshot. You can create freestyle loops on the fly, which allow for immediate feedback and inspiration. The kick and snare are extremely important as the building blocks and foundation of your song. Use your mouse like you would your finger on a hard surface or table top. You can pulsate quickly or slowly.

The other method of previewing your WAV and MP3 files in the FL Studio Browser is using your up and down arrow keys. In this method, you can simply push the keys up or down, and it may feel easier than clicking on each sound with your mouse. The files in any given Browser folder are always listed in an alphabetical order (from top to bottom), so remember to scroll all the way down and start near the end of the alphabet to break the monotony of any given folder.

In order to optimize the way you use your Browser when previewing sounds, you will also need to set your **Preview mixer track** field to whatever track you desire in your Mixer. The FL Studio Mixer is reviewed in *Chapter 6, Using the FL Studio Mixer and Recording Audio*. In this way, you can adjust the volume of the sounds previewed in the **Browser** section and also set EQ, reverb, or any other effect desired. This is crucial when mixing and adding sounds to your project. The following screenshot shows the **Mixer** tab:

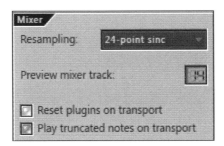

Fig 2.3

In the preceding screenshot, I have set **Preview mixer track** to **14**. This is accomplished by going into the **OPTIONS** menu and clicking on **Audio settings**. In the bottom right-hand corner of **Settings**, there is a small area titled **Mixer**. It is here that you select **Preview mixer track**, which means any sound you preview in the **Browser** section will be funneled into your selected track on the FL Studio Mixer. You can simply drag the number up or down in order to reach the Mixer track you so desire to preview. This is one of the most important things to remember in FL Studio, because you can now add compression to the previewed sounds, add reverb, raise the volume, or lower the volume when previewing sounds in the Browser. When your music production is playing, this will help you see how your previewed sound could potentially be blended with your mix. You will learn how to add reverb and light compression to the preview Mixer in the subsequent chapters.

When mixing your song and having multiple instruments and harmonies playing at the same time, adjusting the volume of the **Preview mixer track** can help you decide whether you want to add a particular sound or discard it. Be cautious of this and set **Preview mixer track** to be at an optimal volume based on your other instruments and tracks playing in the mix simultaneously. Sometimes, the volume varies between folders, but generally speaking, you can set the volume and scroll through most sounds in any given kit adequately, especially if they have all been made by one manufacturer or sound designer.

How it works...

When you find a sound that you like, you can left-click and drag with your mouse, and let go when you reach the lower part of an empty space on the step sequencer. The step sequencer can be opened by pressing *F6*, which we will review in *Chapter 3*, *Working with the Step Sequencer and Channels*, and is the main sequencing section in FL Studio. This will then make a new channel of the sound you desire to use in your project. Every sound you use (from either the **Browser** section or any recorded audio) in your project will have a dedicated channel in the step sequencer. When clicking-and-dragging, you can also replace an existing sound that is already its own channel. If you left-click and drag a sound from the **Browser** section and let go of it on an existing channel, it will light up in orange on the existing channel and subsequently be replaced. When you right-click on a sound in the **Browser** section, you will have additional options, as shown in *Fig 2.4*. The use of these actual channels will be covered in *Chapter3*, *Working with the Step Sequencer and Channels*.

Fig 2.4

The sounds, plugins, presets, history, and parameters of your Browser are directly related to making music. Before recording these sounds into FL Studio, they will be placed as channels inside the step sequencer, and your music project will commence. We will discuss this music-making process in the next chapter. The **Browser** section is your library of WAV and MP3 sounds that differ from VSTs and virtual instrument plugins, which we will also examine later in the book.

There's more...

Let's learn a few things about browsing extra search folders. In cases where you want to specify your own path, store sounds on a drive other than your main drive, or use an external hard drive, you can tell FL Studio to search for that particular path in your **File settings**. This is also a practice used in recording external audio, which we will cover in a later chapter. A widely used practice is to record your vocals and any other audio onto an external drive in order to save space on your computer. You can also use this method for any sounds or files, if you so desire. You will need to click on the **OPTIONS** menu and then go into **File settings**. You may also press *F10* and then click on your **FILE** tab in order to reach the same **File settings** window in FL Studio. An additional way is to click on the small triangle (in the **Browser** options) in the upper left-hand corner of the **Browser** section and then select **Configure extra folders**. The following screenshot shows the **Settings** window:

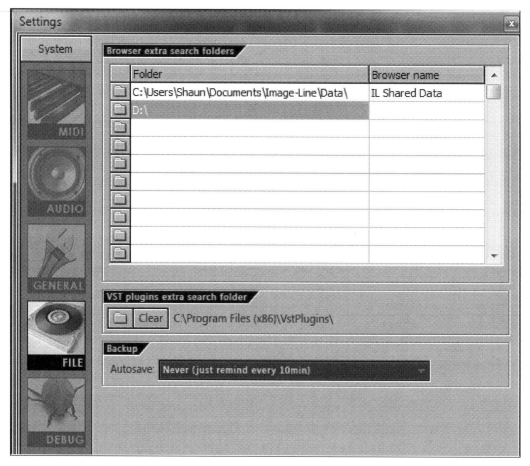

FlO → File →   Fig 2.5

In the preceding screenshot, you can see the **Browser extra search folders** menu. The first row at the top shows automatically when you install FL Studio, as long as you have completed the standard installation. In this **File settings** window on FL Studio, you are able to specify more paths that tell FL Studio what areas to search on your computer in order to bring up the sounds into your project(s). I have added D:\ to the second row as an example. In this example, FL Studio will now search the D:\ drive in addition to any other locations that I specify. In order to actually specify a location for FL Studio, you simply need to click on the folder icon next to each row. Once you click on the folder icon, you will be able to select the path/folder to be added to FL Studio as an extra search folder.

See also

▸ *Chapter 3, Working with the Step Sequencer and Channels*
▸ *Chapter 4, Building Your Song*

Getting new sounds in Browser

This recipe will walk you through the task of finding new sounds on web and importing these sounds into your **Browser** window.

How to do it...

The Browser in FL Studio is directly correlated to the FL Studio installation path on your given computer system. For example, in a PC environment, you can view the FL Studio path at C:\ Program Files\Image-Line\FL Studio 11\Data\Patches. When you arrive at the Patches folder on your actual computer file hierarchy, please keep in mind that on FL Studio, the Browser is directly related to it. You are able to add any WAV or MP3 files that you desire, and you can organize them, name them, and place them in a dedicated folder, like anything else you organize on your computer. Similar to organizing documents, photos, and music, the file path that leads to Patches is where you will organize your wave samples and other pertinent files. As stated previously, it can be a great idea to store WAV or MP3 files on an external hard drive. If you keep all of your files in the FL Studio install directory, they are likely to be overwritten.

Browser = Data Patches
so if you add to data patches it will show in the browser

An easy way to find WAV files, such as percussion, kicks, hi hats, snares, cymbals, or any other type of effect, is to search online by typing in whatever WAV file you desire. There are many free types of WAV files, and you can find whatever you want using your given search engine correctly. For example, if I want to find something like a clock chime, I can simply use an Internet search engine and type `clock chime free.wav` or something of a similar context. Of course, when you are serious about your recordings, you want to have the most high-quality WAV samples you can when working with FL Studio. There are numerous drum packs, sound packs, drum kits, virtual instruments, high-quality loops, and sounds that you can research online and purchase if you so desire. That being said, there are thousands of free wave samples across the Internet, so you may want to test your luck and work with some free WAV files you find online.

When you find a free sound that you want on the internet, there will sometimes be a **Download** button that you can click. Other times, you may need to right-click on a file and select **Save link as** before saving. You want to make sure that the file is indeed compatible with FL Studio, which means it should be an MP3 or WAV file. If you select **Save link as**, and then it tries to save an HTML page, web page, or something of the sort, then you should *not* save that file. The following screenshot shows how a file is saved:

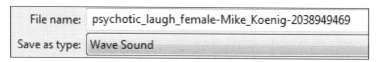

Fig 2.6

In the preceding example, you have right-clicked on the WAV icon for the psychotic female laugh, and your computer recognized that it is indeed a WAV sound. Your computer has also automatically named the file in the manner listed above, next to **File name**. This is the final step before saving your file into the file location of your choice.

Once you have saved your WAV or MP3 file to the proper folder on your computer, FL Studio will recognize this; your new sound will be listed in the **Browser** section and can be previewed when you left-click on the **Browser** section.

There's more...

Let's take a look at the various ways to refresh your Browser. The following screenshot shows the refresh icon:

Fig 2.7

If you are adding sounds to the computer file hierarchy in your `Patches` folder (or external drive) and the FL Studio software is open, you may practice the following two methods:

▸ Click on the third button from the left in the **Browser** section. As shown in *Fig 2.7*, this will **Reread structure**, that is, refresh your Browser, and your new sounds will now be recognized in the Browser.

▸ Press *Ctrl + R*, which is a quick key command that tells FL Studio to refresh the Browser in lieu of clicking with your mouse on the third button from the left.

Additionally, if the FL Studio software is closed—that is, it is not running on your computer—the moment you launch the software, all of your new sounds will show in the Browser, regardless of whether you have refreshed the Browser or not. Refreshing the Browser is probably a little bit easier to do when FL Studio is already running, and it's a nice function to have so you don't have to close and open FL Studio in order to read the folders and new files on your computer. The following screenshot shows the other options in the **Browser** section:

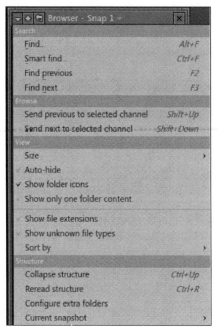

Fig 2.8

If you can't seem to locate a sound that you have previously worked with, you can press the small triangle in the upper left-hand corner of the FL Studio Browser and use the **Find...** button, which is an exact keyword search engine for your FL Studio Browser. You can also press *Alt* + *F*. Alternatively, you may also use the **Smart find...** option, which is *Ctrl* + *F*, because it will most likely find more results while it is not based on an exact phrase. There are also other choices from this small triangle button, including **Search**, **Browse**, **View**, and **Structure**.

To actually scroll through your Browser, it includes two up and down arrows on the FL Studio Browser window in addition to a scroll bar that you can drag. Alternatively, and as a more natural method, you can also use your wheel mouse, wheel mouse optical, or any type of upgraded mouse interface that has an up or down scroll wheel.

See also

> ▸ *Chapter 3, Working with the Step Sequencer and Channels*

3
Working with the Step Sequencer and Channels

In this chapter, we will cover:

- ▶ Gauging fundamental areas
- ▶ Exploring Channel settings
- ▶ Sending a channel to a mixer slot
- ▶ Working with Graph editor
- ▶ Using the Keyboard editor
- ▶ Working with patterns

Introduction

The step sequencer is where you enter your steps. These are the areas on your various channels where you can place MIDI notes and all audio event triggering. You can pull up the step sequencer by pressing *F6* and either finding it in the **VIEW** menu or clicking the **View step sequencer** icon (the second icon from the left in *Fig 3.1*). The steps are arranged in horizontal order in the time scale, from left to right, encompassing grey and reddish-looking square boxes. Directly to the left in every single row on the step sequencer is an FL Studio channel, which is the sound of any given row of steps. The process of entering these steps is accomplished by left-clicking on the enter steps and right-clicking on the erase steps. Also, to the left of every channel are the panning, volume, and solo parameters.

Channel Rack = Step Sequencer

The channels in the step sequencer are the backbone of your entire music production. They will be made up of all of your WAV and MP3 files, virtual instruments, automation, and audio clips. They will change different colors based on the FL Studio default setting, and this will help you recognize certain channels. You can easily rename channels to make your project more organized. You can also filter your channels using the group channels together function. FL Studio, by default, will also group your channels, as seen at the bottom left of the step sequencer. You will also set your beats per bar on the step sequencer and label your patterns. The patterns in the step sequencer will become arranged in your playlist to form your music production, which we will discuss in succeeding chapters.

Also within the step sequencer are the Graph and Keyboard editors; they will allow you to further shape your sound and fine-tune it to your own creative tastes. Within each channel, you have properties that can shape your sound, which are the channel settings that we will review in this chapter. Sounds from the FL Studio browser will be placed into a channel within the step sequencer to add layers of sounds into your project. The step sequencer contains each sound that you are using, and it is the building block of your entire project. When you have your creative juices flowing, you will be able to form your groove or harmonies very fast using the step sequencer. This is almost being "in the zone", so to speak, because you may lose track of time when being extremely creative.

Gauging fundamental areas

The step sequencer contains a plethora of areas that can be clicked on and explored to aid your music production.

Getting ready

In order to get started using the step sequencer, open up FL Studio and press the *F6* key to toggle it. Additionally, go to the **VIEW** menu and then select **Step Sequencer**. When the step sequencer is selected, you will see a small checkbox next to it. A third way is to simply click on the step sequencer symbol. The step sequencer is the second button from the left in *Fig 3.1*. You will also want to have your FL Studio Browser open so you can browse the sounds, which in turn will be sent to your channels. However, you may also load the samples from your **Channel settings** window in the step sequencer or drag them from your computer into an FL Studio channel. You may right-click directly on a channel and then select **Insert** or **Replace**.

Fig 3.1

How to do it...

Let's take a look at the fundamental areas of the step sequencer. This opens up to many other levels and subtopics. The following screenshot shows the step sequencer:

Fig 3.2

▶ **Beats per bar for this pattern**:

The following steps will help you set the beats per bar value for a pattern:

1. Hover your mouse over the small box in the left-hand corner (see the number **4** in *Fig 3.2*). Observe the FL Studio hint bar to see **Beats per bar for this pattern**.

2. Click on **Drag up or down to adjust your beats per bar** and it will adjust the steps accordingly. Release your mouse button when you reach the number you want.

▶ **Pattern selector**:

1. Hover your mouse over **Pattern selector** (where it says **Cookbook Pattern 1** in *Fig 3.2*).

2. Click on it and it will populate the patterns you have used so far. Keep in mind that you can rename each pattern to your own liking; otherwise, the patterns will keep its default labels of the generic patterns 1, 2, 3, and so on.

▶ **Swing**:

Sometimes, it is important that you offset the timing of your groove and make it more human. *Chapter 9, Humanizing Your Song*, is dedicated to doing exactly that. *Fig 3.3* shows the adjustment of the swing slider on the title bar. It shows the beats of your waveform and how their start time is being shifted. It pushes your groove ever so slightly in time to the right, and the areas in red represent the down beat in 4/4 musical time.

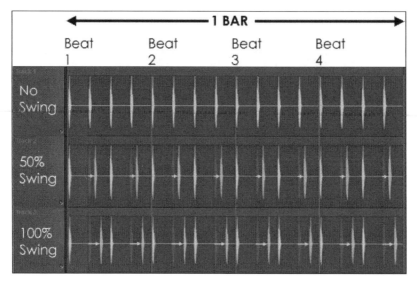

Fig 3.3 Image courtesy: The FL Studio help file

1. Click on the small swing button next to the swing.

2. You may slide the small box to the right and adjust your swing percentage (remember to check the FL Studio hint bar as discussed previously).

▶ **Graph editor**:

The **Graph editor** tab provides the added ability to tweak your various steps. Each note can be moved individually. Take a look at the following screenshot:

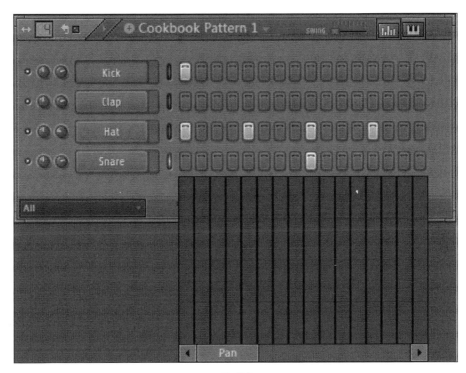

Fig 3.4

1. Click on the first button to the right of the swing slider to bring up the **Graph editor** section. If **Typing keyboard to piano** is turned off (your QWERTY keyboard), you may press the G key to engage **Graph editor**.

2. It will then populate the options from left to right, including **Pan**, **Velocity**, **Release**, **Mod X**, **Mod Y**, **Fine pitch**, and **Shift**. Note that in *Fig 3.4*, the **Snare** channel is selected with the small green light. You must select a channel with the small green light and then click on **Graph editor**. You can then control that particular channel with **Graph editor**. Each row on the parameters correlates to each step on a given channel.

3. Left-click anywhere in **Graph editor** to enter data for steps, which will show up in any given Graph editor parameters. This will show up as a vertical readout in FL Studio.

▶ **Keyboard editor**:

This turns each step into a full-fledged piano turned on its side, as shown in the following screenshot:

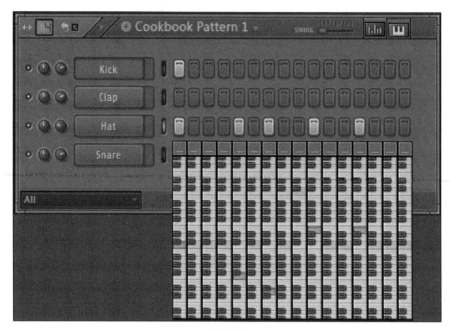

Fig 3.5

1. Click on the mini keyboard symbol in the top right-hand corner of the FL Studio step sequencer.

2. Click on the notes you desire for the steps in your particular channel. When you open **Keyboard editor**, every individual step can be changed into a new note if desired. This is like a piano with all of the keys, but the layout is vertical instead of the regular, horizontal one. If you turn your head to the left, you can see that it is in a piano. You can click inside **Keyboard editor** and your selection will be shown in orange, which will also automatically activate the particular step in question.

3. Scroll up and down with your mouse; you may also click, hold, and drag vertically with your mouse on every column of **Keyboard editor**. This will help you quickly find notes in octaves that are higher or lower on the keyboard. This allows for speedy inspiration and is another useful tool to create music, random melodies, and rhythms. Right-clicking on a note will delete its note data and also leave a faint red color where you last engaged a note.

4. Hold down *Ctrl* when clicking-and-dragging to simultaneously move all the notes up or down in pitch.

▶ **Mute/Solo Button**:

1. Hover your mouse over the small green circle button, shown in the following screenshot, at the far left of a channel in the step sequencer:

Fig 3.6

2. When you left-click on a channel, you can turn a given channel on and off. As a shortcut, simply press numbers *1* to *9* at the top of your QWERTY keyboard to mute on or off. The numbers correlate with the channels from top to bottom.

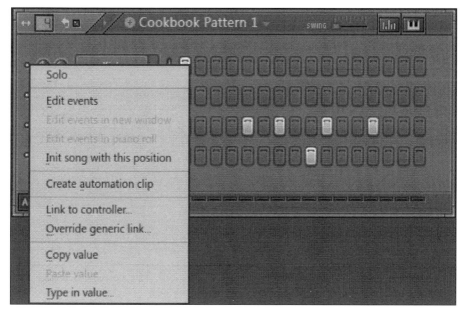

Fig 3.7

3. When you right-click on a channel, it will open up the options in the preceding screenshot.

4. Also, hold *Ctrl + 1* and other numbers at the top of your QWERTY keyboard as a shortcut (again, the numbers correlate with the channels).

5. Select the **Solo** button to mute all of the other channels and only hear the audio from your isolated selection. You can also hold *Ctrl* and click on the green light to make the channel a solo selection.

6. We will review the creation of automation clips in *Chapter 10, Recording Automation*.

7. Note that in the previous option of **Link to controller...**, you may use a MIDI controller to turn the **Solo** button on or off or control the volume and panning knobs. Please review the recipe *Working with MIDI controllers and MIDI pads* in *Chapter 4, Building Your Song*, for more details. There are many physical knobs and sliders that can be utilized in MIDI controllers if you enjoy using the feel of your hands in lieu of clicking with a mouse. Essentially, any parameter on your computer screen can be controlled using a MIDI controller.

▶ **Channel panning knob**:

1. Hover your mouse over the knob directly to the right of the **Mute / solo** button in *Fig 3.6*. The hint bar will tell you that it is, indeed, the channel panning parameter. You will also see a small FL Studio symbol that represents how far left or right you are pushing your sound.

2. Left-clicking, holding, and dragging up or down correlates with a right/left crossfade, respectively. Hold down *Ctrl* to make the knob move slowly. You may place certain instruments to the left, right, or somewhere in between based on your creative taste. Although a fundamental property of all music productions, panning can have a huge impact on your final mood, mix, and production.

3. Right-click to select additional options. You may reset the knob here to return it to FL Studio's default position. *Alt* + left-click will also reset it.

4. Right-clicking will also give you the automation clips and the **Link to controller...** options, both of which will be covered later in the book.

▶ **Channel volume knob**:

1. Click on the volume knob and pull up or down to adjust the level of your channel. Directly to the right of the channel panning is the **Channel volume** knob in *Fig 3.6*. FL Studio will also show a small readout of the volume setting when the volume knob is engaged.

2. Hold down *Ctrl* before engaging your mouse button to have more control over the volume. This will enable you to adjust your level in small steps rather than large steps and may help in cases where only a small tweak is needed.

3. Right-clicking will allow you to reset the volume to FL Studio's default position, create an automation clip, or link to a MIDI controller (using **Link to controller...**).

4. This is arguably the most important aspect of music production—the relative volume of one instrument or part to another. They should not be clipped or set too high, which could cause distortion. The step sequencer makes it very easy to adjust the volume as the volume knob is included directly to the left of every channel. We will review other volume adjusters later in the chapter.

▶ **Channel**:

1. Left-click on a channel to bring up the **Channel settings** window. We will review this in the next recipe of this chapter, titled *Exploring Channel settings*.

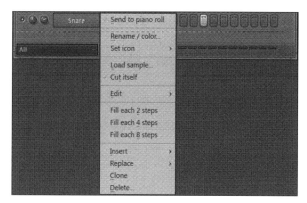

Fig 3.8

2. Right-click on a channel to open up the additional options. In the preceding screenshot, we right-clicked on the **Snare** channel.

3. Select **Fill each 2 steps**, **Fill each 4 steps**, or **Fill each 8 steps** to command FL Studio to automatically fill your steps in the channel that you have selected. This may help when you are testing out hi hats, shakers, and percussion, or in any creative way that you can think of.

4. Select **Rename / color...** to better organize your project to your individual system. A quicker shortcut is pressing *Shift* + click.

5. Select **Set icon** to help with the organization if necessary.

6. Select **Clone** to make an exact copy of your selected channel. This will not include the steps or the Piano roll information, but cloning a channel will produce the same parameters as the original channel that is being cloned. This means that the panning, volume and all the knobs within the **Channel settings** window will be cloned. The cloned channel will then appear directly below the original channel that is being cloned. This is very useful when you want to make a variation of an existing instrument that you are using and don't want to lose the original.

▶ **Channel select**:

The **Select** tab is the small green slit to the right of the kick channel in *Fig 3.6*.

1. Left-click on the green slit button currently engaged to select all the channels, and have the green slit button highlight all of your channels in your given pattern.

2. Right-click to select the additional channels, which includes your currently selected channel. Alternatively, you may press *Shift* and click on the desired channels.

3. Right-clicking on a channel select will also remove the channel selection.

4. Knowing which channels have been selected is crucial to understanding how to copy and paste channels or patterns and when you will send certain channels to the FL Studio Mixer. We will review these details in subsequent chapters. Also, multiple samples can be triggered at once via multiple MIDI triggers or controllers.

▶ **Steps**:

Left-click or right-click on the steps in the step sequencer (grey or reddish blocks) to trigger your sound or virtual instrument (refer to *Fig 3.2*).

How it works...

The beats per bar set the number of steps in each step sequencer pattern. When working your beats per bar with a standard 4/4 time pattern (which is mostly used in popular music genres such as Indie Rock, Pop, Alternative, EDM, and Hip Hop), you can set this number to **4**, **8**, **16**, **32**, or **64**. This will enable you to have a standard beats and bar pattern, and after engaging the Space bar while in pattern mode, your pattern will loop around to form a seamless loop. If you are working with a 3/4 time pattern, you may set your beats per bar for this pattern to the number **6** or **12**. The loop you form can happen very quickly, and that is a reason why FL Studio is one of the easiest programs to use.

Each pattern may have a different and individual beats per bar. You may set the number of beats per bar in the **GENERAL** settings of the song project (press *F10* and then go to **Project | GENERAL**). By using the Piano roll, you will eradicate this entire issue of setting individual beats per bar values because you will be able to stretch your notes infinitely.

You may have up to 999 patterns using FL Studio, and each pattern will incorporate as many channels as you desire.

Using the space bar is vital to working with the step sequencer in all phases of your music production. This will enable you to stop your current loop and restart it from the beginning so that you can revise the steps you have entered at the start of the sequence if you wish to do so. Alternatively, you can let the loop play through, and it will cycle back to the beginning.

You may add as many channels as you want to whichever patterns you desire in the step sequencer. Remember that these patterns will later be used to arrange and build your song in the FL Studio Playlist, which is covered at the start of *Chapter 5, Using the Playlist*. For example, pattern 1 may include only your kick drum pattern, and you may rename it to `Kick`; pattern 2 may include only your hi hat pattern, and you may rename it to `Hi Hat`; pattern 3 may be your virtual instrument violin pattern, and you may rename it to `Violin`; and pattern 4 may be a guitar bassline, and you may rename it to `Bassline`.

A key function in all of this is copying and pasting channel data in addition to cutting channel data (erasing the channel data in the step sequencer). Channel data is anything to the right of a channel. This can be MIDI data, audio, a Piano roll, automation data, controller data, and so on. You will want to use the channel **Select** button (small green slit) on the channel in question. For example, let's pretend you have many channels and many steps filled in the step sequencer, all within pattern 16. In an example of pattern 16, you could have a cymbal channel, a piano channel, and a shaker channel, all on separate channels, but within the same pattern 16.

In order to separate the sounds from the pattern, which will later be used in the FL Studio Playlist (*Chapter 5, Using the Playlist*) when building your song, you will want to use the channel **Select** green slit, press *Ctrl + X* to copy and delete it's sequencer data (because you are moving it elsewhere), navigate to a new pattern, and finally press *Ctrl + V* to paste it in. You may do this with multiple channels at once. You will not have to adjust the channel **Select** button in this process. It will remain in place on your given selected channel or channels. Using this method will allow you to work with one pattern of your choice when adding sounds and instruments and let you be creative with it. You will then have to separate the individual pieces and parts of your production by cutting and pasting channels or using the **Split by channel** feature covered later in this chapter. You can copy, paste, and cut channel data like you would with text in a Word document. Using the beats per bar and pattern selectors is all up to the user. How you divide your pieces and parts and arrange them is another crucial piece of the music production process.

The key features of working with the **Graph editor** are **Velocity** and **Shift**. The Graph editor can also adjust the panning and fine-tuning of the music file – using the **Fine pitch** function can make slightly flat instruments sound really cool. When working with the step sequencer, using the **Velocity** tab allows you to adjust the volume for each individual step on the step sequencer. **Velocity** is a tremendous tool for virtual instruments, guitars, and pianos because the lower the volume, the more soft and gentle the notes are conveyed. When you move the **Graph editor** to adjust the value of **Velocity**, you will be able to adjust the orange columns on each step in the step sequencer on a given channel. This will make things less robotic and add a human feel. Feel free to experiment with the velocity of your music in the **Graph editor**, and make sure you have the channel **Select** button engaged on the channel data that you want to adjust with the **Graph editor**. Another key feature is something you will find when you slide the **Graph editor** function all the way to the right. There you will find the **Shift** function, which offsets the timing of the notes ever so slightly. At a maximum **Shift** value, it will play the next step. Again, you will be able to adjust the columns of the **Graph editor**, which in this case will show in a blue column. The key reason for using the **Graph editor** is to adjust individual notes or events in lieu of working globally and affecting them all. The step sequencer is extremely intuitive when used this way because everything is located on one screen, and you don't have to navigate very far to make considerable adjustments to your music project. It's unbelievably powerful in its own right—just look under the proverbial hood!

Using the **Keyboard editor** on the step sequencer also makes it easy for the user to make quick changes to their music project. If you are using this, you are dealing with the tone and key of your sounds in any given channel. As discussed earlier, the **Keyboard editor** is a piano that has been turned on its side, and you may enter the piano notes by simply using your mouse. Note that using the **Keyboard editor** can come in handy when dealing with a multitude of sounds. You can adjust the key of your percussion or virtual instruments. Changing the pitch of an audio sample will adjust the playback speed. Changing a virtual instrument note will adjust the MIDI note value. Any note placed in the steps of the step sequencer can be manipulated with the **Keyboard editor**. Also, remember that each note that you press using your mouse in the **Keyboard editor** will automatically place a step in the step sequencer on your given channel.

Using the **Mute/Solo** button is something that is done during the mixing process. In FL Studio, the moment you start using the step sequencer, you are immediately immersed into the mixing process because you have control over the mute/solo feature, panning feature, and volume. Muting or soloing your channel can provide you with access to hear what your project sounds like with your channel, without your channel, and with only your channel. Soloing a channel can help when you really need to hear what is going on with your audio and in the cases of a vocal performance. Sometimes, you may hear a pop or click noise in your music project, and soloing something allows you to "find the culprit," so to speak. Soloing is also used when making equalization adjustments, which we will discuss when reviewing the FL Studio Mixer. When mixing, you will want to hear how your tracks/channels sound by themselves and also in the context of the entire mix. The content of your entire mix is incredibly important, so you may use muting or soloing, as you see fit, to build your music project and for the process of choosing your arrangement.

The channel panning and channel volume features are also crucial elements in any musical project. Panning will allow you to and interest to your song and place instruments tactfully to the left or right to make all of the elements of your song sound harmonious. You may also automate panning whenever you want to. We will review automation in *Chapter 10, Recording Automation*. The volume is arguably the most important part of mixing instruments because you want each channel to be at an optimal volume relative to all of your other channels. This also goes for when you have vocal tracks or any external instrument. Your vocals will need to "sit" well with all of the instruments in your project. Mixing instruments and vocals also includes additive or subtractive **equalization** (**EQ**), which will be reviewed in *Chapter 6, Using the FL Studio Mixer and Recording Audio*. You also want your percussion and all of the instrument channels to be set at the proper volume. Decreasing or increasing the volume on given channels is up to the musical creator and their creative taste. Holding down the *Ctrl* button while moving up or down with your mouse allows you to adjust the volume in smaller increments with more control.

Using the steps in the step sequencer gives you immediate feedback of the steps you have placed. This is all about left-clicking to input data and right-clicking to erase a step. You may also click-and-drag with either mouse button to easily fill or erase successive steps.

Note that your main project tempo in FL Studio is directly correlated to the steps in the step sequencer. If you have a drum beat with MIDI data, this can be slowed down or sped up by adjusting your project tempo.

You may also use the *Alt* + up/down arrow key to move your selected channel(s) up or down in the step sequencer. This may help organize your project. You can find this option under the **CHANNEL** menu in the main window of FL Studio. The options will show **Move selected up** or **Move selected down**.

There's more...

Often, you may want to start your project by adding channels with percussion and starting your drum beat. This means that you may add channels that include a kick, hi hat, snare, cymbal, and other percussion and enter the steps as you see fit. After this, you may add virtual instruments, sounds, and then a bassline. On the other hand, it is also handy to start with a MIDI part or harmony, add some other instruments, and lastly make your drum beat. In this fashion, you can really pick percussion that fits your existing harmonies and bassline. Nevertheless, some people enjoy starting with the drum beat and adding their harmonies and notes later on. Of course, you can record live music to a click track with many instrument players to develop the human chemistry and vibe. Again, there are no true rules in music production; use whatever method works best for you.

 Keep in mind that many people prefer to use the **Piano roll** option after adding channels in the step sequencer. We will review the **Piano roll** in *Chapter 4, Building Your Song.*

See also

▸ *Working with the Graph editor*

▸ *Using the Keyboard editor*

▸ The *Using the Piano roll* recipe in *Chapter 4, Building Your Song*

▸ The *Using patterns to build a song* recipe in *Chapter 5, Using the Playlist*

Exploring Channel settings

Working with FL Studio channels and the settings inside them allows you to tweak your sounds with a plethora of options and quick presets. Generally, a **Sample/shape properties** tab (**SMP**), an **Instrument properties** tab (**INS**), a **Miscellaneous** tab (**MISC**), and a **Special tools & functions** tab (**FUNC**) is visible when you click on a given channel. When you are working with virtual instruments, virtual plugins, or any type of software synth, you will find a **PLUGIN** tab, that is, the plugin properties. In this tab, you will be working with the settings and parameters of your third-party plugin; this means that you will be able to use software synths and virtual instruments from multiple manufacturers and sources, including the free **Virtual Studio Technology** (**VSTs**) available online. With third-party plugins and free plugins, you will see that a screen readout pops up when you click the **PLUGIN** tab, and it generally allows you access to presets, parameters, knobs, and the virtual keybed or keyboard. The free plugins are designed by coders, geeks, underground designers, and those that believe in freeware. Most VST plugins and software synths are .dll files. There are always exceptions to the rule as VST3 plugins use a .vst extension. We previously reviewed how to install virtual plugins and effects in *Chapter 1, Configuring FL Studio*. With plugins that are part of the FL Studio factory installation, you will have access to the **PLUGIN** tab, which has immediate parameters and control modifiers.

Getting ready

As discussed earlier, your channels are the backbone of your music project and contain all of the sounds that you are using. Press *F6* to bring up the step sequencer, or go to the **VIEW** menu and select **Step sequencer**. A third way to bring up the step sequencer is to use your mouse and click the second button from the left in *Fig 3.9*. It shows the tiny square steps inside the step sequencer. In order to bring up the channel settings and subfolders, click directly on a channel.

Fig 3.9

How to do it...

Let's take a look at the channel settings inside the channels on the step sequencer, which can be considered subtabs.

> **The SMP tab**:
>
> The **SMP** tab is the place where you will use audio manipulation tools such as pitch shift, time stretching, normalizing, and reversing. The following screenshot shows all the **Channel settings** tab options:

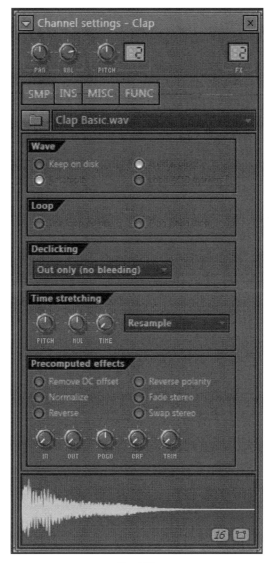

Fig 3.10

1. Click on a channel in the FL Studio step sequencer. If the channel is an audio sample, it will default on the **SMP** tab as shown in the previous screenshot. With virtual instruments, it will default to **PLUGIN**.

2. Use the panning (**PAN**), volume (**VOL**), and pitch (**PITCH**) knobs based on your creative taste. Again, with the volume, make sure your level is not clipping. These knobs may be automated like any other knob in FL Studio, which we will review in *Chapter 10, Recording Automation*.

3. In the *Fig 3.10*, the channel has the name `Clap Basic.wav`. Click on the folder symbol directly to the left of that to bring up your computer file hierarchy to see where your given sound is located. Also, use the folder symbol to change the sample.

4. Click and explore the precomputed effects at the bottom of the window and the color of the small circles will change to orange when selected. They require no computational power to be played, which makes them super useful. You can hear the changes while viewing the visual feedback of your given waveform at the bottom of the **SMP** section. Since they are precomputed effects, you cannot automate these knobs. Automation will be covered in *Chapter 10, Recording Automation*.

5. Click and explore the knobs at the bottom to shape your wave form readout and modify your sound. Many of these knobs create sounds and chords that are much smoother. These knobs can be automated by being drawn with your mouse movements or using a MIDI controller.

6. Adjust the knobs under the **Time stretching** area. These knobs can speed up, slow down, or change the pitch of your waveform. We will review crucial tools involving time stretching in *Chapter 7, Sampling Using Edison*. Right-click on **TIME** to automatically apply a specific bar length to your sample.

7. Click on the waveform to hear a preview of your current sound properties.

8. Right-click on the waveform to bring up the additional options.

▶ **The INS tab**:

The **TIME** section of the **INS** tab has the shape and envelope of your sine wave samples—you may also adjust it to **TNS** (tension). The following screenshot explores this option:

Fig 3.11

1. Click on the **INS** (instrument) tab within your channel settings. It will default to the volume properties of your sound envelope. A red drawing will be visible, which you can adjust or right-click to toggle between **TIME** and **TNS**. The **TNS** screen will display a from drawing and adjust the curve between the points, as shown in the following screenshot:

Fig 3.12

2. In *Fig 3.12*, you can see the **TIME** mode, which has turned the **DEL**, **ATT**, **DEC**, and **REL** knobs all the way to the left. This will help with triggering samples when you press and hold them on a MIDI keyboard, with your mouse, or in the Piano roll. When you press the knobs quickly and briefly, the sample should cut off completely. This means that you also have this cutoff ability in the FL Studio Piano roll, which will be reviewed in *Chapter 4, Building Your Song*. Be sure to look at the subtab and envelope values of **PAN**, **VOL**, **CUT**, **RES**, and **PITCH**. The small orange light in the left-hand corner must be engaged to make each envelope active. The **PAN** option does not support an envelope.

3. The envelope of your sine wave in the **TIME** mode includes **Attack, Decay, Sustain, and Release** (**ADSR**). Attack is the time it takes to go from the minimum to the maximum. Decay is the time it takes to go from the maximum to the sustain level. Sustain is the level you stay at for as long as you hold the key (or sustain pedal). Release is the time it takes to go from wherever you are to the minimum.

4. Envelope parameters are modified over time per event.

5. Click on **TNS** to adjust the tension with the same knobs. You can also right-click on either the **TIME** or **TNS** knob to select either. In the tension edit mode (**TNS**), you can adjust the curves of the purple sine wave drawing.

Further shape your sound using the **Low Frequency Oscillator** (**LFO**) and Filter areas. This will modulate your sound. An LFO modulating an oscillator will produce vibrato, which is a frequency modulation. An LFO modulating a filter will produce an auto wave effect, which is a timbre modulation. An LFO modulating an amp will produce tremolo, which is an amplitude modulation. You may choose between sinc waves, triangle waves, and square waves.

The filter section controls the lows, mids, and highs of the given sound. In the real world, this is the reason you can hear the bass and thumping from a neighbor's apartment or a dance club on the street. When the doors to a dance club are opened, the music's high end is released. Standing outside, it is only thumping that you will hear. Mod X is the filter cutoff frequency that can cut the highs with a low pass filter and cut the lows with a high pass filter. After the cutoff point, the filter will start doing its job. Mod Y is the filter resonance that controls the ringing of the frequencies at the cutoff. In LFOs, these parameters are modified over time, periodically.

▶ **The MISC tab**:

The following steps will show you the settings for the MISC tab:

1. The **VOL** knob under **Levels adjustment** can amplify your sound, in addition to all of the other volumes. The step sequencer volume knob goes up to 100 percent. This knob in the **MISC** tab goes up to a whopping 200 percent. The **Levels adjustment** area is handy for automation, which will be reviewed in *Chapter 10, Recording Automation*. The following screenshot shows the **Levels adjustment** tab:

Fig 3.13

2. The **Cut by** feature is found in samplers such as the MPC, software samplers such as the FPC, and Battery. Usually, notes will roll into each other. Click on **Cut** to make the signal stop and cut it off when the next note hits.

3. Multiple notes are handled through the **Polyphony** section. This is the maximum amount of voices/notes that you can use simultaneously. If you lower this number, you will save CPU power and increase computer performance.

4. On the keyboard at the bottom, you can change the channel root note to something different from the main project by right-clicking on the seekbar (the main project always defaults to **C5** at a specific place). Set the key range by clicking-and-dragging the seekbar.

Let's see how to get a note that glides/slides into the next note using the following steps:

1. Engage the Mono button under the **Polyphony** area, and the small circle will turn orange. Mono makes it so only one note can be played at a time (no chords).

2. Adjust the **SLIDE** knob to the right of the **Mono** button.

3. Hold down a note with your left finger and then simultaneously click on another note(s) with your right finger to hear the effect you have just added. You may use your QWERTY keyboard or a MIDI controller to trigger your notes.

4. Move the **SLIDE** knob further to the right in order to have a more drastic effect between keys/notes.

▶ **The FUNC tab**:

Let's take a look at the **FUNC** tab, which includes many options to process and shape your sound, as shown in the following screenshot:

Fig 3.14—presets for Echo delay / fat mode

1. Click on the small triangle sign in *Fig 3.14* next to **Echo delay / fat mode**. This will populate some presets to further shape your sound.

Fig 3.15

2. Explore the **Arpeggiator** area. An arpeggiator will automatically add a specific sequence of notes to your instrument, generally in an ascending or descending order. It could help inspire you if you are not the best keyboard player in the world. You may click next to the **CHORD** area, and FL Studio will populate it with multiple chords, which you will be able to choose for arpeggiation. When using a chord, the arpeggiator will focus on that particular key range and apply an automatic sequence of notes. Explore the areas next to the **OFF** button, in addition to the **Slide**, **TIME** (in the hint bar it is shown as **Arpeggio time**), and **GAT** (in the hint bar it is shown as **Arpeggio gate**) buttons.

3. Select from the choice of chords first and then experiment with the arpeggio directions, which can go up and down your keyboard in various fashions. The arpeggio directions can be clicked by selecting any option directly next to the **OFF** button.

4. Use the **OFS** (offset) button to fine time shift your sound, which will move things over in time ever so slightly. This can help with your groove and make things less robotic. This is under the **TIME** area at the bottom left.

▶ **The Plugin Tab (third party)**:

The **PLUGIN** tab will appear on plugins purchased from FL Studio, third-party software purchased from any manufacturer, or free plugins found online. It will also pop out on a graphical interface, as shown in the following screenshot, and then explore steps for the **PLUGIN** tab after that:

Fig 3.16

1. Click on the **PLUGIN** tab after loading a VST channel. You can load a channel by selecting **Add one** from the main **CHANNELS** menu or by right-clicking on an existing sequencer channel and selecting **Insert** or **Replace**.

2. Your virtual interface will pop up and you will be able to press any keybed with your mouse, QWERTY keyboard, or MIDI controller.

3. Use the **MISC** and **FUNC** tabs like any other channel according to your creative taste.

4. In *Fig 3.16*, you have clicked on the regular **PLUGIN** tab in your FL Studio Channel settings, after which the **Sytrus** interface will appear. Sytrus is an available upgrade for FL Studio, but you could download a demo version too.

► **The Plugin tab (default)**

Factory virtual instruments are included in FL Studio's default installation. The **PLUGIN** tab will not pop out on a graphical interface, but the functions and parameters , shown in the next steps, can be tweaked directly from the **PLUGIN** tab as shown in the following screenshot:

Fig 3.17

1. Select the **CHANNELS** menu (the main window in FL Studio) and go to **Add one | 3x Osc** to make a 3x Osc channel. You can also right-click on an existing sequencer channel and select **Insert** or **Replace**.

2. When you click on the channel, the **PLUGIN** tab shows immediate access to the keyboard, settings, and parameters.

3. Use the FL Studio Browser and open up the folder Channel presets.

4. Click on the 3x Osc folder to open up the various presets of sounds for the 3x Osc virtual instrument.

5. Right-click on the preset or patch to send the preset you want to the **3x Osc** channel. You may also left-click, hold, and drag the preset directly on top of the **3x Osc** channel or let the preset go directly on top of the parameters shown in *Fig 3.17*.

6. The same method will work for the TS404 bassline synthesizer.

How it works...

The **SMP** tab is the tab that shows your waveform, file hierarchy, and time stretching information. We will review key ways to work with time stretching in *Chapter 7, Sampling Using Edison*. The precomputed effects on the **Sample** tab are quite handy because you can normalize and reverse your sound. Normalizing will boost the volume (or normalize the volume so the peaks are at the same level) of any given sample or sound, and may help when you need to beef up your sound. Reversing is an awesome tool, which can be used based on your creative taste. When you right-click on the waveform in the **SMP** tab, you are able to further edit your sound using Edison. When you select edit after right-clicking on your waveform, FL Studio automatically opens up Edison. You may also use the knobs above your waveform to tweak it and view immediate feedback about your changes on the waveform image.

The **INS** tab is where the true audio engineers will go, although all you really need are good ears and a willingness to experiment with different parameters. You can come up with some truly interesting sounds here. This allows you to shape your sound based on how long you hold down a note for and when you let go of it.

The **MISC** tab has your levels, **Cut by**, and **Polyphony**. The **FUNC** tab has interesting effects for echo and delay, in addition to a very intuitive arpeggiator. All four of these areas allow the user to modify their sound and use it in creative ways. The **PLUGIN** tabs are used to open up virtual instruments and add harmonies and sounds to your music project.

There's more...

You can experiment with sounds by right-clicking on a channel and selecting **Clone**. In this way, you can keep your original channel, mute it, but then see how it sounds with other parameters engaged.

If you have adjusted many channel parameters and want to keep your adjusted sound, knobs, and settings to be used at a later date, you may select the small triangle at the very top of any **Channel settings** window. This will allow you to save your channel by clicking on **Save channel state as...**, and you may then save it in the `Channel presets` folder in the FL Studio Browser. In this manner, you can bring up the sound that you really liked within any project in FL Studio and then tweak it from there yet again (refer to the top-left corner in *Fig 3.10*). All channel settings automatically save on the current music project you are working on. This enables you to create a collection of sounds that you are proud of.

Also, remember that you can *group* your channels to bunch certain ones of the same sort together based on your music project. FL Studio also does this for you automatically, which will show in the bottom left-hand corner of the step sequencer.

See also

▸ The *Sending a channel to a mixer slot* recipe

▸ The *Adding virtual instruments* recipe in *Chapter 4, Building Your Song*

Sending a channel to a mixer slot

Although you have seen the plethora of options included in the FL Studio channel settings, sending a channel to a mixer slot will allow superior control over your sound. The FL Studio Mixer will allow you to use gain, equalization, compression, reverb, delay, and a multitude of other FL Studio factory effects or third-party effect plugins. When you want to group instruments together, you can send them all to one mixer slot, thereby creating common gain control. Equalization is very important because you can add (boost) or subtract (cut) certain frequencies to make certain elements of your song stand out and be clearer for your listeners. We will review this in detail in the *Adding effects and your effect chain* recipe in *Chapter 6, Using the FL Studio Mixer and Recording Audio*. The FL Studio Mixer will also allow you to view the level of all your pieces and parts in a more organized way.

Getting ready

You will want to have the step sequencer open so you can view your channels. To view the FL Studio Mixer, you may press *F9*. Alternatively, you may use the **VIEW** menu to select the **Mixer** option or click on the furthest symbol on the right, as shown in *Fig 3.18*. This icon represents the levels of your different channels / tracks / audio stems / FX slots in the FL Studio Mixer.

Fig 3.18

How to do it...

Let's have a look at the different methods to send a channel to a mixer slot.

▸ **Standard method**:

1. Click on a channel in the step sequencer to open up **Channel settings** as shown in the following screenshot:

Fig 3.19

2. Look to the upper right-hand corner of your given channel setting where you will find a small box labeled **FX**.

3. Hover you mouse over the **FX** area, and click, hold, and drag up or down to adjust the number of the **FX** slot/number.

4. In *Fig 3.19*, we adjusted the **FX** slot number to represent the number **1**.

5. The level/volume of the kick channel will now show up in the column **Insert 1** of the FL Studio Mixer.

6. Right-click on your column in the FL Studio Mixer, and select **Rename** to rename your FX slot as you see fit. We renamed Insert 1 to Kick in *Fig 3.19*.

A quicker shortcut for this whole process is to double-click and then hold the **FX** button, which will automatically pull up the FL Studio Mixer. At this point, you can drag the **FX** button to find an open slot. If your channel is already in a mixer slot, double-clicking the FX slot will allow you to quickly pull the channel up on the mixer.

▸ **Alternate method – one channel at a time**:

1. Select the channel you want to send to the mixer by clicking on the channel **Select** (small green slit).

2. Click on the mixer slot that you want the channel to be sent to.

3. Hold down *Ctrl + L* to automatically send the channel to the mixer slot that you have selected.

4. FL Studio will automatically give the mixer slot the same name as your selected channel.

▸ **Alternate Method – multiple channels in succession for organization and quickness**:

The following screenshot and the steps after it describe how to send multiple channels to the mixer at once:

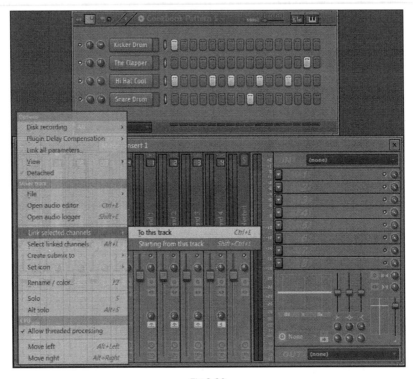

Fig 3.20

1. Use the channel **Select** (small green slit) and highlight more than one channel by right-clicking on it.

2. Click on the insert slot you want to start/match up your channels.

3. Click on the small triangle in the upper left-hand corner of the FL Studio Mixer.

4. Select **Starting from this track** and FL Studio will automatically add your selected channels in succession on the FL Studio Mixer.

5. You may also use the *Shift + Ctrl + L* function, as shown in *Fig 3.20*, in lieu of using your mouse.

In *Fig 3.20*, we selected the four channels with the green slit and then clicked on **Insert 1**. When we use the **Starting from this track** option in *Fig 3.20*, FL Studio will automatically send the said channels starting at **Insert 1**. This means **Insert 1** will be **Kicker Drum**, **Insert 2** will be **The Clapper**, **Insert 3** will be **Hi Hat Cool**, and **Insert 4** will be **Snare Drum**. The succession of channels from top to bottom in the step sequencer matches the horizontal succession (left to right) in the FL Studio Mixer. If you haven't already renamed any insert tracks, the name of your channels will automatically be carried over to the FX slots in the FL Studio Mixer.

How it works...

Sending a channel or channels to mixer slots allows you to control each part of your project more precisely. During the creative process, you may add lots of channels to the step sequencer and enter data inside the step sequencer steps or piano roll. Because the creative process happens very quickly, you may not have the time to separate each track in the FL Studio Mixer. This is where the **Starting from this track** functionality comes into play. It can come in very handy if you wish to consecutively send and automatically separate your channels when you are ready to send them to the mixer. The **Starting from this track** option does the "manual labor" out of sending one channel at a time to the FL Studio Mixer, but there are no true rules. The way you send channels to the FL Studio Mixer is based on your personal workflow.

If you know that your workflow usually follows the same trend, you can also save an FL Studio project as a file/template of your choice. In this manner, you can set up as many channels as you want and have them routed/sent to wherever you want in the FL Studio Mixer. You can then adjust the sounds you are using by changing/replacing them and then saving your project as a new name. This will result in a streamlined template for your workflow, but the actual music project will vary differently from project to project. A template will allow you to make a fundamental skeleton and could help aide in the process. You can save a template as an `.flp` file, like any other FL Studio project file.

There's more...

If you like to use your mouse and scroll through the different numbers in your channel settings that match up / to the FX slots in the FL Studio Mixer, you will see the highlighted area (visual feedback) in the FL Studio Mixer change as you scroll your mouse on a given number. You will want to have both the **Channels setting** window and FL Studio Mixer open at the same time to view the visual feedback. Otherwise, you can use the quick tip of double-clicking on an **FX** button, which automatically brings up the mixer.

You can also click on the small triangle in the upper left-hand corner of the FL Studio Mixer, select **Detached**, and drag/move the FL Studio Mixer to a separate monitor/screen/TV/ display. This will give you a large view of the FL Studio Mixer, and you will not have to open and close it within one screen any longer. This will help with your workflow and organization. In order to automatically assign your channel to an available mixer slot, click on the upper left-hand triangle (**Channel options**) on any channel settings window and select **Assign free mixer track**.

See also

▶ The *Adding effects and your effect chain* recipe in *Chapter 6, Using the FL Studio Mixer and Recording Audio*

▶ The *Perfecting equalization* recipe in *Chapter 6, Using the FL Studio Mixer and Recording Audio*

▶ The *Export your audio stems* recipe in *Chapter 8, Exporting and Rendering your Project*

Working with the Graph editor

Within the step sequencer, there is a very powerful tool called the Graph editor. This means that you will have access to change individual steps on the step sequencer by adjusting the panning, velocity (volume), release, filter cutoff, filter resonance, pitch, and time shifting. This is a great tool if you want to change the sound of the drums and percussion. You can greatly enhance the mood of your music by adjusting these nuances within the drums and percussion.

Getting ready

To get started with using the Graph editor in the step sequencer, you only need to have the step sequencer open with some channel data for your steps.

How to do it...

1. Open up a step sequencer by pressing the *F6* key, or simply browse with your mouse to the **VIEW** menu and select **Step sequencer**. You will want to have data in your steps which are generally drums or percussion based. The following screenshot shows the **Graph editor**:

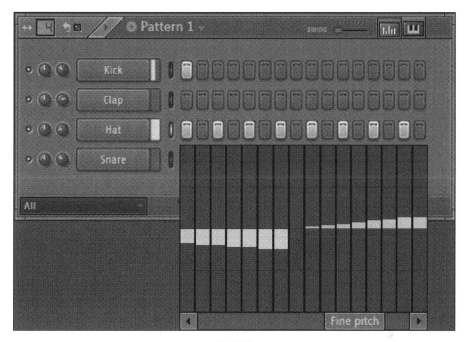

Fig 3.21

2. Click on the small box in the upper right-hand corner of the step sequencer. This is the graph-like image in between the **SWING** and small piano symbols.

3. Adjust the event properties by moving the bottom slider. Click on the columns to adjust your given steps

4. Hold *Ctrl* while clicking-and-dragging the columns to interpose values. Right-click inside the editor to engage an incremental adjustment and drag your mouse to draw ascending or descending steps.

5. Make sure you have engaged the channel you want to edit with the Graph editor. In *Fig 3.21*, you will be working with the **Hat** channel. The right-click method has been used to create "value ramps."

How it works...

When you have access to pan (left-hand side and right-hand side of your speakers or headphones) every piece of data in the step sequencer, you can immediately tweak your song, which will give you interesting results. Panning will allow you to separate your instruments and/or percussion to have a well-balanced music production.

Velocity, also known as volume, will add a human feel to your project and make the level of your channel varied when it needs to be. Velocity will also add an aggressive or soft feel to instruments such as the piano and guitar. It is the power at which a note is struck and not just the volume. For example, when using a guitar instrument, a very high velocity will add a strong pluck sound while a low velocity will make it sound like strumming. This is easy to distinguish when using a MIDI controller with touch-sensitive keys. The hard or soft manner in which you press the keys will add certain distinctions as you work with the same sound patch.

Using the Mod X and Mod Y functions can help you add filter effects and sweeping frequencies. Mod X is the filter cutoff and Mod Y is the filter resonance. For example, on a snare or clap channel, try lowering the Mod X between 7 percent and 50 percent and then adjust the Mod Y to around 25 percent. Fill in every single step on the step sequencer so you can hear the changes. The Mod X and Mod Y columns are very sensitive, so the simplest adjustment could considerably change the sound. The pitch property is used mostly for drums and percussion, but you may try to adjust other instruments with the fine pitch property (for other instruments, you can simply use **Keyboard editor** or **Piano roll**). Another great way to add a human feel is to adjust the time shift with the **Shift** parameter. Adding all these properties in the Graph editor is vital to connecting to your music project and having it connect to your listeners.

There's more...

When you are working with a kick drum, you may want to use the **Shift** parameter to shift the sample to the right, in the time scale. This means that you will add a tiny bit of the blue color to the given column when you use the **Shift** parameter on a kick drum in the step sequencer. Small adjustments that change the timing of when the step sequencer plays your samples can be the difference between a good song and great song. You can also easily change the feel of an entire song just by adjusting the timing and velocity of the kick drum. The same goes for all percussion, which means that there are no rules. The more experimenting you do with the Graph editor, the better you will be at knowing how to shape your sounds based on your creative vision.

See also

- ▶ The *Guaging fundamental areas* recipe
- ▶ The *Sending a channel to a mixer slot* recipe

> ▶ The *Working with MIDI controllers and MIDI pads* recipe in *Chapter 4, Building Your Song*

> ▶ The *Humanizing with the OFS knob* recipe in *Chapter 9, Humanizing Your Song*

Using the Keyboard editor

The Keyboard editor will allow you to have quick access to each note/pitch value in the step sequencer when working with "steps."

Getting ready

To get started with using the Keyboard editor in the step sequencer, you only need to have the step sequencer open with some channel data on your given steps.

How to do it...

1. Engage the channel **Select** button (small green slit) or click on a channel as shown in the following screenshot:

Fig 3.22

2. Click on the small box that looks like a piano key in the upper right-hand corner of the step sequencer.

3. Click on the note/pitch that you want to use for your given channel.

4. Use the channel **Select** (small green slit) to change the channels and still have the **Keyboard editor** open.

5. Click on the small box above each column of the piano notes to engage a slide/portamento effect. When engaged, it will show a small symbol that looks like half a triangle. In the previous figure, the portamento effect has been engaged on three notes in the Bell channel.

6. Hold down *Ctrl* to drag all of the notes at once. They will stay relative to each other, and you will be able to drag all of them up or down at the same time.

7. Left-click and drag on the piano columns up or down to find notes/pitches further up and down the piano.

8. Right-click to erase the data in the Keyboard editor and associated step.

How it works...

The Keyboard editor will work for any virtual plugin, drums, or percussion. You can change the pitch/notes of the data currently being entered as "steps," or you can click on a piano note and it will automatically add the step in your associated column. You can click-and-drag on each column and hear the sound output of each note as you drag up or down. This allows for immediate variations of notes without the need to open up the FL Studio Piano roll.

See also

▸   The *Gauging fundamental areas* recipe

▸   The *Adding virtual instruments* recipe in *Chapter 4, Building Your Song*

▸   The *Using the Piano roll* recipe in *Chapter 4, Building Your Song*

Working with patterns

The actual arrangement of your music project in FL Studio is based on the use of patterns. Patterns are, of course, made up of all your different channels and sounds in the step sequencer. Once you have differentiated all of your different patterns, the arrangement of these patterns will be placed into the FL Studio playlist, which will be reviewed in *Chapter 4, Building Your Song*.

Getting ready

To start working with patterns, you will only need to have your step sequencer open. You may do this by pressing the *F6* key.

How to do it...

1. Enter data for any of your given channels on a specific pattern. In *Fig 3.23*, **PAT 1** is being worked on. You can observe this by looking at the area next to the right of the **TEMPO** information or by looking at the top of the step sequencer where it reads **Pattern 1**.

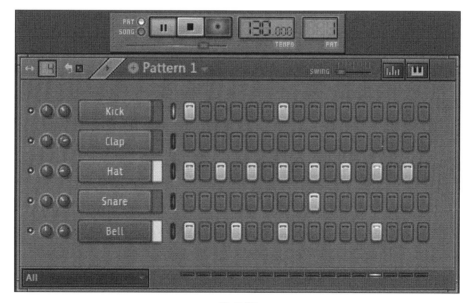

Fig 3.23

2. Press the space bar or click play in FL Studio. At the very bottom of the step sequencer, you will see a small orange area, which the hint bar refers to as a "playing step." This will scroll left to right and then repeat/loop as your pattern returns to the start. The playing step helps you to visually see which pattern, if any, is currently playing. The preceding screenshot explores these details.

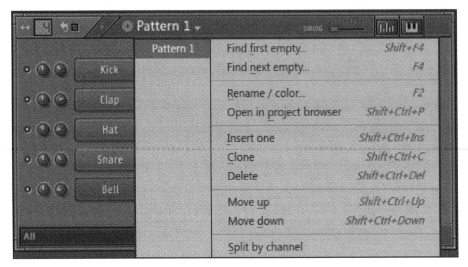

Fig 3.24

3. Click on the drop-down menu to bring up the additional options. You have clicked the text titled **Pattern 1** at the top of the step sequencer, as shown in *Fig 3.24*.

4. Select **Split by channel** to split each channel into a separate pattern.

5. If we select **Split by channel**, it will separate all of the channel data in the current pattern into subsequent patterns from top to bottom.

6. In *Fig 3.24*, all the channel data is currently on **Pattern 1**. If we select **Split by channel** while on **Pattern 1**, FL Studio will make **Pattern 1** include only the **Kick** data, **Pattern 2** will now only have the **Hat** data, **Pattern 3** will only have the **Snare** data, and **Pattern 4** will only have the **Bell** data.

7. After using the **Split by channel** function, as listed in *Fig 3.24*, **Pattern 1** in the drop-down box will now show **Kick**, **Hat**, **Snare**, and **Bell** per the figure below. FL Studio will automatically rename your patterns based on the channel names (from top to bottom) and automatically split the channels into successive patterns. The following screenshot explores these options:

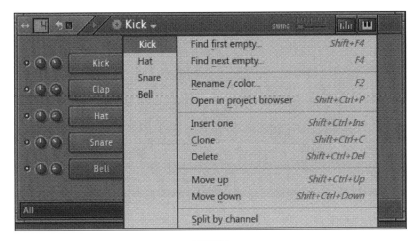

Fig 3.25

How it works...

Patterns are copied and pasted or the **Split by channel** functionality is used basically for one purpose: to separate the many pieces, parts, and sounds of your music project in order to make a full music production. This will happen when you arrange your different patterns in the FL Studio playlist and engage the **SONG** button under the **PAT** button near your main play button. We will review this more in depth *in the Using patterns to build your song* recipe in *Chapter 5, Using the Playlist*. You may choose to work on one single pattern at the onset of the creative process because you may be adding many channels very quickly and coming up with percussion or instrument parts. After this, you can use **Split by channel** or manually cut and paste your channel(s) to separate patterns. In this manner, you can create sections for your intro, verses, chorus, bridge, outro, or any sections that you deem fit for your music project.

See also

- ▶ The *Comparing pattern and song mode* recipe in *Chapter 4, Building Your Song*
- ▶ The *Using patterns to build your song* recipe in *Chapter 5, Using the Playlist*

4

Building Your Song

In this chapter, we will cover:

- ▸ Working with rhythm and percussion
- ▸ Adding virtual instruments
- ▸ Working with MIDI controllers and MIDI pads
- ▸ Comparing pattern and song mode
- ▸ Using the Piano roll feature

Introduction

Building your song in FL Studio allows you the freedom to add drums, harmonies, sounds, and instruments. This will usually come in the form of virtual instruments, MP3 files, WAV files, software plugins, and the like. You will be adding all of these elements as channels in the step sequencer, as discussed in previous chapters. There are many ways to record your data into the step sequencer. You can use your mouse and draw your chosen notes into the **Piano roll** feature, physically play and perform a melody using a MIDI keyboard, press the keys on your actual computer (QWERTY) keyboard, or manually enter each step within the step sequencer. The step sequencer also has the added functionality of using the **Graph editor** and **Keyboard editor**. Some people prefer to perform their melodies using a MIDI keyboard because of the hands-on feel and touch sensitivity of the keys, which can later be edited and quantized if certain notes are slightly out of sync.

Working with rhythm and percussion

Although each part of your song is tremendously important to the final outcome, working with rhythm and percussion is debatably the most important part of your song. If your drums, kicks, snares, hi hats, and other percussion are weak, you song won't stand the test of time and won't sound very good to your listeners. Rhythm and drum samples can sound very different from genre to genre, so you want to pick these properly. That being said, you can also experiment with a fusion of sounds and mix genres to create your own sound.

Getting ready

To get started adding rhythm and percussion, you will want to have the step sequencer and FL Studio browser opened. Press *F6* to bring up the step sequencer, or go to the **VIEW** menu and select **View step sequencer**. A third way to bring up the step sequencer is to click on the second button from the left in the console shown in the following screenshot. It shows the tiny square steps inside of the step sequencer. You may press *F8* to bring up the FL Studio Browser, or go to the **View** menu and select **Browser**. A third way to bring up the **Browser** window is to click on the fourth button from the left in the console, as shown in the following screenshot:

Fig 4.1

How to do it...

The following steps will explore the important functions required to work with rhythm and percussion:

1. Go to the main **OPTIONS** menu and then to **Project general settings**. There, under **Time division**, you may set your main **Bar** and **Beat** for the entire music project, as shown in the following screenshot:

Fig 4.2

2. If you need to override your main **Bar** and **Beat** settings with a different scaling, set **beats per bar for this pattern** for your specific pattern. In *Fig 4.3*, this is set to **4** and shown in the upper-left-hand corner of the step sequencer.

> A song structure in 4/4 time (most popular song signature) is usually by 4, 8, or 16 bar loops. If you want a longer drum loop with more variation, you should set it to 16 bars. Nevertheless, the drum loop can actually last as long as you need when sending channels into the FL Studio Piano roll. This is reviewed in the final recipe of this chapter, *Using the Piano roll feature*.

3. Set your FL Studio project tempo, which is signified as **Beats Per Minute** (**BPM**). The BPM tempo adjuster is located to the right of the transport controls, which are the play, stop, and record buttons. The following screenshot shows the options for the **Percussion** menu:

Fig 4.3

4. Add channels to the step sequencer. This will usually be a kick, snare, hi hat, shaker, bongo, cymbal, sound effects, or any type of sound you want to utilize as percussion. You may drag samples from the browser to the gray, blank area on the step sequencer to add them. You may also right-click on a sample inside of the browser and select **Open in new channel**.

5. Right-click on a **Hat** or **Shaker** channel as per *Fig 4.4* and select **Fill each 2 steps**.

6. Fill in your step data for **Kick**, **Snare**, and **Percussion**. The following screenshot shows the step sequencer entries:

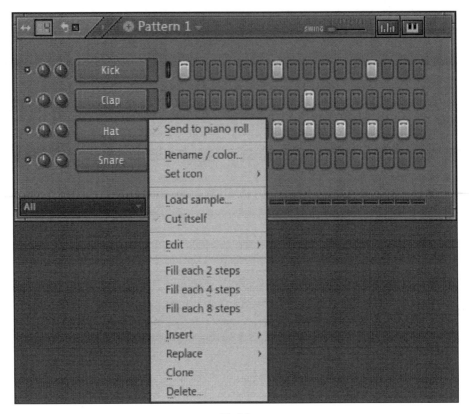

Fig 4.4

Once you have step data on any percussion channel in the step sequencer, there are two ways to swap and replace the data with a new sound. These two ways are mentioned in the upcoming steps. The following screenshot shows the FL Studio Browser:

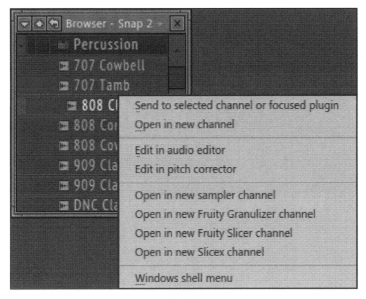

Fig 4.5

7. Swap current data in any channel with a new sound from the FL Studio in order to test the different options. This is done by right-clicking on a sound in the FL Studio Browser or you can just engage any channel by clicking on the small green slit areas. selecting **Send to selected channel or focused plugin**, as shown in *Fig 4.5.*

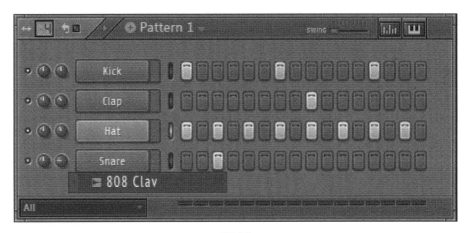

Fig 4.6

8. Another way to swap current data in a channel is to left-click on any sound in the **Browser** window and drag it to the channel you want to swap. In *Fig 4.6*, we dragged a sample from the **Browser** window and were about to swap it with the **Hat** channel. When you hover your mouse over the channel you want to swap, it will show the channel in orange and then you can release your mouse button. The **808 Clav** WAV sound will replace the **Hat** channel. Step data will remain unchanged, but the actual sound will be replaced/swapped.

9. Press the Space bar to start and stop your current pattern.

How it works...

You may add as many channels as you want for your percussion and rhythm. It helps with the creative process to "go with the flow" and keep adding elements to your music project in a single pattern. You may then use the **Split by channel** method, as discussed in *Chapter 3, Working with the Step Sequencer and Channels*, in order to separate all of these elements for your song arrangement. You will also want to set your **Preview mixer track** as discussed in *Chapter 2, Using Browser*. This will help to test out sounds before adding them as a channel to the step sequencer. You can also just simply click on sounds in the **Browser** window to test them out, but the **Preview mixer track** will help you to at least adjust the volume on previewed sounds. Please remember to work with the various parameters in **Graph editor** as well as **Keyboard editor**. This will allow you to enhance and fine-tune individual notes of percussion and rhythm—not just a global adjustment. Also remember to open up your **CHANNEL** settings on any given channel in order to modify and alter your sounds. If you are constantly starting with the same processes in your workflow, you can save your project as a template. In this manner, you can take some of the tedious nature out of the equation. Remember to clone channels (right-click on a channel for the **Clone** option) if you want to experiment with different options of the same sound as well as copy and paste data from one channel to the next.

There's more...

The rhythm and percussion section of your music production is the backbone of your music production. This can drastically alter the mood and genre of your music. Once your drums and rhythm are established, you will have a nice base to work with and then you can add your bass line, instruments, and other harmonies such as the piano, violin, guitar, and various synthesized sounds. That being said, sometimes you will want to do the opposite. You may start with an extremely simple hi hat or shaker that acts as a metronome and then begin your instrument melodies. Once you have some melodies in place, it can be very rewarding to add a kick and snare that compliments the mood and tone of your melody. If you enjoy adding your kick and snare later, make sure your melodies are at a suitable volume. If you start with a harmony that is too low in volume and then add your rhythm, the volume may not be loud enough. That is why you must start with the kick, snare, and hi hat first—so you can set it at a suitable volume and then add your instruments. Nonetheless, do what you feel is right during your creative process. Your volume level is crucial here because after you start with one sound, you will be building other sounds around it.

See also

▶ The *Getting new sounds in Browser* recipe in *Chapter 2, Using Browser*

▶ The *Exploring Channel settings* recipe in *Chapter 3, Working with Step Sequencer and Channels*

▶ The *Sending a channel to a mixer slot* recipe in *Chapter 3, Working with Step Sequencer and Channels*

▶ The *Perfecting equalization* recipe in *Chapter 6, Using the FL Studio Mixer and Recording Audio*

Adding virtual instruments

Adding virtual instruments, software sounds, and software plugins allow you to make inspirational harmonies in your music production. Usually, you will find presets that you can scroll through in any given virtual instrument plugin. You will also find knobs that affect the sound parameters. Virtual instruments mean sounds that are based in software. You will be able to control these sounds using your QWERTY keyboard, MIDI controller, your mouse (preview only), or by using the FL Studio Piano roll. The actual installation of virtual instruments and effects to be utilized in FL Studio was covered in *Chapter 1, Configuring FL Studio*. There is a wide array of virtual instruments, from low quality to high quality. For example, Hans Zimmer uses certain virtual instruments when composing scores for film, so there are many high-quality orchestral and sample libraries. NATIVE INSTRUMENTS and EASTWEST are two companies known for high-quality virtual instruments. The quality will be based on the coding and algorithms of software designers. Usually, the most realistic sounding virtual instruments are hybrids of high-quality recordings and programming. The drawback is that they are also pricey, but may be worth it depending on your needs. You may also find free virtual instruments by searching on the Internet.

Getting ready

To get started using virtual instruments, you will simply need to have the step sequencer opened. Your virtual instruments will appear as a channel in the step sequencer. With FL Studio default virtual instruments such as 3x Osc and TS404, the **PLUGIN** tab will give you immediate access to the parameters. Other times, your **PLUGIN** tab will be a graphical pop-out interface that will vary in appearance depending on the plugin designers.

How to do it...

The following steps will guide you through the process of adding virtual instruments:

1. Right-click on a channel in the step sequencer as shown in *Fig 4.7*.

2. Select **Insert** and then bring up the software instrument you want to use. FL Studio allows you to use their factory plugins, 3x Osc, TS404 bassline synthesizer, Fruity DX10, BooBass, and FL Keys, among others as instrument plugins. If it says **DEMO** after opening or trying to save a project, it is only a demo plugin. You can test out demo sounds but cannot save them to your project.

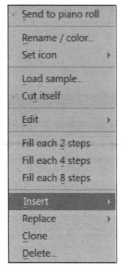

Fig 4.7

3. Alternatively, you may use the FL Studio Browser. Right-click on a sound and select **Open in a new channel**. *Fig 4.8* shows a right-click on a sound within the 3x Osc folder. You may also use the main FL Studio **CHANNELS** menu and then select **Add one**.

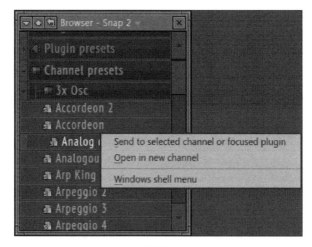

Fig 4.8

4. Use the FL Studio step sequencer and **Keyboard editor** to enter the notes of your instrument. You may also right-click on a channel and use the Piano roll, reviewed later in this chapter.

5. Use your MIDI controller, mouse, or QWERTY keyboard to preview the sounds of your instrument plugin. Hold down *Ctrl* and click on a channel name to play a previous C4 note.

6. *Fig 4.9* shows the graphical pop out of an instrument plugin when you click on the **PLUGIN** tab in your channel settings:

Fig 4.9

7. When an instrument plugin has an actual pop out and a software graphical readout, you may scroll through presets using the left and right arrows at the upper right-hand corner of the plugin. It will list the name of your preset on the upper-left of your plugin. *Fig 4.9* shows we are working with the instrument called **eFlute**, within the **Fruity DX10** plugin. Right-click on the left or right arrow to display a list of all available sound patches of your plugin.

 Right-click on the left or right arrow to display a list of all available sound patches of your plugin.

8. To see how many presets are present within a given instrument plugin, look at the FL Studio hint bar. In the following screenshot, we see that **eFlute** is the 11th patch/sound out of 59 presets:

Fig 4.10

9. There are two main ways to engage your QWERTY keyboard to function as a basic controller. The keys on your actual computer screen will control the notes in FL Studio. This is in cases where you do not have an actual computer keybed or MIDI controller, or when you are mobile with a laptop but no MIDI controller.

Fig 4.11

10. To use your QWERTY keyboard to record or preview notes, you will want to select **Typing keyboard to piano** in the **OPTIONS** menu or simply engage the orange light on the small keyboard in *Fig 4.11* (on the top left-hand side). If you decide to use **Metronome**, you can click the symbol underneath the keyboard sign in *Fig 4.11*. Right-click to select different sounds of your Metronome.

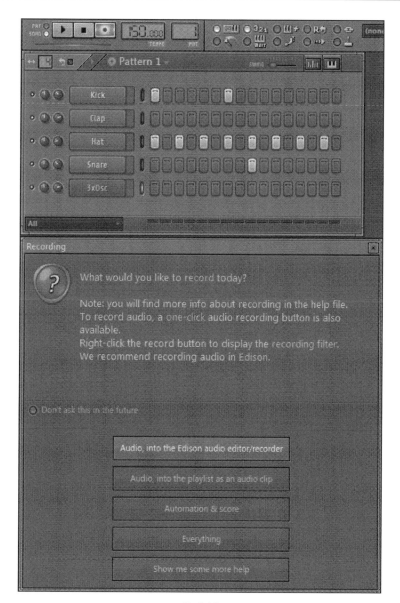

Fig 4.12

Recording using a MIDI controller/keyboard or a QWERTY computer keybed

1. Engage the channel you want to record with the channel select button (small green slit next to the **3xOsc** channel in *Fig 4.12*).

2. Right-click on the **3 2 1** button to select your precount duration.

3. Click on the recording button in the transport controls and it will turn orange.

4. Select **Automation & score**. This means your MIDI data and notes will be recorded into the step sequencer. MIDI isn't actual audio—it is simply note data, duration, and how hard you pressed a particular key (note velocity). You can change and cycle through various sound patches once MIDI data is recorded.

5. Click on the play button to begin your countdown.

6. Record your performance and your channel will now show data in the FL Studio Piano roll. The following screenshot shows the transport controls used for recording purposes:

Fig 4.13

How it works...

Once you have your instrument plugin in a channel within the step sequencer, you have many options with regard to how to get your data recorded and saved in the step sequencer. Working with the Keyboard editor can be handy if you are on the go and you only have access to a mouse and your computer. If you have a MIDI controller and you want to actually perform your notes as your pattern plays, you will use the recording method from *Fig 4.12*. You will be recording **Automation & score** because your score means the notes you are playing. Using virtual instruments within your computer means you are not actually recording audio per se—you are recording the MIDI notes within your software plugin. Once recorded, you can replace your sound patch. You may also paint or draw notes directly into the Piano roll, which we will review later in this chapter.

The area next to the transport controls (play, stop, and record) is crucial when working with virtual instruments, recording, and using the step sequencer. If you engage the button to the right of **3 2 1**, you will find the hint bar tells you it is the **Blend recording (overdub)** button (highlighted with a red circle). When using the overdub button in conjunction with the **Loop recording** (the button with the R and an arrow icon) button, your pattern will loop back around and you can continue to add notes/data to your given channel without pressing stop. You can also switch to different channels and continue to record. This is a remarkable function of FL Studio because your creativity can expand as your project continues to play. Be careful during the blend recording process because everything you do (besides recording MIDI data) will be recorded, for example, tempo and volume knob tweaks.

If the overdub button is turned off and you still have the **Loop recording** button engaged, your notes/data will be replaced by whatever notes you choose to play. During this process of overdubbing or loop recording, you can actually move from channel to channel by using the channel select button, and FL Studio will continue to record. You can also add new channels, sounds, and plugins while FL Studio continues to record! This allows you to get very creative and add parts on the fly, which you can edit later.

See also

▸ The *Using the Piano roll* recipe

▸ The *Installing virtual instruments and effects* recipe in *Chapter 1, Configuring FL Studio*

▸ The *Sending a channel to a mixer slot* recipe in *Chapter 3, Working with Step Sequencer and Channels*

▸ The *Adding effects to your effect chains* recipe in *Chapter 6, Using the FL Studio Mixer and Recording Audio*

Working with MIDI controllers and MIDI pads

Working with MIDI pads, controllers, and keyboards allows you to have a hands on feel when working with FL Studio and opens up many doors for the creative process. You may find that you have more creative control when turning physical knobs instead of a mouse or drawing in automation curves. It is extremely helpful when working with keyboards because you have 10 fingers instead of one mouse click. Working with pads can help when working with percussion samples and coming up with percussion grooves. You may also have faders/sliders that can control the faders/sliders (volume control) in the FL Studio mixer. In this manner, you can adjust the volume of multiple mixer tracks at the same time, similar to a standard analog mixer, but in this case you are using a MIDI controller to control software.

Many keyboards and MIDI controllers are also touch sensitive, which means the volume output will vary depending on how hard or how soft you press the keys. This also helps with creativity and building your song. Additionally, MIDI keyboards come in all sizes. You may have a small, transportable keyboard when you are on the go, or a full size 88-key MIDI controller at your home studio. There are also many different types of MIDI pads, touchscreens, and knob configurations. Using a physical MIDI controller may make you feel like you are more involved with your music project because using a mouse can become boring and tedious. MIDI signals can now be recognized by simply using a USB chord, which makes them very easy to use with your computer.

Getting ready

You usually want to connect your MIDI controller before launching FL Studio. However, if you connect after launching, you may press **Rescan MIDI devices** as shown in *Fig 4.14*. You may use a USB chord that connects to your computer or MIDI cables that will connect to your audio interface.

How to do it...

The following steps will show you how to work with MIDI devices using FL Studio:

1. Plug your MIDI device into your computer. If you are connected to the Internet, your device will usually automatically install the proper MIDI drivers/software for your computer. However, sometimes the manufacturer may have a MIDI driver that unlocks more features of the device. At other times, you may have an installation disk. This may work, but keep in mind the manufacturer's website usually has the most recently updated drivers.

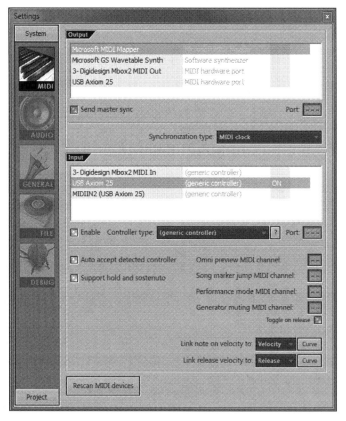

Fig 4.14

2. Press *F10* to open up your MIDI settings, or go to the **OPTIONS** menu and select **MIDI settings**.

3. Click on your desired device in the **Input** section so it shows up in blue, as shown in *Fig 4.14*.

4. Click on the **Enable** button as shown in *Fig 4.14*. When engaged, it will turn orange.

5. Click on the **?** (question mark) tab while connected to the Internet for more information on linking MIDI controllers to your device.

6. Click on the **(generic controller)** to view MIDI devices that are preconfigured to work with FL Studio. You may also use a generic controller, that is, something not in the list, and configure it to your liking.

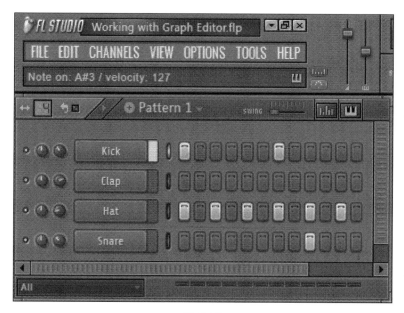

Fig 4.15

7. Press a key on your MIDI controller. If it is operating correctly, you will see MIDI activity, which is apparent due to the orange glow of the MIDI button, as shown in *Fig 4.15*. The hint bar will also display which key you have pressed and how hard you have pressed it. (**velocity: 127**) If you have a channel engaged (green slit), it will show the volume activity in white (kick activity). When acting on other MIDI inputs, such as moving a knob or a slider, the MIDI signal will light in green instead of orange.

8. If your device is not operating correctly and FL Studio has been launched, you may select **Rescan MIDI devices**, as shown in *Fig 4.14*.

Fig 4.16

9. You will also see a screen readout of the key you have pressed on your MIDI controller when you open up your channel settings or virtual instrument plugin. In *Fig 4.16*, the C key was pressed on your physical MIDI key and the **C5** key symbolizes this. The physical keys on your MIDI controller will parallel your graphical images in FL Studio. This generally holds true for any instrument plugins that pop out into a graphical keyboard interface.

10. Let's look at the connecting knobs, sliders, and any physical parameter on a MIDI controller (not preconfigured). Have a look at the following screenshot:

Fig 4.17

11. Move your mouse to any parameter, knob, or slider in FL Studio.

12. Right-click on the knob or slider you want to control with your MIDI controller and then select **Link to controller...**, as shown in *Fig 4.17*.

13. The **Remote control settings** dialog box will appear as shown in *Fig 4.18*.

 Simply move a knob, slider, or any physical control on your MIDI controller, and it will now be controlling the parameter you previously right-clicked on in FL Studio. Make sure the **Auto detect** parameter is activated in the **Remote control settings** window; otherwise, this method will not work.

Fig 4.18

Connecting multiple knobs, sliders, and any physical parameter on a MIDI controller (not preconfigured)

The following steps explain how to connect multiple knobs, sliders, and any physical parameter on a MIDI controller:

Fig 4.19

1. Click on the **Multilink to controllers** button, which is the button on the bottom right-hand side of the preceding screenshot.

2. Click and move, one at a time, the parameters you want to control with your mouse in FL Studio.

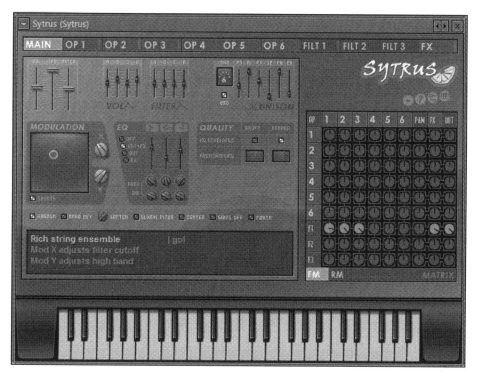

Fig 4.20

3. In the preceding screenshot, we have clicked and moved the **X** knob with our mouse, and then we have clicked and moved the **Y** knob with our mouse. This must be done in the order you specify, because FL Studio will remember which knob, slider, or parameter you have moved and in what order. This will then match up to the physical knobs your move with your fingers and hands.

Fig 4.21

4. When we move any parameter with our mouse, FL Studio will show a brief hint next to the **Multilink to controllers** button. In *Fig 4.21*, the hint titled **2: Sytrus - Main - Modulation Y** has appeared after we moved the Y knob in *Fig 4.20*. This is because it was the second parameter we moved. The first parameter we moved was the **X** knob.

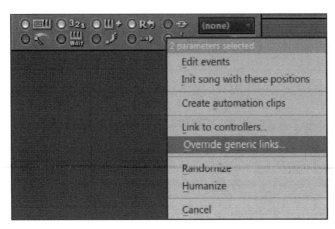

Fig 4.22

5. Right-click on the **Multilink to controllers** button.

6. Select **Override generic links...**. Note that it also says that two parameters are selected because we have clicked and moved two parameters with our mouse, the **X** and **Y** knob.

7. Finally, move the knobs, sliders, or physical control on your given MIDI controller in the exact order you want to specify, based on the order you engaged with your mouse in *Fig 4.20*. The first/primary knob or control you physically turn with your finger or slide with your hand (this can be any knob or button you desire) will control the X knob because it was clicked first in the example on *Fig 4.20*. The second knob or control you physically turn with your finger or slide with your hand will control the **Y** knob because you clicked it second with your mouse, as shown in *Fig 4.20*.

How it works...

When you are selecting **Link to controller...** or **Multilink to controllers**, you are selecting whatever physical control you desire to move with your hands instead of clicking with a mouse. Many times, people enjoy using sliders on their MIDI controller to control the sliders in the FL Studio mixer. You may also control any knob within the channel settings on any FL Studio channel. The creative possibilities of using your MIDI controller are unlimited; many times, using the functionality of MIDI control will enhance your studio productions as well as your live performances. If you can see the **Link to controller...** button on right-clicking a knob, slider, or parameter, it means that you can control it via MIDI control. Many times, these controls are used to control low pass or hi pass filters, which can add intrigue and suspense to your music projects. You can also use other physical tools on your MIDI controller, such as the pitch bend.

Many DJs and EDM producers use the functionality of MIDI at live venues, but MIDI control is friendly to all genres of music, including Rock, Jazz, and Pop. MIDI pads or keys can also control your mute and solo buttons in FL Studio, in addition to your volume and panning. You can also use a MIDI button as an on/off switch to toggle effects. When performing live, it allows you to have much more flexibility. For many, using MIDI control is the final piece of the puzzle, because it allows you to have fun while creating music instead of just using your mouse. You may have a better feel and control for your FL Studio parameters when moving MIDI controllers instead of clicking-and-dragging with a mouse. With regard to using MIDI keys on a keyboard, it basically replaces older types of synthesizers, which produce their own sounds. The only caveat is that you need to have a powerful computer when using a MIDI keyboard, which controls your virtual instruments.

See also

- ▶ The *Adding Effects to your effect chain* recipe in *Chapter 6, Using the FL Studio Mixer and Recording Audio*
- ▶ The *Using automation on virtual instruments and effects* recipe in *Chapter 10, Recording Automation*

Comparing pattern and song mode

Pattern/song mode is the basis of understanding how to arrange your song in FL Studio. A pattern is simply a slice of time that will last a couple of seconds, loop back to the beginning, and repeat. Of course, a final song will usually last between a couple minutes to eight minutes or so. When we arrange our patterns into the FL Studio playlist using song mode, we are able to incorporate various patterns to form a full production. We may also separate all of our pieces and parts in patterns in order to utilize them in the FL Studio playlist in song mode. In song mode, we can arrange our pieces and parts (patterns) to form our intro, verse, chorus, bridge, outro, and so on depending on our musical requirements.

Getting ready

In order to get started, we need to have the FL Studio step sequencer opened as well as the FL Studio playlist. The step sequencer can be opened by pressing *F6* and the playlist can be opened by pressing *F5*. Press *Tab* to toggle between these windows. We will also want access to the transport controls (play/pause, stop, and record) next to the **TEMPO** information because that is where we specify pattern or song mode.

How to do it...

The **SONG** button is very crucial with regard to arranging your song in the FL Studio playlist! The following screenshot shows the area where you can find the **PAT** and **SONG** functions:

Fig 4.23

The following screenshot is an example of the **Split by channel** function, which was reviewed in *Chapter 3, Working with the Step Sequencer and Channels*:

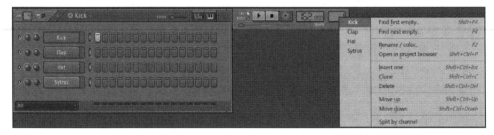

Fig 4.24

The following steps will explain you how to the compare pattern and song mode:

1. Insert steps or data on a single pattern. In *Fig 4.24*, we have entered steps on the **Kick**, **Clap**, **Hat**, and **Sytrus** channels. You cannot see data on each channel because we have already used **Split by channel**.

2. Click on whatever pattern incorporates all of your original data, as per *Fig 4.24*, and select **Split by channel**. In *Fig 4.23*, we click on the pattern name at the top of the step sequencer **Kick** or right-click on the **PAT** box once your pattern is selected.

3. As reviewed in *Chapter 3, Working with the Step Sequencer and Channels* the **Split by channel** function will automatically transfer each channel data to its own pattern. This takes the "manual labor" of cutting and pasting out of the equation. After using the **Split by channel** functionality, the **Kick** steps/data will remain on **Pattern 1** because it is vertically the uppermost channel in the step sequencer. The **Clap** step data will be moved to **Pattern 2** because the **Clap** channel is vertically below the **Kick** channel. The **Hat** steps will be moved to **Pattern 3** because the **Hat** channel is vertically below the **Clap** channel in the step sequencer. Finally, the **Sytrus** data will be moved to **Pattern 4** because it is the bottom-most channel in the step sequencer. Four channels are equal to four patterns, and the **Split by channel** functionality splits it out for you.

Fig 4.25

4. Click on the small circle beside **SONG** underneath the **PAT** button, as shown in *Fig 4.25*. This will engage your FL Studio playlist and the orange triangle will now be located at the top of the playlist. This orange triangle will move in time with the location of the playback of your song. Engaging the **SONG** button is essential in order to be able to arrange a full length song!

Fig 2.25

5. Scroll with your mouse onto whatever pattern you desire to paste into the FL Studio playlist.

6. Click on the FL Studio playlist and your selected pattern will be pasted to the timeline of your song.

7. In *Fig 4.25*, we have started our song with the **Hat** pattern for two measures, and after the **Hat** pattern, we have pasted the **Kick**, **Clap**, and **Sytrus** patterns, which will all now play at the same time.

8. FL Studio allows for 999 patterns, so you have the liberty to be very creative.

How it works...

In *Fig 4.25*, we have clearly separated the **Hat** pattern, and it plays by itself at the beginning of the song. You may also paste a multitude of patterns on track 1 if you so desire, as well as right-click on the track names (**Track 1**, **Track 2**, and so on) in order to rename them. Each track can have various patterns located on a single row if you so desire. Pasting patterns into the FL Studio playlist lets you specify exactly what you want to happen at specific moments in time. You can also click-and-drag when you are clicking in the playlist in order to quickly paint in the same pattern over and over if desired. This may help with quickness and workflow. Sometimes you will want to separate your percussion parts on different patterns in order to add or remove them at certain parts of your song. You may select solo tracks in the playlist by right-clicking on the small green light next to **Track 1**, **Track 2**, and so on. A left-click will mute or unmute tracks. You will also be able to control (specify location, paste, and move) pattern harmonies, virtual instruments, audio recordings, and automation clips in the playlist. Any data you have in any channel in any pattern can be pasted into the FL Studio playlist. Using the playlist is how you build your song based on your music project and what you want to occur. Once you are done arranging all of your parts in the playlist, you will also be able to export your song. Once exported, it will play back as an MP3 or WAV file on MP3 players, the Internet, a CD, or any media device. The playlist is where you move song elements around to produce the coolest arrangement.

See also

▸ The *Using patterns to build your song* recipe in *Chapter 5, Using the Playlist*

▸ The *Recording external audio* recipe in *Chapter 6, Using the FL Studio Mixer and Recording Audio*

▸ The *Exporting an MP3 or a WAV file* recipe in *Chapter 8, Exporting and Rendering your Project*

Using the Piano roll feature

The FL Studio Piano roll feature is very useful when crafting bass lines and melodies in your music production. When you open up **Piano roll**, you have a large graphical interface where you can see the beats, bars, measures, notes, and note durations of your given FL Studio channel. Although it is used for harmonies when working with synths, virtual instruments, pads, and so on, it is also useful for any sound in any conceivable channel including but not limited to hi hats, kick drums, and snares. The piano roll has a larger piano area where you can toggle between real-world piano note values or images of a keyboard. You can slice your notes and perform complex edits at the click of a button. This is sometimes preferred over the step sequencer and Keyboard editor, although a mixture of both can be a great music production tool.

Getting ready

In order to use the FL Studio Piano roll, you simply need to have a channel of any sound or virtual instrument inside of the FL Studio step sequencer.

How to do it...

Let's examine how to use the all-powerful FL Studio Piano roll.

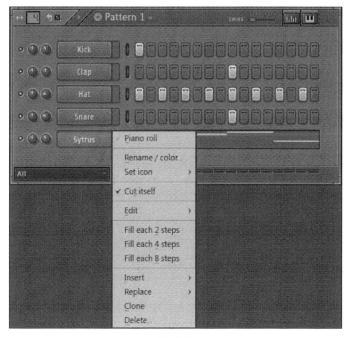

Fig 4.27

1. Right-click on a channel in the step sequencer. In *Fig 4.27*, we have right-clicked on the **Sytrus** channel, which happens to be a virtual instrument. Next, select **Piano roll**.

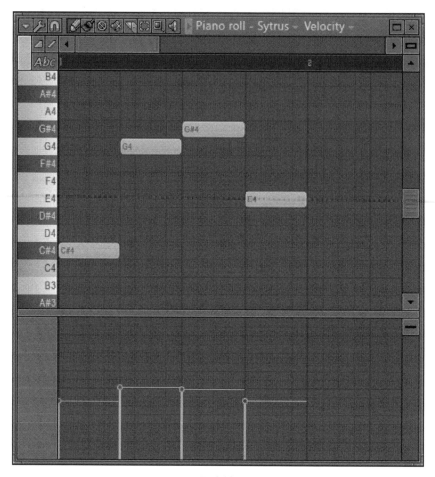

Fig 4.28

2. Left-click on **Draw** (the pencil icon in the preceding screenshot) or **Paint** (the paintbrush icon in the preceding screenshot) in your notes for your channel to explore drawing or painting functions. Right-click to erase and remove notes.

3. Adjust the length of notes by hovering your mouse over the end of your note until you see a horizontal adjustment mouse maneuver.

4. Move notes up, down, left, or right by hovering your mouse in the center of your notes until you see a vertical and horizontal cursor icon.

5. If you have a scroll wheel on your mouse, hover on top of the black bar next to **Abc**, as shown in *Fig 4.28*, and you will be able to zoom in or zoom out using your scroll wheel. This helps to focus the area you are working on. You may also have to adjust the horizontal scroll bar as shown in *Fig 4.28* based on how you are zooming in or zooming out.

6. Hover your mouse over any part of the Piano roll window's exterior in order to resize the piano roll graphical interface to your liking. You may hover your mouse over the top, right, bottom, or left hand sides as well as the top-left corner, top-right corner, bottom-right corner, and bottom-left corner in order to resize. The cursor icon will change based on how and where you want to resize.

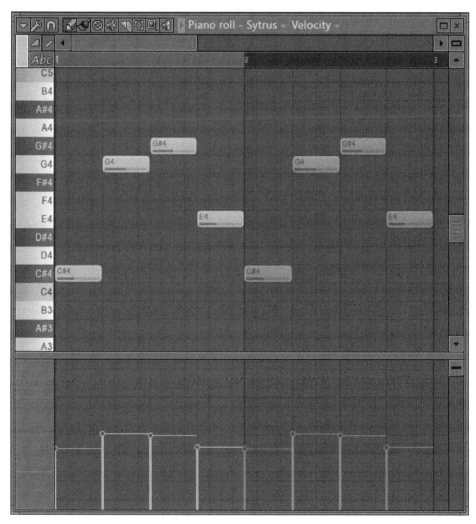

Fig 4.29

Now, let's try copying and pasting notes within the Piano roll feature. Perform the following steps:

1. Press *Ctrl* + *A* to select all current notes.

2. Press *Ctrl* + *C* to copy notes.

3. Press *Ctrl* + *V* to paste notes.

4. Hold *Shift* + right arrow key to move the notes to the right. Alternatively, once you have pasted the notes, you can use your mouse to hover over the notes and drag them to the right.

5. The pasted material will show in red, as shown in *Fig 4.29*, until you click elsewhere.

A handy tip is to hold *Ctrl* and click-and-drag your mouse to select notes of your choice. Then hold *Shift* and drag the notes with your mouse and the area you have selected will automatically be copy-pasted. Clicking on an empty area will duplicate your last note length. Pressing *Shift* and clicking on an empty area will duplicate your last note value and simultaneously allow you to change its length. Holding down the *Alt* key will allow you to toggle the **Piano roll** grid on and off, allowing you to slide certain notes away from the grid if necessary. Click and hold the right mouse button in order to automatically bring up the **Slice** tool.

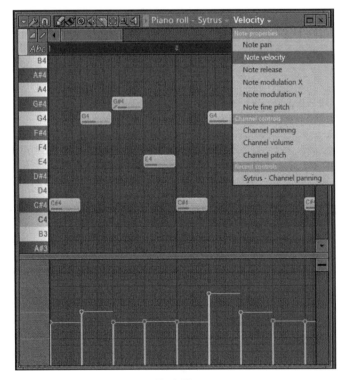

Fig 4.30

6. The bars at the lower portion of the FL Studio **Piano roll** window correspond with each **Note velocity** (volume).

7. Click on the bars and drag up or down to adjust the volume of the corresponding notes directly above them.

8. Click on **Velocity** at the top of the **Piano roll** window to bring up additional options. You may select whatever option you need and then the bars will be engaged as per your selection and you can adjust them from there. You may double-click on any note in the **Piano roll** window to bring up options for your double-clicked note, as shown in *Fig 4.31*. We have double-clicked on **C#4** in *Fig 4.31*. Make changes as you desire and click the space bar to preview those changes. Click on **Accept** to accept the parameters you have changed. This also works for any selection of notes. Select as many notes as you desire, double-click, and you will then be able to adjust their **Note properties** on a global scale/mass edit. The pop-out properties icon will then read **Note properties – selection**. Additionally, with chords, some notes can be excluded by keeping them out of your selection.

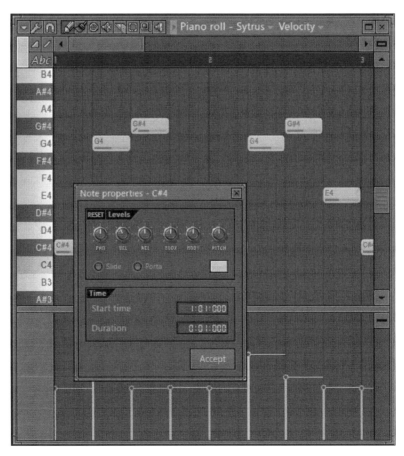

Fig 4.31

How it works...

The **Piano roll** feature is a very powerful tool within FL Studio. It is styled after popular MIDI editors. You may draw or paint as many notes as you desire and copy and paste them, as shown in *Fig 4.27*. This can help when you want the exact same notes in the next measure or when you want a similar note pattern that you want to tweak a bit after copying and pasting. Please note that your **Piano roll** data can be expanded way past the length of your beats per bars in the step sequencer. This means you may want to move your **Piano roll** data to a separate, dedicated pattern and then use the playlist to arrange your pattern. Your **Piano roll** data can stretch as far as you like, so you can make changes and variations within one channel if you so desire.

You can also record piano roll data while in pattern mode. Sometimes, this is advantageous when making bass lines and harmonies. The way in which you use the FL Studio **Piano roll** is based on your own preferences. Some users like to keep adding notes in the **Piano roll** section past measure three or four and get all the way up to measure eight or longer. In this manner, you have your variations already set in place and you don't have to make new data in new patterns or copy and paste from pattern to pattern. The length on one single Piano roll can stretch to three or four minutes or longer. However long your piano roll stretches may be, it will be clearly represented when you paint your given pattern into the FL Studio playlist.

Once you right-click on a channel and open up the **Piano roll** feature, your channel data and graphical readout will change when viewing the step sequencer. It will no longer show steps in the step sequencer. It will show each note in your Piano roll as per the **Sytrus** channel in *Fig 4.27*. You can then simply click on the green lines (which are your notes) from the step sequencer to open up the **Piano roll** window. You can also copy and paste your Piano roll data between channels or between patterns. In this manner, you can copy your exact data into a new channel with a new sound and test options for how you want the mood of your song to progress. For example, let's say you made a great piano roll riff while using a synth patch. At that point, you can copy and paste the data and test out new sounds like a violin, piano, or any sound you think may enhance your project.

There's more...

Please remember to experiment with the top three options in the upper-left-hand corner of the **Piano roll** window. These are **Options**, **Tools**, and **Snap to grid**. Look at the FL Studio hint bar when hovering your mouse over these options. There are a plethora of options here, including the **FILE** option, where you can import MIDI files. This means you can import note data from a variety of sources, including websites such as `http://mididb.com/`. The MIDI notes you import will be imported as note data in the **Piano roll** feature, and you can specify how you want them to sound by using virtual instruments in FL Studio. You can import popular songs to review the notes that were used and it can be a tremendous learning tool. You can also use this when composing cover songs and remixes. The possibilities for working with MIDI files and importing their data into the FL Studio **Piano roll** feature are enormous.

The **Snap to grid** option will adjust the length of your grid within the **Piano roll** window. The entries, drawing, and paint buttons will snap to the grid you specify here. This can be handy when you are working with percussion and hi hats and when you want to have them sound very fast. The way a rock drummer does triplets is the basis of how you can manipulate the **Piano roll** feature. This is almost like another adjustment of the beats per bar for this pattern on the step sequencer. The snap to grid within **Piano roll** tells FL Studio how to break down the pieces and parts of each beat. This can give you more control and tweaking ability. For example, when adjusting the **Snap to grid** option to **1/6** steps, you will find how small each step can be in **Piano roll**. This is not limited to hi hats and percussion; this is for any type of audio you have in **Piano roll** and the creative possibilities are endless. It can be a little bit tedious to paste in all of your notes on a 1/6 step, so you can copy and paste a small section then continually double your selection. You can also save the score as **...** in the **FILE** menu on the **Piano roll** window to save your particular note arrangement.

There are also many options within the **Tools** button, including but not limited to the **Quick Chop** and **Chop...** buttons. You may select any note on **Piano roll** or select all notes with *Ctrl + A* followed by any chop option to see how it adjusts your notes. This can be handy for hi hats in your music production. Another handy option is to explore the **Chord** option in the **Piano roll options** button. You can find these options by clicking on the **Piano roll options** button (a small triangle in the upper-left-hand corner) as shown in the following screenshot:

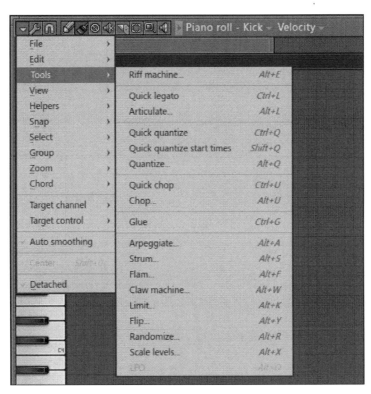

Fig 4.32

You can select the chord you want to use and with a single mouse click your chord will be pasted into the **Piano roll** window. The **Strum** option within the **Tools** options can humanize your chords. When you are physically playing your performance with a keyboard or MIDI controller, your performance may be a tad off in time due to human error or latency time on your computer. If you notice that your performance is a little bit shaky but the basic idea is laid down, you can use the **Quantize...** option. This will snap your performance back in time with your grid. Just like how some people enjoy using physical faders and knobs, using a MIDI keyboard is preferred by many people to record/play in their notes instead of clicking with a mouse. Please look at the many options to tweak your **Piano roll** data under the **Tools** button.

See also

- The *Working with rhythm and percussion* recipe
- The *Adding virtual instruments* recipe
- The *Introducing the step sequencer* recipe in *Chapter 3, Working with Step Sequencer and Channels*
- The *Using Patterns to Build Your Song* recipe in *Chapter 5, Using the Playlist*

5
Using the Playlist

In this chapter, we will cover the following topics:

- ▶ Using patterns to build a song
- ▶ Comparing patterns and audio
- ▶ Using markers and snap
- ▶ Viewing the playlist

Introduction

By pasting patterns in FL Studio, you can arrange the many pieces and parts of your production. You may also paint automation curves and record external audio in the playlist. Automation will be covered in *Chapter 10, Recording Automation* and in the *Recording external audio –keyboards, vocals, guitars, turntables, and devics* recipe in *Chapter 6, Using the FL Studio Mixer and Recording Audio*. The playlist is where you can specify which patterns are played (or not played) at which point in time. As discussed previously, you can actually make a full-length song with one pattern by using the Piano roll and by continually adding more beats and bars with data. Thus, beats per bars is the area where you can distinguish between an intro, verse, chorus, bridge, outro, or any type of section of your song. It is all up to the individual artist using FL Studio to decide their particular musical arrangement. This is shown in the first recipe *Using patterns to build a song*.

You must use patterns that were made in the FL Studio step sequencer in order to build an original musical production from scratch. In this way, you build, overdub, and continually layer in order to come up with an original work. You may also insert full-length WAV or MP3 files and function exclusively as a recording studio, where you would then record vocals on top of the completed instrumental. You can chop any type of material (patterns or audio) in the playlist. So, in the end it may be a true fusion, mixture, and mash up of digital music. All files exist as channels, as reviewed in *Chapter 3, Working with the Step Sequencer and Channels*.

Using patterns to build a song

If you were a writer who is writing a novel, you would start with a blank document and build your story with words and paragraphs. If you were a painter, you would start with a blank canvas and use markers or a paintbrush to build your creative vision. When working with FL Studio, you will be pasting your various patterns in the step sequencer in the FL Studio playlist.

Getting ready...

In order to start using the playlist, you need to have some data entered in your *steps* within channels and patterns on the step sequencer. You can press *F5* or use the **VIEW** menu to bring up the playlist. Press *Tab* to toggle between the various windows that are open in FL Studio.

How to do it...

Let's look at two quick start methods to paste/paint patterns into the playlist:

> ▸ **Quick start**: Hover your mouse over the **PAT** box and drag it up/down to select a pattern number. Click on the playlist (*F5*) to paint it in. In *Fig 5.1*, the **PAT** box is shown to the right of the **TEMPO** button, with a value of 162.000.

> ▸ **Alternative method**: You may also click where it says **Kick**, next to the word **Playlist** in *Fig 5.1*. Not only will it bring up a list of patterns, but also show a list of all the automation clips and audio files created in the current project. Right-click on the same area to open up a really cool **PROJECT PICKER** window, where you can select your patterns or channels laid out in an awesome interface.

Let's take a look at the multiple patterns being arranged using the following steps:

1. Select a pattern in the step sequencer.

2. Make sure you select the **SONG** mode, next to the transport controls in *Fig 5.1*. This will make your music project enter the **SONG** mode, and **Play Position Marker** (a small, orange-colored triangle) will be engaged when you press the Space bar to stop or play your project.

3. Click with the **Paint** tool in the desired area in order to paste the pattern you have selected. You may also click-and-drag to the right with the **Paint** tool in order to smoothly paste the same pattern over and over again.

4. Use the right-click button to erase patterns.

5. The following screenshot shows that anything pasted in the **Playlist** section is like a small graphic of any given pattern in the step sequencer and the information inside it. You can see that the **Hat** and **303ish 2** patterns come in at bar **5**. The **303ish 2** pattern shows Piano roll data because we have entered Piano roll data using a virtual instrument on that particular pattern. When you enter notes in the Piano roll on a given channel or pattern, the **Playlist** window will reflect this in order to help you see and organize your arrangement. The following screenshot shows the **Playlist** window:

Fig 5.1

6. Click on the small square button next to the name of your pattern and then select the source pattern to populate and choose available patterns as per Fig 5.2. Once your patterns are pasted into the **Playlist** window, you will have the option to toggle between your patterns present in the list, as shown in the following screenshot:

Fig 5.2

7. In the following screenshot, we have opened the pattern selector under the step sequencer by hovering our mouse on **Kick**. Your cursor will turn into a hand when you hover over **Kick** or any generic pattern name, indicating that the drop-down menu will get populated.

Fig 5.3

How it works...

By pasting your patterns (which have your channel steps or notes) in the playlist, you can form a full music production project. This happens when you click on the **SONG** mode, and the small play-position marker is engaged at the very start of the playlist on bar **1**. Now, when you press the Space bar key, any pattern you paste into the playlist will be in time from left-to-right, and you can see the position pointer move along while highlighting the grid in time. A regular pattern when operating in the **PAT** mode will simply play your data and loop back to the beginning. You can stretch patterns to extremely long lengths by using the Piano roll, but you still have to paint your given pattern into the playlist. The area where you paste your patterns in the playlist will also be the area that is used to export your project into the rendered audio, which we will review in *Chapter 8, Exporting and Rendering Your Project.*

There's more...

You may also use the **Slice** tool directly (hover your mouse on the various tools at the upper left-hand corner of the playlist and look at the hint bar) in order to slice particular patterns and then edit or move them. Slicing is also exceedingly useful in the FL Studio Piano roll. If you select the **Make unique** option (shown in *Fig 5.2*), it will automatically create a new, unique pattern in the step sequencer. This can be handy if you want to tweak a pattern without navigating back to the step sequencer. This is also a great tool to remove part of your drums or incorporate a short silence to bring variety to your arrangement. Many times, you may want to slice off a certain part and then make it unique so that it becomes its own separate entity that you can mix later on. You can do this by pressing the Pattern clip drop-down box in *Fig 5.2*. This can prove handy because your song arrangement is affected and changed immediately. This method is used on any type of audio or samples. When working with vocals, you may want to make some of your pieces unique in order to change the volume of a specific word or add a different effect in the mixer.

You may also paste any pattern you want, even if it has no steps or notes yet. This means that you can paste a blank pattern in the playlist; you can go to this pattern while your arrangement is playing and add your notes later. The longer you stretch your notes in a channel/pattern, the longer will your pattern automatically stretch in the playlist. If your pattern is currently playing or being triggered in the playlist, you will clearly see the LEDs of the playing step (orange slits) at the bottom of your step sequencer.

A tremendous option when working with your arrangement is to double-click and drag your pattern where you see the numbers that represent the measures in your playlist and where the play position marker is located. When you do this, your selection will become in red color, and you can highlight the measure/sections that will be played and looped back around. This is handy to specify a particular area that you want to play back, which can then be edited and fine-tuned without listening to the whole song. If you only want to edit the intro, you can click-and-drag your mouse to highlight this area only. This feature allows you to specify which part of your song will play back and is helpful when adding/changing/revising/experimenting with pieces and parts, recording vocals, and drawing automation curves.

See also...

- ▸ The *Using markers and snap* recipe
- ▸ The *Comparing pattern and song mode* recipe in *Chapter 4, Building Your Song*
- ▸ The *Recording external audio – keyboards, vocals, guitar, and devices* recipe in *Chapter 6, Using the FL Studio Mixer and Recording Audio*
- ▸ The *Exporting an MP3 or WAV file* recipe in *Chapter 8, Exporting and Rendering Your Project*
- ▸ The *Using automation on virtual instruments and effects* recipe in *Chapter 10, Recording Automation*

Comparing patterns and audio

The patterns that you paste into the FL Studio playlist reflect how you manage/arrange your project and decide which parts will play or not play during your song. This is easy to see on the FL Studio Playlist, where you will have a graphical readout of your patterns, audio, and automation clips. Audio clips will be shown on the playlist in a waveform readout, as will any type of MP3 or WAV file. As discussed earlier, patterns in the playlist can stretch very far if your Piano roll is extended.

Getting ready...

In order start using the **Playlist** section and patterns, you need to have some data entered in your *steps* within the channels and patterns on the step sequencer. You may press *F5* or use the **VIEW** menu to bring up the playlist. We will be working with a recorded vocal file. Recording an external audio will be covered in *Chapter 6, Using the FL Studio Mixer and Recording Audio*, because, in some cases, your recording can show up directly on the FL Studio Playlist.

How to do it...

We will review the different types of patterns that are seen as specific images on the playlist using the following steps:

1. Press the space bar key or click on play with your mouse on the FL Studio transport controls while in the **SONG** mode.

2. Paste your patterns as discussed in the previous recipe of this chapter, *Using patterns to build your song*.

3. If you have data in your steps and have not used the Piano roll on that channel, the data will be read out like the **Hat** pattern shown in *Fig 5.4*.

4. If you have a channel/pattern that used a Piano roll, it will be similar to the **303ish 2** pattern in *Fig 5.4*.

5. If you have vocals, an MP3 file, or a WAV file, it will show the audio data, as shown in *Fig 5.4*, next to **Track 5** titled **Vocals track 1** in the header.

6. When working with automation clips, you will see automation curves and shapes as seen in the example in *Fig 5.4*. The topic of automation will be covered in *Chapter 10, Recording Automation*.

Fig 5.4

How it works...

The readouts on various channels, patterns, audio data, and automation curves are a friendly way to keep your project organized and see exactly what is happening at specific moments (bars and beats) in time. You can use all of the features described in the previous recipe of this chapter, *Using patterns to build your song*. If you need to paste the same pattern multiple times in a row, you can use the paint tool and click-and-drag the pattern to the right. You can also use the **Maximize / restore** button to drag FL Studio's main window and drag audio files directly into the playlist. This restore button is shown in the following screenshot, directly to the left of the exit icon. You may click-and-drag an audio file from your desktop (or anywhere on your computer) into the FL Studio Playlist. The following screenshot shows the **Maximize / restore** button:

Fig 5.5

See also...

▸ The *Using patterns to build your song* recipe

▸ The *Viewing the playlist* recipe

▸ The *Recording external audio – keyboards, vocals, guitar, and devices* recipe in *Chapter 6, Using the FL Studio Mixer and Recording Audio*

▸ The *Using automation on virtual instruments and effects* recipe in *Chapter 10, Recording Automation*

Using markers and snap

Using markers in your FL Studio Playlist is a great way to organize your pieces and parts and to label what is happening in certain sections. The basic idea is to label these with intro, verse, chorus, bridge, outro, or whatever you want depending on your workflow. It helps to have these markers because they remind you of what is going on with your song and also help when you are selecting areas in the playlist. Snap is the setting that dictates how your patterns can be moved around and locked to the playlist timeline. These can be adjusted to certain beats, bars, and fractions of time.

Getting ready...

To start using markers, you need to have the FL Studio playlist open. You do not need to have any patterns pasted in the playlist to add markers. When you have patterns in your song, the markers can be added, moved, renamed, or deleted; so the modification of the markers depends on your own organizational habits.

How to do it...

The following steps you show how to use markers and snap, and *Fig 5.6* shows the basic view of the playlist:

1. Press *Alt + T* when viewing your playlist and a marker will be created. You can then name your marker and press *Enter*. The following screenshot shows the markers, titled **Intro** and **Verse 1**, that have been added to the playlist:

Fig 5.6

2. Alternatively, you can add a marker by using the **Playlist** option's drop-down box (triangle at the upper-left corner), which is shown in *Fig 5.7*. Your markers, options are populated once you scroll down to the **Time markers** option.

Fig 5.7

3. Once you have a marker in the playlist, you can right-click on the marker in order to add another one, delete it, or rename it. This is shown in *Fig 5.8*.

4. To move or slide markers to different sections of your song, hover your mouse over to the beginning (left-hand side) of your marker. A horizontal slide cursor will appear.

Fig 5.8

How it works...

The use of markers is up each individual user and depends on how your current music project is organized. You can add markers wherever you desire; you can move, delete, and even rename them. Even though you can see what is happening in the playlist with your patterns, markers are a great function that help with organization. Label them as you wish so that you are reminded of the parts that are currently triggered.

There's more...

The **Snap to grid** settings in your playlist are directly correlated with your ability to slide your markers, patterns, audio, and automation clips (shown in *Fig 5.9*). You will also find the **Snap to grid** button in the **Piano roll** and **Event editor** sections. If your grid is set to **Cell**, your markers and patterns will be locked in time with the cells on the playlist when clicking, dragging, and inserting. If your grid is set to **(none)**, you can freely slide your marker without any grid constraints. The grid can be toggled on and off by pressing *Alt* when dragging . When you have audio on your playlist, the grid setting allows you to chop, slice, or edit your audio in fine, exact increments. The same rules apply to automation clips and patterns. The following screenshot shows options in the **Snap to grid** button:

Fig 5.9

Your **Snap to grid** setting is the governor of the time values that your patterns are locked to. As mentioned earlier, you can momentarily ignore the grid by pressing the *Alt* key while dragging.

Selecting **Main** in any of the **Snap to grid** settings will make all the applicable windows (**Piano roll**, **Playlist**, and **Event editor**) use the default **Main** value. You can set the default value by clicking on **Line** (above the magnetic snap symbol in *Fig 5.10*) or the value currently displayed, generally located at the top in the main window of FL Studio. This **Main** value will govern the **Main snap**, **quantization**, and **step edit** steps. **Snap to grid** simply shows how your parts of music are magnetized to the grid.

Fig 5.10

See also...

▶ The *Using patterns to build your song* recipe

▶ The *Comparing patterns and audio* recipe

▶ The *Recording external audio – keyboards, vocals, guitar, and devices* recipe in *Chapter 6, Using the FL Studio Mixer and Recording Audio*

▶ The *Exporting an MP3 or WAV file* recipe in *Chapter 8, Exporting and Rendering Your Project*

Viewing the playlist

Viewing the playlist is an organization tool that helps you to work on certain sections of your song. Generally, the more pieces and parts you have, the more often you will be resizing your playlist.

Getting ready...

To start viewing the playlist and to change the vertical and horizontal zoom parameters, you simply need to have the playlist open with patterns inserted inside it. An easy way to bring up the playlist is to press the *F5* key.

How to do it...

Let's look at how to zoom in and out of the playlist while looking from left to right:

1. Using the horizontal scroll bar directly correlates with the amount of patterns that you can view from left to right. *Fig 5.11* and *Fig 5.12* show the same playlist window zoomed out and in, respectively.

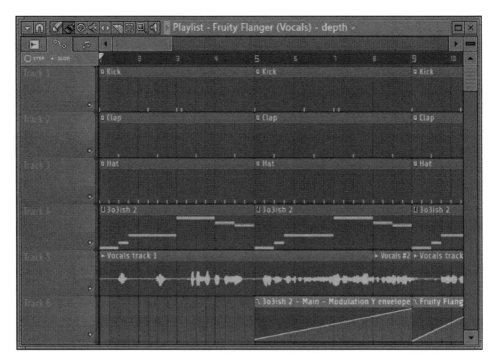

Fig 5.11

2. To zoom in or out horizontally, hover your mouse over the left or right edge of the horizontal zoom bar. This zoom bar is directly above the bar count area. In *Fig 5.12*, you can see that you can hover your mouse over the area above bar **27**. This is the right-most side of the zoom bar. Once you see the cursor change to an arrow, you will click-and-drag your mouse to change the zoom.

Fig 5.12

3. Alternatively, you can zoom in or out using a scroll wheel on your mouse. You can do this by hovering your mouse in the black area with the numbers (bar count), scroll up to zoom out, and scroll down to zoom in. This is shown in the following screenshot. You may use this functionality once you have hovered your mouse over the bar numbers in the black area, and it will work when your cursor turns into a hand. The following screenshot shows the bars in the **Playlist** window:

Fig 5.13

A handy tip is to press *Ctrl + Shift*, click directly on the scroll bar, and then click-and-drag to the right or left. Also, try pressing *Ctrl + Alt* while clicking-and-dragging up and down directly on the scroll bar. The *Alt* method allows us to zoom the grid in when scrolling up and out when scrolling down.

Let's take a look at the vertical view of the patterns in the playlist using the following steps:

1. To change the view of your playlist to vertical view, hover your mouse over the upper right-hand portion of the playlist, directly underneath the exit button.

2. In *Fig 5.14*, we clicked-and-dragged the **Change clip size** functionality up, which makes each track and correlating pattern stretch vertically on a global level. We did this using the **Change clip size** functionality, which will be shown in the FL Studio hint bar. Also, in *Fig 5.14*, notice that the box (directly underneath the exit button) looks like a square now. To do this, we clicked-and-dragged the **Change clip size** functionality up. We can see up to **Track 2** and a little portion of **Track 3**.

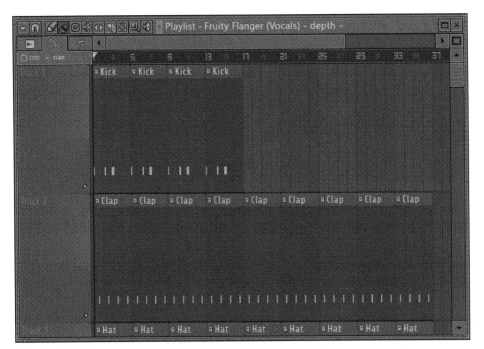

Fig 5.14

3. In *Fig 5.15*, we did the exact same thing. However, we dragged the **Change clip size** box down this time. Now, in *Fig 5.15*, we can see up to **Track 23** and all of our correlating patterns are vertically squashed. This allows you to see more patterns and increases the screen real estate of the playlist window. Notice that the **Change clip size** box now resembles a very thin line.

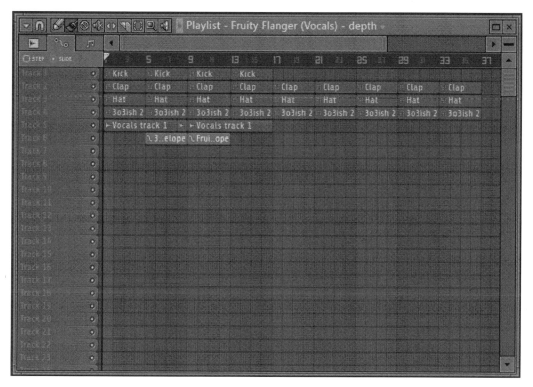

Fig 5.15

4. When using the vertical zoom function, you can also look at the FL Studio hint bar. The numbers will change from **Zoom level 0** to **Zoom level 134**. *Fig 5.15* is actually at **Zoom level 0**. The following screenshot shows how the hint bar will look:

Fig 5.16

5. Hover your mouse over any line that separates the track names on the left-hand side of the playlist. Your mouse will then turn into an up/down arrow selector, where you can adjust individual track sizes to your liking. The global box reviewed above will maintain your adjustments when stretching tracks up and down.

How it works...

In *Fig 5.11*, we dragged the horizontal scroll bar to the left. Notice that the scroll bar in *Fig 5.11* is smaller because we zoomed in. You can also see up to the bar **10**. In *Fig 5.12*, we clicked-and-dragged the scroll bar to the right. We can now see more patterns and up to bar **37**. The actual playlist window has not been adjusted or resized. We have simply used the horizontal zoom in (drag to the left) or zoom out (drag to the right) functionality. Pressing *Ctrl + Shift* or *Ctrl + Alt* is quick and super handy when dragging the scroll bar.

The examples that we just discussed show you how to use the horizontal and vertical zoom functionality. You can also highlight certain sections of your playlist by highlighting and dragging a selection on the bar count area. This selection will show up in red color, and you can now zoom in or out accordingly. Sometimes, you will be dealing with small parts of your song and focusing on one particular area. Other times, you will want to zoom out and get a feel of how things look for the entire arrangement. Like any window in FL Studio, you can also maximize the window or resize it by hovering your mouse over the top, bottom, on the left, right, or corners of the playlist window until you see your cursor change to an arrow.

There's more...

As noted above in a tip, you can also change the vertical dimensions of individual tracks by hovering your mouse between each track on the left-hand side of the playlist. For example, if you hover your mouse between **Track 2** and **Track 3**, your mouse will turn into an arrow and you can then resize **Track 2** exclusively.

You may also mute certain tracks directly in the playlist by clicking on the small green circle next to each track name. Next, right-click on the green circle to solo the track. Right-click on a track name and select the **Set** icon to choose from a handy list of music-related symbols, which automatically label and rename your track.

Use the **Playlist options** drop-down box (upper left-hand corner), select **Detached**, and then drag your playlist to a separate computer monitor. This can help with organization and can give you a clear view of your playlist instead of the need to open and close the many parameters and windows of FL Studio. Detaching is also used with the FL Studio Mixer, reviewed in *Chapter 6, Using the FL Studio Mixer and Recording Audio*.

See also...

  ▸ The *Using patterns to build your song* recipe

  ▸ The *Recording external audio – keyboards, vocals, guitar, and devices* recipe in *Chapter 6, Using the FL Studio Mixer and Recording Audio*

  ▸ The *Exporting an MP3 or WAV file* recipe in *Chapter 8, Exporting and Rendering Your Project*

6

Using the FL Studio Mixer and Recording Audio

In this chapter, we will cover:

- ▶ Using send tracks in the mixer
- ▶ Recording external audio – keyboards, vocals, guitars, turntables, and devices
- ▶ Adding effects and your effect chain
- ▶ Perfecting equalization
- ▶ Understanding master tracks and loud wars
- ▶ Getting the best out of your mixer
- ▶ Recording with or without effects

Introduction

Using send tracks in the mixer, recording external audio, adding effects, adding equalization, mastering your song, and recording with or without effects are all crucial in the mixing process. The FL Studio Mixer offers a consolidation of all of these processes. We have already seen the vast capabilities of FL Studio with regards to rhythm and harmony multitracking; the FL Studio Mixer allows even more control over your sounds and shapes the final sonic landscape for your audience.

Using send tracks in the mixer

Using send tracks in the mixer allows you to free up your computer load and easily add an effect to multiple mixer slots.

Getting ready

In order to start using send tracks, you will want to have the FL Studio Mixer open as well as have your channels in the step sequencer sent to the mixer slots. This is done by setting the FX number, as reviewed in the *Sending a channel to a mixer slot* recipe in *Chapter 3, Working with Step Sequencer and Channels*.

How to do it...

The use of send tracks is a well-known practice on both analog mixers and mixers inside of DAWs. Perform the following steps to learn to use send tracks in these mixers:

1. Open up the FL Studio Mixer. This can be done by pressing *F9*.

2. Look at the far right of the mixer. You will see four send mixer slots titled **Send 1**, **Send 2**, **Send 3**, and **Send 4**.

3. Click on one of the previous send channels, either 1, 2, 3, or 4. In *Fig 6.1*, we have selected **Send 1**.

4. Select an effect from the effect slots. These are labeled 1 through 8 and can be selected using the triangle drop-down icon and by hovering on **Select** or **Replace**. For our purpose, we will select an effect called **Fruity Reeverb 2**. In *Fig 6.1*, we have engaged **Send 1** and picked **Fruity Reeverb 2** in the first effect slot on the right-hand side.

5. Rename the send channel to your liking. In this case, we will rename the channel `Reverb Send` because we know we are working with a reverb effect, as selected in step 4. This is done by selecting the send channel and hitting *F2* to rename it.

 Press *Shift* + click on a channel to rename it.

Fig 6.1

6. Click directly on the insert slot that you want to tweak with the send channel. You must engage the audio you want to adjust. In our case, we will click on a **Snare** channel in the mixer, which is shown in *Fig 6.2*. We have the **Snare** channel audio here, as discussed in the *Sending a channel to a mixer slot* recipe in *Chapter 3, Working with Step Sequencer and Channels*. Once you click on the **Snare** channel or any channel in the mixer, it will be faintly highlighted.

7. Finally, adjust the reverb send knob to your liking. Bear in mind that you need to select/highlight the **Snare** channel first, and then you need to turn your send knob. In *Fig 6.2*, we have the **Snare** slot highlighted, but we only turn the small send knob near the bottom of the mixer in the same column as the **Reverb Send** channel. When you turn your send knob to the right, you will see a graphical vertical readout of the amount applied as well as the FL Studio hint bar, which will show the percentage, from 0 to 125 percent.

Fig 6.2

8. Turning the **Reverb Send** knob allows the **Snare** mixer slot to send its signal to the **Reverb Send** track, which then applies the effect to the signal and sends the affected signal to the master track. You will also see that regular inserts in the mixer display a very small **INS** slot at the top of the mixer. These are channels sent to the mixer from the step sequencer. The four send slots in *Fig 6.2* say **SND**.

How it works...

When you have a full-scale music project, you will have many channels on various inserts (**INS** or **FX** slots) in the mixer. When you set up a send channel, you can add a little bit of the send effect to multiple mixer inserts, without having to add the same reverb effect individually. The send slot equates to a global effect. If you want to send some reverb (or any effect you desire) to your hi hat mixer slot, you can simply engage your hi hat insert and then adjust the send knob to your liking. If you want to send some of the same reverb send to your percussion or bongo insert, then you can adjust it again with the same send knob. If you want to apply the same send effect to your virtual instrument harmonies, you can use the same send knob again. It is up to you how much you want to apply. Again, your send knob goes from 0 to 125 percent, so you are able to specify how high you want to go in each individual insert slot. You can set up your four send slots and apply them to any mixer slot you desire. Generally, sends are used for reverb and delay, but there are no rules in music production. If you think outside the box, your creative possibilities are boundless. It's all about finding your own sound.

There's more...

You can also create automation clips (reviewed in *Chapter 10, Recording Automation*) and use physical knobs on a MIDI controller to control your send knob. Additionally, you can add more effects (1 through 8 in the vertical region of the mixer) to shape your send sound. You may also want to cut out your low-end frequency when your send slot is actually highlighted or engaged and you are working with reverb. This will help open up your reverb send and take away the "muddy" and unclear sound. Panning your instruments or sounds left and right also helps a great deal with creating your own sonic space. Please remember that you can still tweak all of your parameters on any given effect as well as scroll through the presets. In this recipe, we can see our virtual effect and all of its parameters by clicking on the **Fruity Reeverb 2** effect in *Fig 6.1*.

See also

- ▸ The *Adding effects and your effect chain* recipe

- ▸ The *Sending a channel to a mixer slot* recipe in *Chapter 3, Working with the Step Sequencer and Channels*

- ▸ The *Using automation for virtual instruments and effects* recipe in *Chapter 10, Recording Automation*

- ▸ The *Creating automation clips* recipe in *Chapter 10, Recording Automation*

Recording external audio – keyboards, vocals, guitars, turntables and devices

The recording of external audio is done through the FL Studio Mixer. Please refer to the *Knowing your sound cards and audio interfaces* recipe in *Chapter 1, Configuring FL Studio*, with regards to engaging your audio device. No matter what type of external sound you want to record, you will have to select your sound card or audio interface in your audio settings by hitting *F10* and understanding the basic signal flow.

Getting ready

To get started with recording external audio, you need to have your FL Studio Mixer open. This can be done by hitting *F9*. A prerequisite for recording external audio is to have your correct sound card or audio interface selected in your audio settings by hitting *F10*. This was reviewed in *Chapter 1, Configuring FL Studio*. Note that if your microphone is near your speakers, you will need to turn your speakers or studio monitors off before recording into a microphone to avoid feedback. The best practice is to turn your speakers all the way down or off before recording and to use headphones to hear your mix. The output of your speakers into the microphone is definitely a bad practice and can cause unwanted feedback and damage to your microphone, so turn your speakers off before recording vocals.

How to do it...

All external audio recordings include the exact same steps. You simply have to select the input that your audio device is plugged in to on your audio interface or ASIO4all framework. In this example, we will be working with a condenser microphone and recording vocals using the following steps:

1. Click on any mixer slot in the FL Studio Mixer. This will be the path for your audio to travel. You need to pick a mixer slot that is free of any audio. In *Fig 6.3*, we have selected mixer slot **20 (INS 20)** and renamed it to read MBox mic.

2. While your external audio mixer slot is still engaged, click on the IN dropdown of your FL Studio Mixer. This is a dropdown of your available audio inputs; it is based on the sound card you previously selected in your *F10* audio settings. In *Fig 6.3*, we can see that we have selected **MBox2 In 2**. In this example, our real-world XLR condenser microphone is plugged into Input 2 on our MBox2 audio interface. This drop-down box directly correlates to the inputs on your audio interface.

3. Right-click on the small disk icon at the very bottom of **INS 20**. This column correlates to **INS 20**. It will bring up your computer hierarchy, where you can specify the exact location that you want to save your file in.

This is the point where you can organize your recorded audio. You can name and save this vocal track to an external hard drive, which can contain folders of all your music projects. This helps to save file space on your actual computer hard drive because WAV files are large byte files. Another option is to simply left-click on the small disk icon, but it will not allow you to specify where you want your audio recording saved. Rather, it will simply automatically save your audio recording to the default folder within FL Studio, titled `Recorded` in the browser.

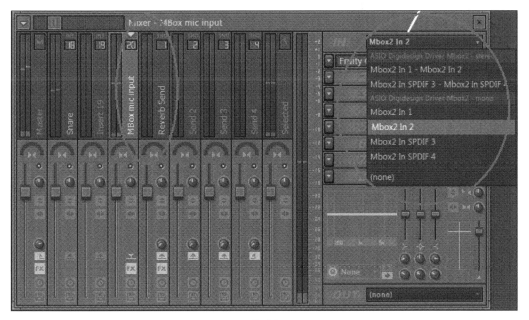

Fig 6.3

4. Bring up your playlist (by hitting *F5*) and highlight the measures you want to record on. Generally, you can highlight an area of your verse, chorus, intro, bridge, or outro. This way, you are specifying where you want to record instead of just recording from the beginning and losing your breath along with your performance. However, if you are a singer-songwriter and want to capture the mood of a straight through performance that lasts 3 to 4 minutes or longer, you can highlight a larger chunk of time. We have double-clicked and dragged our mouse on the measures from 1 to 9 as shown in the following screenshot:

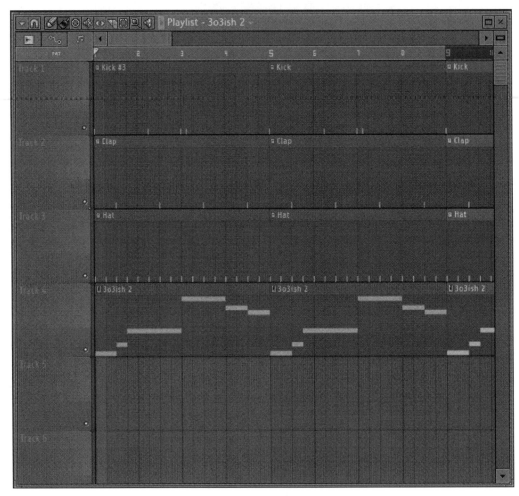

Fig 6.4

5. Click on the recording button on the transport controls as shown in *Fig 6.5*. The transport controls are play/pause, stop, and record.

6. Select **Audio, into the playlist as an audio clip**.

7. Click on the play button, and your recording will count down based on your **3 2 1** countdown setting shown to the right of the transport controls. You can also right-click on the **3 2 1** parameter to select the 1 bar or 2 bars countdown before recording. This will help you prepare before the recording and give you a little time to set up. The following screenshot shows the **Recording** window:

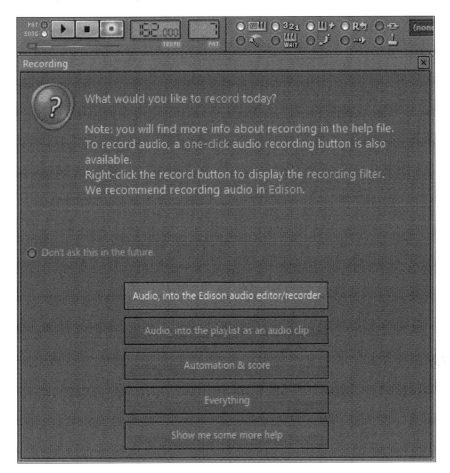

Fig 6.5

8. Your audio recording will now show up in the playlist in the exact section that you previously highlighted before recording. In *Fig 6.6*, it shows as **Vocal 1_4**, and you can see the waveform readout. It also automatically goes to the next available track in the playlist, which happens to be **Track 5**.

9. This track can now be treated like any type of audio in the playlist. You can move, cut, copy, paste, and rearrange your audio recording as shown in the following screenshot:

Fig 6.6

Your audio recording is now also its own dedicated channel in the step sequencer, as shown in the following screenshot:

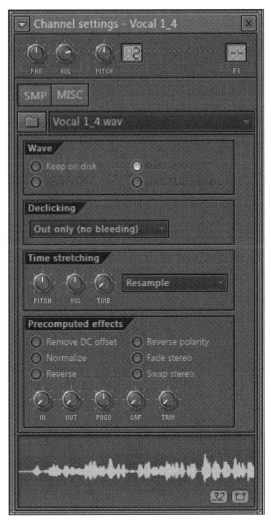

Fig 6.7

10. Once you find your new audio channel in the step sequencer (it will also be defaulted to a new step sequencer group called **Audio Clips**), it can be treated like any other WAV sample, MP3, or virtual instrument channel. You can send this to a mixer slot to gain more control and tweak your vocals further.

11. When you are done recording the vocals, go back to the FL Studio Mixer and select **(none)** on the insert slot where you selected your audio input (as shown in *Fig 6.3*). In this manner, you won't hear any audio coming through your interface or background noise being picked up from your microphone, and you will be able to mix cleanly again.

How it works...

Using the FL Studio Mixer allows you to pick a mixer slot for your audio path and select the input on your sound card or audio interface. You can record one microphone or audio input at a time or multiple inputs at the same time depending on your audio interface. For example, if your audio interface has eight inputs, you will need to go through each mixer slot one at a time and then select the input you want from the input drop-down box. This can help those who are in a band and depends on human chemistry and vibe to bring out the best in their recordings. It can also help singer-songwriters because they can use one microphone input for an acoustic guitar and another microphone input for the vocals. If you only have one microphone and one input, you can lay down one piece of the input at a time, which equates to overdubbing one recording after the next. The overdubbing technique is the best way to layer vocals for singers or rappers. Artists can double their vocals to add emphasis to certain words, and the second layer of vocals is where artists usually find their harmonies.

There's more...

Proper cables are extremely important when recording external audio. If you need 1/4 " cables, make sure you get balanced cables that will reduce the noise and boost your sound to an optimal level. This balanced 1/4 " cable is shown in the following image; it can be recognized by two rings near the tip, which may be black or metallic:

Fig 6.8

When working with condenser microphones, most of the time you will need phantom power, which is usually offered on mixers and audio interfaces, as well as an XLR cable as shown in the following image:

Fig 6.9

You are able to test the level of your audio the moment you select its input from the drop-down box on the FL Studio Mixer, so make sure you have everything set to a good level before recording.

You need to have a very quiet room before recording vocals and even have noise-canceling headphones that won't "bleed" or seep into the microphone. With live artists or a band recording, sometimes a small amount of bleed into the microphone can be considered good because you are capturing the sound of your room. When recording a live drum set, the bleed from one microphone to another is inevitable, and it is up to the producer or engineer to mix the various parts in the best way.

Soundproofing your room makes it so no one on the outside can hear your ruckus. Sound treatment is a whole other animal; it means adding materials (construction, flooring, carpet, doors, windows, bass traps, and monitoring isolation pads) that make your room optimal for mixing. This means that your mix will translate as what you hear and what it sounds like on entertainment systems, on CDs, on online streamed material, and on all devices. When recording vocals, you usually want to be in room that deadens the space; your level and signal will now be that much clearer and focused. Usually, a pop filter is used in front of the microphone so that sharp annunciations are not clipped. Great recordings have come from using closets as recording booths (try the song *Bird's Eye View* by *Statik Selektah*), so you may get lucky in the spaces you find! Good audio recording is, nevertheless, subjective and depends heavily on the type of sound you want to create.

See also

> ▶ The *Recording with or without effects* recipe
>
> ▶ The *Knowing your sound cards and/or audio interfaces* recipe in *Chapter 1, Configuring FL Studio*
>
> ▶ The *Sending a channel to a mixer slot* recipe in *Chapter 3, Working with the Step Sequencer and Channels*

Adding effects and your effect chain

The adding of effects in your effect chain takes place in the FL Studio Mixer. The purpose of an effect is to monitor or tweak your audio signal. When you engage each **Insert** slot in the mixer, you have the option to add up to eight effects in your chain. You can always add more effects by creating submixes to further mixer channels.

Getting ready

In order to start using effects on your mixer tracks, you have to have your audio signal sent to actual mixer inserts. This is reviewed in the *Sending a channel to a mixer slot* recipe in *Chapter 3, Working with Step Sequencer and Channels*.

How to do it...

1. Send a channel in the step sequencer to a mixer slot by double-clicking on the **FX** box (upper right-hand corner) in your **Channel settings**. This was reviewed in the *Sending a channel to a mixer slot* recipe in *Chapter 3, Working with Step Sequencer and Channels*.

2. Press *F9* to bring up the mixer.

3. Press the Space bar to start your project's playback.

4. Click on a mixer slot to engage the slot/column of the mixer. In *Fig 6.10*, we have engaged **INS slot 1**, which we renamed as **Kick**, and it is faintly highlighted. *Shift* + click on a slot to quickly rename it.

5. When you have your mixer slot engaged (it will be faintly highlighted), the mixer vertical hierarchy on the right of the mixer will correlate directly to the audio signal you engaged.

6. Click on the small, drop-down triangle next to the slot you want to enter an effect on.

7. Hover your mouse over **Select** to select the effect you desire. It will say **Replace** if an effect currently exists. It will populate a list for you, as shown in *Fig 6.10*.

 Right-click on the small triangle to bring up **PLUGIN PICKER**, which is a neat function that allows you to select plugins based on their picture and audio category.

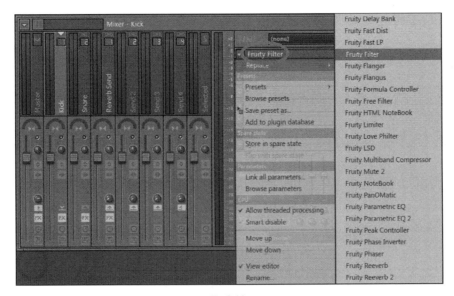

Fig 6.10

8. Click directly on the name of the effect, which is now in the slot you selected, to bring up the vast parameters of the effect.

9. When you click on the name of the effect in your slot, it will bring up the graphical plugin you added. In this case, we have added the **Fruity Filter** plugin, which will adjust the frequency ranges of your given sound.

10. Click on the small arrows on the upper right-hand side of your plugin while looking to the hint bar or right-click on the arrows to bring up the list of presets. *Fig 6.11* shows that we are on the preset **Party next door**, which is number 2 out of the four available presets. Presets are like a collection of parameters named by the plugin designers. From that point on, you can still tweak your parameters and save them as your own preset.

Fig 6.11

11. Add more effects within the same mixer slot/effect chain if you desire. We are still engaged on **INS 1**, which was renamed to read **Kick**. **Fruity Filter** is the topmost effect that we choose, as shown in *Fig 6.12*, and we now have the option to add 2 through 8. The same principles apply to every insert slot on the FL Studio Mixer. They are all independent from one another. Be cautious as to which mixer slot is currently engaged/faintly highlighted because the vertical hierarchy of each chain will only apply to the slot that is engaged.

Fig 6.12

How it works...

When working with our effect chain, we are affecting the exact mixer slot that is engaged. This is completely different from what we reviewed regarding the four send tracks in the mixer. You may have a better understanding of how send tracks work now, because when you work with independent mixer slots, they all have eight effects in their respective chains. With send tracks, you can send a little bit of your effect to whichever slots you desire.

When you are working on each mixer track, like we did in this recipe, each added effect will add to the workload of your computer. Also note the green mute button and knob directly to the right of each effect slot. The mute button will turn the effect on and off, and right-clicking on it will enable you to automate the muting. We will review automation in more detail in *Chapter 10, Recording Automation*. The knob to the right of the mute button will adjust the level of your effect. This can go from 0 to 100 percent. You can also automate any of the parameters within your graphical effect plugin by right-clicking on any knob in the plugin and selecting **Create automation clip**. In *Fig 6.11*, you will be able to automate the **Cutoff freq**, **Resonance**, **Low pass**, **Band pass**, **High pass**, and **x 2** buttons. Please remember that your effect chain is directly affected by the slots below it. You need to be aware of this when adding effects beneath other effects.

There's more...

Keeping with the principle that each effect is affected by what is beneath it, FL Studio allows you to move effects up or down in your chain. In *Fig 6.10*, after you click on the small triangle, you also have the option to move up or down. This can have a drastic effect on your audio signal. The best way to discover what happens when you move effects up or down is to experiment. Your ears will tell you what is likable versus what is unpleasant. If you have a weak processor on your computer and your project starts to pop, click, and glitch when you add a multitude of effects, you have one more option. You can highlight the section of your song with the effects in the FL Studio playlist and export that section only.

When you export something out of the playlist, it will render down all of the effects that are part of that sound. You will also want to mute all of the other channels or simply solo your mixer track that includes the effects. Once it is rendered down and exported into a WAV file, it will have the effects embedded inside of it and be one solid file. You can then import this file back into your project and remove the effects in your chain that were bogging down your computer. This can be a bit tedious but is sometimes the only way to help your computer process all of the information. It's important to ensure that memory-and CPU-hogging applications are not running concurrently with FL Studio.

See also

- ▶ The *Understanding master tracks and loud wars* recipe
- ▶ The *Exporting and re-importing a WAV file* recipe in *Chapter 8, Exporting and Rendering Your Project*
- ▶ The *Using automation for virtual instruments and effects* recipe in *Chapter 10, Recording Automation*

Perfecting equalization

Equalization means dealing with the frequencies of your instruments and percussion. **Hertz (Hz)** is the measure of the pitch, also known as the frequency; dB is the volume. Equalization helps you shape the sonic landscape when your music is played back on headphones, speakers, loud speakers, or any type of media device, or even when it is streamed online. You have probably seen the basic controls on entertainment systems and within your automobile radio. The basic controls are simply low, mid, and high. There is a fine line between knowing what to adjust and what sounds good just the way it is! The best advice is to trust your ears and get feedback from others in order to recognize the techniques that work for you. A pitch-to-frequency chart will help you understand the exact frequencies that correlate to the pitches, as shown in the following screenshot:

Pitch to Frequency Chart

PITCH	OCTAVE 0	1	2	3	4	5	6	7	8
A	27.5	55	110	220	440	880	1760	3520	7040
A#	29.13	58.27	116.54	233.08	466.16	932.32	1864.65	3729.31	7458.62
B	30.86	61.73	123.47	246.94	493.88	987.76	1975.53	3951.06	7902.12
C	32.7	65.4	130.81	261.62	523.25	1046.5	2093	4186	8372
C#	34.64	69.29	138.59	277.18	554.36	1108.73	2217.46	4434.92	8869.84
D	36.7	73.41	146.83	293.66	587.33	1174.65	2349.31	4698.62	9397.24
D#	38.89	77.78	155.56	311.56	622.25	1244.5	2489.01	4978.02	9956.04
E	41.2	82.4	164.81	329.62	659.25	1318.51	2637.02	5274.04	10548.1
F	43.65	87.3	174.61	349.22	698.45	1396.91	2793.82	5587.64	11175.3
F#	46.24	92.49	184.99	369.99	739.98	1479.97	2959.95	5919.9	11839.8
G	48.99	97.99	195.99	391.99	783.99	1567.98	3135.96	6271.92	12543.8
G#	51.91	103.82	207.65	415.3	830.3	1661.21	3322.43	6644.86	13289.7

Values above are measured in Hz or CPS

Fig 6.13

Getting ready

To start using EQ as an effect in the FL Studio Mixer, you will need to have some sort of audio sent to a mixer track. This was previously discussed in this chapter as well as in the *Sending a channel to a mixer slot* recipe in *Chapter 3, Working with Step Sequencer and Channels*. Once you have audio on any given mixer track, you are ready to start using equalization. You may press *F9* to bring up the FL Studio Mixer.

How to do it...

1. Send your audio to a mixer slot.

2. After your mixer slot is engaged or faintly highlighted, click on the triangle drop-down box next to the first effect slot in your mixer.

3. Select the **Fruity Parametric EQ 2** effect, as shown in *Fig 6.14*. Also note that the ninth mixer slot is engaged (faintly highlighted) and has been renamed to read `Alien Synth`. The dropdown will read **Replace** or **Select** based on whether an effect currently exists in a slot.

Right-click on the triangular drop-down box to bring up your list of plugins from the very cool **PLUGIN PICKER** feature.

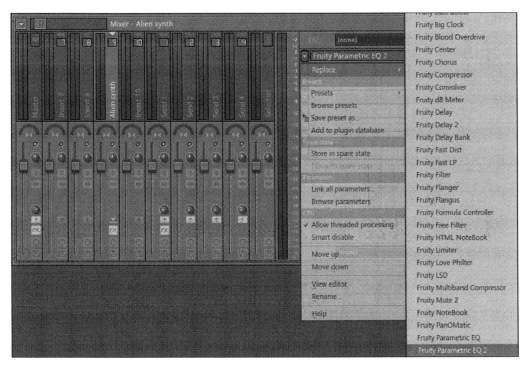

Fig 6.14

4. You will see the audio show up in purple and red visual feedback as shown in *Fig 6.15* on your EQ effect plugin. The leftmost side goes all the way to 20 Hz (low), and the rightmost side goes to 20000 Hz (high). Certain sounds and instruments sit in certain frequency ranges. Low bass is where 808s and kick drums sit, while vocals and percussion tend to stay between the mid-high range of frequencies.

5. Look to the right-hand side of your EQ plugin effect and focus on the yellow column.

6. Click-and-hold with your mouse on the small box of the yellow column and drag it up slowly. If you notice the dB numbers on the plugin, the range is from **-18** all the way up to **+18**. For general purposes and as a fundamental approach, you should raise this between **+6** and a little bit above **+12**. In *Fig 6.15*, we have raised up that particular frequency band to around +10.5 dB. This is the gain box.

7. As you drag up your yellow column, you will see that the circled number 4 in yellow will be pushed up on the EQ readout section of your plugin. When you use the square box in the column, it is locked to a vertical adjustment; it can only go straight up or straight down.

8. Look to your yellow column again and adjust the yellow circle / half circle at the bottom, which is next to **FREQ**. In this manner, you can sweep your frequency left and right until you hear something pleasing to your ears.

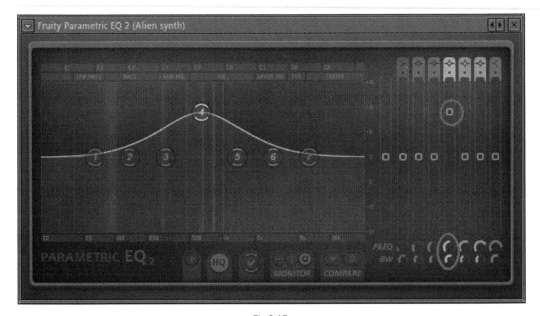

Fig 6.15

9. Look at the extreme bottom of your yellow column and you will see another circle that you can adjust. This is the bandwidth control, which is in the **BW** row at the bottom. When you adjust this knob, it will adjust how wide a range you are dealing with, from narrow to broad. Note that the only change we are making is to the bandwidth. The frequency and dB have not changed at all. The only difference between the previous and following screenshot is that the bandwidth is narrower in the latter.

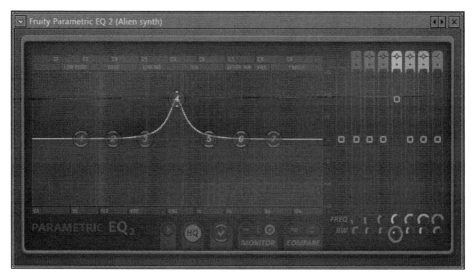

Fig 6.16

10. Once you find something pleasing to your ears, adjust the square box (dB) that goes straight up or down all the way back to **0**. This will not adjust your frequency or the bandwidth you have already set, so do not worry. It will only bring your dB back to zero.

11. Slowly, bring up the dB scale to taste. You will want to slowly bring it up vertically until you hear it kick in. You want to raise it up in a delicate manner. You will not raise this all of the way up to where it was earlier in step 6, but you will raise it ever so slightly. In the following screenshot, we have brought our dB back down to zero and then raised it up to our final position, which is around +2.5 dB:

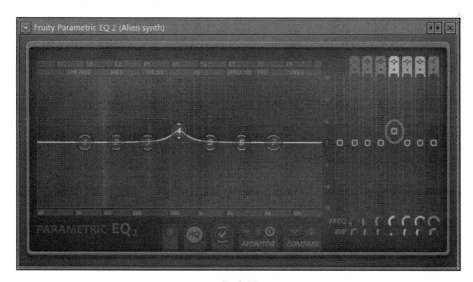

Fig 6.17

How it works...

The process we just described is called additive equalization. It boosts specific frequency ranges, but the downside is that it leaves the rest of your music content / mixer tracks down in volume from the area being boosted and reduces headroom. To do this, bring up the gain of a frequency range and sweep the frequency knob back and forth until you hear something you like. When you find a pleasing frequency range, bring the gain back to zero and then add it back until you have just enough for your tastes. This tends to yield a more hyped sound, which is sometimes the desired effect. For example, a kick drum can sound much bigger than it really is! Remember to use your ears in order to distinguish what is too much or too little. Using too much or too little EQ can make or break a song quite easily. Sometimes, the hardest thing to do is to leave instruments that already sound good alone.

A method that is used by prominent engineers is called subtractive equalization. In this method, you will basically do the same thing, but you will remove your displeasing frequency. Turn the gain of one of your frequency bands up by about +5 to +10 dB and sweep the frequency back and forth until you find an area that sounds displeasing to your ears. Then, you can return the gain back down to zero and lower it a little bit. This is regarded as a more natural-sounding use of equalization because it leaves most of the original content intact.

There's more...

You can also hover your mouse over the top portion of each column in the **Fruity Parametric EQ 2** effect until you see an arrow appear. This will change the type of filter, and you will be able to scroll through a low pass filter, band pass filter, high pass filter, notch filter, low shelf filter, and high shelf filter. A low pass filter will cut off the high frequencies, and you will hear the lows. You will be rolling off the highs and can choose how sharp you want a roll-off slope to be and how extreme that slope is. No dB adjustment will be available. Low pass is the noisy neighbor bass. A band pass filter focuses on the band you want to hear, and no dB adjustment will be available. A high pass filter will cut the low frequencies without dB. You will hear the highs. You will be rolling off the lows and can choose how extreme or sharp a roll-off slope you want. The higher you bring the high pass frequency, the more AM radio sounding it can be!

A notch filter takes out a certain frequency with no dB. Shelving equalizers amplify or satisfy the main frequency selected, plus all of the frequencies beyond that point. Shelving equalizers are good at making an instrument sound a little brighter or darker overall, without affecting any one specific frequency. Shelving EQs have a dB and can work pretty well. Shelving can give more bass or less bass across the board. It can give more treble or less treble across the board. Shelving is an overall boost or an overall removal.

To make your mix less muddy, you may want to remove 75 Hz and below on all instruments and all vocals. This is a tactic that is practiced by some of the best engineers. You can do this by selecting a high pass filter on band 1 (purple column) in **Fruity Parametric EQ 2** and adjusting the frequency to around 75 Hz. This is also a good trick for hi hats and percussion sounds that need to be clear in your mix. Most of the time, you don't need these low frequencies (75 Hz and below) on most your instruments besides bass, so you can roll them off and add more clarity to your mix. However, in cases where you desire to keep some of the darkness in your hi hats or instruments, you can try panning to either side so it has its own sonic space.

Using an equalizer to boost higher frequencies can give the illusion of an instrument sounding closer, while removing higher frequencies can make an instrument sound farther away.

Be mindful of your panning and volume throughout the EQ and mixing process. The greater the difference in the volume on one side (panning), the farther to that side is the sound from the center. So, raising the volume and panning a certain sound could open up the mix a bit.

Also, remember that you can use a MIDI controller to adjust the many knobs and parameters on your EQ plugins and on any type of effect in FL Studio. As always, you can also create automation clips by right-clicking on a given parameter.

Also, beneath your entire tree of effects in your effect chain (1 through 8), there is a basic low-, mid-, and high-frequency selector for your given mixer track on the FL Studio Mixer. This can come in handy for quick adjustments if you don't want to open up **Fruity Parametric EQ 2** and is great in cases where you want to totally cut off the low end. If you want to cut off the low end, simply bring the low shelf slider all the way to the bottom, that is, to -18 dB. You can also adjust the mid and high frequencies with this handy, basic EQ controller. Note that this EQ is like a ninth slot, and thus, it will affect the sound after all of the other slots in the chain. This is the final adjustment right before the output of the track.

See also

- The *Adding effects and your effect chain* recipe
- The *Sending a channel to a mixer slot* recipe in *Chapter 3, Working with the Step Sequencer and Channels*
- The *Using automation for virtual instruments and effects* recipe in *Chapter 10, Recording Automation*

Understanding master tracks and loud wars

Loud wars refer to the trend of increasing your songs main output. There are loud wars everywhere you look. If your YouTube video is not as loud as someone else's, the instant you press play, the average listener thinks it is not as good. When you are watching TV and a commercial comes on, it becomes much louder than the program you are watching. Anything that is streamed online must be extremely loud because your average listener truly believes that louder is better. Most producers and artists have to join this battle—if you can't beat them, join them.

The only issue with mastering is that the definition of mastering has changed dramatically over the years and it is still changing today, depending on who you talk to. In the 60s and 70s, when records were made on vinyl, you wanted your whole album to be uniform and flow smoothly from track to track in sequential order. Albums were like a story. They were there to be enjoyed. Mastering engineers, at the time, had the job of deciding which track went in what order, in addition to making sure that the levels and EQ flowed smoothly through the vinyl. This was still practiced with cassettes and CDs because these also told a story, and the mastering process involved picking the song order and making each song flow smoothly from one to the next.

The digital age, the Internet, iTunes, Napster, MP3 compressed files, and the release of singles instead of albums have changed the definition of mastering. Sure, it's awesome that everyone can share their songs worldwide through e-mail and the internet, but we are now dealing with MP3 files, which can be equated to compressed music. If you are simply releasing a single, you don't need someone to pick the album's song order. Picking the song order is irrelevant. Basically, when it comes down to it, your only concern is how loud your song is compared to other commercial releases.

While you don't have to be concerned with this, and you can do whatever you want with your music, loud wars put a good amount of pressure on artists, engineers, and producers. If you are producing pop, electronic, dance, or hip hop, you almost have to join the loud wars. This can be viewed as a good thing as well. This means that your track is loud, punchy, clear (yet hard hitting), and will hopefully include the many frequency ranges that are pleasing to listeners. Loudness while having clarity is what really wins the battle. It is extremely helpful to have a reference track close by, so that you can compare your song to a similar artist or genre you like, to note how the production quality differs.

Getting ready

To get started with mastering your project, it is imperative that you have your sequencing and mixing completely finished. During mastering it, you will only be dealing with the master track on the FL Studio Mixer, which is the first mixer track on the left-hand side. You want to make your complete production sound as good as is humanly possible, before you get to the mastering stage. Your levels, EQ, panning, sequencing, vocals, harmonies, and song arrangement should all be complete. You can also adjust the EQ when mastering, but it will only be adjustable on the master track. To bring up the FL Studio Mixer and the master track, you can press *F9*.

How to do it...

1. Bring up the FL Studio Mixer (by hitting *F9*) and click on the track titled **Master**.

2. While the master track is engaged, select **Fruity Parametric EQ 2** in the effect's first slot. You can do this by clicking on the small triangle, hovering your mouse over **Select** or **Replace**, and selecting your plugin from the list as shown in *Fig 6.18*.

 Right-click on the small, triangular dropdown to bring up the awesome **PLUGIN PICKER** feature.

Fig 6.18

3. The master volume slider at the top of your FL Studio project (the leftmost slider) should always be set at 100 percent, as shown in *Fig 6.19*. The same goes for your master track fader in the actual mixer as shown in *Fig 6.18*. This should always be at 100 percent. The reason for setting both of these at 100 percent is to avoid clipping. We will raise the volume through two effect plugins, not through these tools.

If either of these important sliders are changed, *Alt* + click or right-click and select **Reset** to return them to their default positions of 100 percent. *Alt* + clicking to reset the levels also applies the setting to most knobs and sliders in FL Studio.

Fig 6.19

4. Click on the **Fruity Parametric EQ 2** effect name in the first effect slot to bring up the graphical interface. We will only be using this plugin to bring up the volume a little bit.

5. In **Fruity Parametric EQ 2**, look at the column directly to the left of the purple column. Hover your mouse over the small box on this column, and note whether the FL Studio hint bar reads **Main level**.

6. Click-and-drag this column up until you reach about +3 dB in the FL Studio hint bar. You can also use the graphical plugin dB numbers as a guide. In *Fig 6.20*, you can see that the first slider is around +3 dB. There is a straight, white line in the EQ section that represents the main level. Again, we are not using this plugin for any EQ purposes at this particular juncture. This is simply a trick to raise the main level.

Fig 6.20

7. Bring up the **Fruity Compressor** plugin, which is directly underneath **Fruity Parametric EQ 2**. This will be on the second effect slot in the master effect chain as shown in the following screenshot:

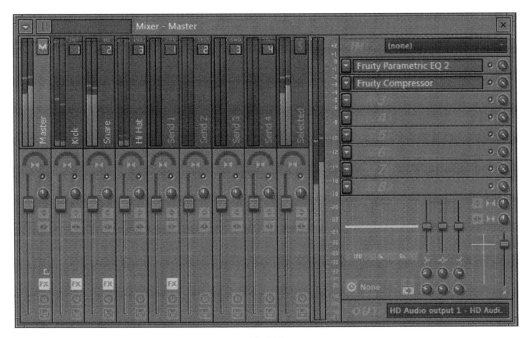

Fig 6.21

8. Click directly on the **Fruity Compressor** name in the second slot to bring up the graphical parameters, as shown in *Fig 6.22*.

9. For now, keep the **Threshold** and **Gain** knobs at **0.0**. At the current juncture, this means that the **Threshold** knob will be turned all the way to the right and the **Gain** knob will be directly in the middle.

10. Adjust your ratio to **3.0 : 1**.

11. Leave **Type** as **Hard**.

12. Turn the **Attack** and **Release** knobs all the way to the left, which will result in an attack time of **0.0 ms** and a release time of **1 ms**.

13. Press the Space bar to hear your project's playback. You will be using your ears during this process.

14. Turn the **Threshold** knob until you reach about **-4.0 dB** (negative 4.0 dB).

15. Turn the **Gain** knob slowly (while holding down *Ctrl* for smaller increments) until you hear the volume boost. This will be right around **4.0 dB** or something close to it. This could be around **3.0 dB** to **4.0 dB** or slightly higher. Use your ears because you do not want to induce any distortion or clipping. You can experiment and move the **Gain** knob way past **4.0 dB** to realize how far you can go without clipping.

Fig 6.22

How it works...

With regards to the threshold, values above the dB level of the threshold will be compressed in accordance with the ratio. The gain will boost the overall value of the ratio to compensate for the volume reduction. The amount of gain reduction is determined by the ratio. A ratio of 3:1 means that if your input level is 3 dB over the threshold, the output signal will be 1 dB over the threshold. It is the dBs your input signal will need to increase to produce a 1 dB gain in the output signal.

The **Type** tab affects how gradually compression kicks in above the threshold. The **Attack** tab refers to how quickly the signal triggers compression to kick in. The **Release** tab sets the time that the compressor takes to stop acting after the level has dropped below the threshold. This method described previously helps you join the loud wars. You will find that it works great once you export your project, burn a CD, and listen to it in the car while comparing it to other commercial releases. It will also sound great everywhere, including on entertainment systems, MP3 players, your studio monitors, and online streamed material.

What we have done is turned the **Fruity Compressor** effect into a brick wall limiter. (Generally, a ratio of 10:1 is considered for brick wall limiting, but the way we adjusted the attack and release times makes it function as a limiter.) Be mindful of your **Peak meter** option in the FL Studio Mixer. This shows your dB level on your master track, and it should not go past 0.0 dB. Dynamic processors such as compressors and limiters are devices used to control the volume of a signal. Some are used to bring loud signals closer to the volume of quieter signals. Others extend the difference between loud and quiet signals.

A limiter could be compared to a governor, where signal peaks do not exceed a certain value. Typically speaking, a ratio above 8.0:1 is considered to be limiting. Limiters typically employ very fast attack times with fast release times and high thresholds. We have shown an example using the 3.0:1 ratio to demonstrate how powerful this brick wall limiter can be, without having to use the 8.0:1 ratio. Feel free to experiment with different thresholds, ratios, and gain levels.

There's more...

While mastering, you may also want to use EQ and adjust your frequency ranges. The high-shelving EQs do a nice job of opening up your track and letting air into the high-end spectrum. You may also want to test out multiband compressors; they allow you to focus on each band and then compress or limit as you see fit. Instead of one large compression on the entire song, you can focus on the bass and then compress, focus on the mid-levels and then compress, and finally, focus on the high end and then compress.

Remember that you may also want to master after you have rendered your completed music project, directly before mastering. This greatly helps your CPU load because your entire project will be rendered down to one WAV file. Then, you can close your project, open up a blank project, and import your WAV file into it. Your WAV file will be the only audio file in your entire project in FL Studio. At that point, you can use plugins to master your project.

The method we just used that involves **Fruity Parametric EQ 2** (for the main level only) and **Fruity Compressor** (which was turned into a brick wall limiter) will hold its own against any mastering process out there. You can now win against any producer in the loud wars. You may also want to purchase plugins from `www.waves.com`, `www.izotope.com`, `www.fabfilter.com`, or `http://mcdsp.com/`. We will review how to install these types of plugins as well as free plugins found on the Internet in *Chapter 1, Configuring FL Studio*.

See also

▶ The *Install virtual instruments and effects* recipe in *Chapter 1, Configuring FL Studio*

▶ The *Export your audio stems* recipe in *Chapter 8, Exporting and Rendering Your Project*

▶ The *Exporting and re-importing a WAV file* recipe in *Chapter 8, Exporting and Rendering Your Project*

Getting the best out of your mixer

Since each mixer track in the FL Studio Mixer can have its own chain of effects, there are ways to save your work and develop your own templates over time. FL Studio also has some defaults to get you going and improve your understanding of certain mixer chains. Remember that each mixer slot can have its own chain from 1 to 8 in the vertical list.

Getting ready

To get started with using your mixer to the best of your abilities, you simply need to have audio enabled on any of the mixer tracks. This was reviewed in the *Sending a channel to a mixer slot* recipe in *Chapter 3, Working with Step Sequencer and Channels*. You can press *F9* to bring up the FL Studio Mixer.

How to do it...

1. Bring up the FL Studio Mixer and engage a mixer track.

2. Choose your chain of effects. In *Fig 6.23*, we have engaged / faintly highlighted the **Snare** mixer track (**INS 2**) and selected **Fruity Compressor** on the first slot, **Fruity Parametric EQ 2** on the second effect slot, and **Fruity Flangus** on the third effect slot. In this example, we have already tweaked each of the plugin parameters and we are satisfied with the result.

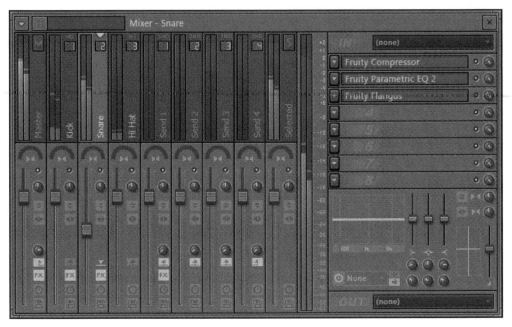

Fig 6.23

3. Select the small triangular drop-down box in the left-hand corner of the FL Studio Mixer as shown in *Fig 6.24*.

4. Hover your mouse over **File** and then click on **Save mixer track state as...**.

 When selecting **Save mixer track state as...**, you can click, hold, and drag it to any other mixer track in order to copy-and-paste the effect chain from one track to another.

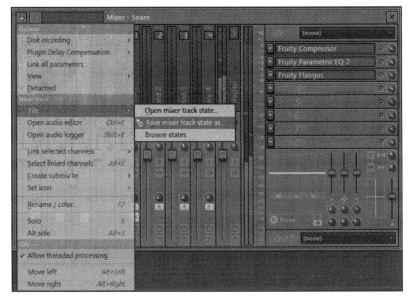

Fig 6.24

5. You will be able to save your effect chain for this given mixer track as shown in *Fig 6.25*. This action will save your effect chain and all of the parameters within each plugin in the chain.

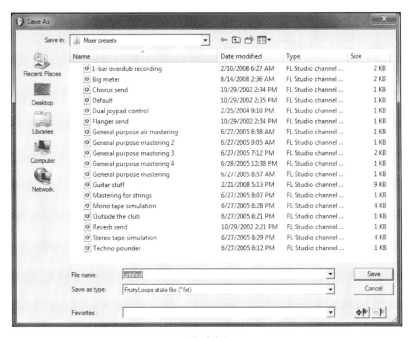

Fig 6.25

6. If you are working with two screens or monitors, you can move the FL Studio Mixer to a new screen using the triangular drop-down box in the left-hand corner of the mixer.

7. Click on the triangle and make sure that **Detached** is clicked. You can now slide your mixer to a new screen to create more screen real estate and organization for your project.

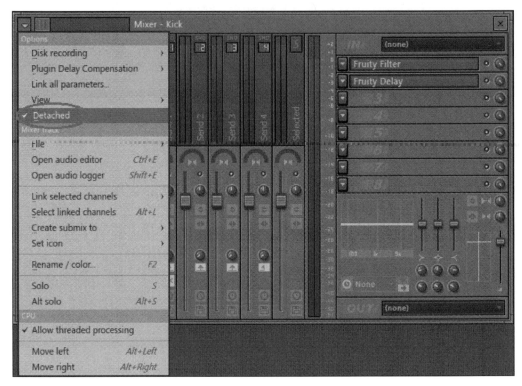

Fig 6.26

How it works...

The reason for saving your mixer track state is so you don't have to carry out the same manual process time and again. Sure, each project will have its own sounds and concepts, but saving your mixer track state will basically create a template of the mixer track, which you can bring up for quick recall. From that point on, you can tweak it to your liking, but the fundamental settings are apt, or at least close to what you desire. You can rename these mixer track states to whatever you like. This can save hours of time in the long haul.

Additionally, FL Studio includes presets to help you get started. Use the triangular drop-down box, hover your mouse over **File**, and select **Open mixer track state...** to test some of FL Studio's mixer states. Anything you previously saved on your own will also be populated in this area.

There's more...

When you are mixing your song and have a multitude of instruments and sounds on many mixer tracks, you can right-click on the **Mute / solo** button in order to solo any mixer track you desire. You want to hear your mix in the context of all of the sounds at once, but sometimes you may want to solo a mixer track in order to finely tweak the sound and ensure that it is crisp. The mixing process takes time, and you will get better with experience. The best way to learn how to mix by ear is through experimentation. Listen to other mixes that you consider successful and break down why they are deemed a good mix/master. Rename your mixer track by pressing *Shift* + clicking on a track or highlighting a track and then pressing *F2*; doing so helps to organize the mixer.

As always, you can use a MIDI controller with physical knobs and sliders to adjust the parameters on the mixer instead of using a mouse. You may also automate many of the controls on the mixer, which will be reviewed in *Chapter 10, Recording Automation*.

See also

▶ The *Sending a channel to a mixer slot* recipe in *Chapter 3, Working with the Step Sequencer and Channels*

▶ The *Working with MIDI controllers and MIDI pads* recipe in *Chapter 4, Building Your Song*

▶ The *Using automation for virtual instruments and effects* recipe in *Chapter 10, Recording Automation*

▶ The *Installing virtual instruments and effects* recipe in *Chapter 1*, Configuring FL Studio

Recording with or without effects

Recording with or without effects relates to the external audio you are recording. The recording of external audio was reviewed earlier in this chapter and relates to vocals, guitars, keyboard synthesizers, turntables, and any audio that is recorded with a microphone. When you are ready to record external audio in FL Studio, you can adjust your sound before recording. This means that your sound inside FL Studio will then hold the parameters and audio signal you tweaked before recording. The audio will be rendered inside FL Studio and may be difficult to change and adjust. The other method is to record your audio signal dry. This means that you will not have any compression or EQ changes on your signal, and you can then edit your audio after the recording. This gives you more freedom and flexibility to shape and change the sound you want inside the box, which means inside your computer program—FL Studio.

However, there is a slight middle ground here. You want to have the clearest and cleanest audio signal possible before recording audio in FL Studio, especially for vocals. This means that you can use an external preamp or compressor, which will amplify your sound, give you a lot more gain, and provide more character to your tone.

Getting ready

You want to follow the same principles that were reviewed in *Recording external audio* earlier in this chapter.

How to do it...

1. Engage a mixer track on the FL Studio Mixer.

2. Select your audio input from the upper right-hand **IN** dropdown in the FL Studio Mixer. This will correlate directly to the inputs on your audio interface.

3. Select the disk icon at the bottom of the FL Studio Mixer on the mixer track you have engaged for recording. You may right-click on it to save it to a path you specified or simply left-click to save it in the FL Studio default path.

4. At this point, you can add effects directly on your effect chain while your mixer track is engaged for recording. This will adjust your sound before it is recorded and your adjustments will play back once the recording is complete.

5. Engage the record button in the FL Studio transport controls and then press the play button to begin your recording. You can also use the **3 2 1** countdown before recording.

How it works...

Before recording, you can add effects in your effect chain to shape your sound. If you are using an audio interface, you can adjust your gain and get your level suitable for recording. If you are using an external preamp or compressor, you can adjust the settings on your hardware before recording. Most of the time, the raising of the gain is well practiced. The question that comes into play is whether or not you are going to add extra compression and EQ to your recorded signal directly before recording it in FL Studio. Generally, the adding of the EQ and compression is practiced before recording vocals. If you have vintage or external analog gear with quality EQ controls and electronics, you may want to give your EQ a try.

All audio interfaces have an onboard preamp; if you are using a vintage piece of gear as your preamp, you will turn your audio interface preamp gain all the way down. In this manner, your gain/EQ will be handled by your vintage preamp; the interface is simply the place for your signal to travel back and forth on your computer. Look for audio interfaces with a good analog-to-digital converter, which will provide as little latency as possible. For example, a great microphone preamp is the Daking Mic Pre One. You could use this piece of gear to amplify your vocals before recording, but make sure to turn your audio interface gain all the way down. Find out more about Daking at www.daking.com. The same principles apply when working with external EQs or compressors.

There's more...

You can also monitor your recording with reverb in order to enhance your vocal performance, but the reverb will not actually be rendered in the audio recording. The reverb is set up only to add a nice sonic quality for your vocals during performance. Usually, a vocalist or performer can perform better with a slight reverb effect on their audio signal. You can also do this with other effects. This is referred to as monitor routing.

Fig 6.27

Take a look at how to monitor your vocals using the following steps:

1. You will want to engage or faintly highlight a track for recording. In this case, it is **INS 1**, which is titled **To Disk**. Select your audio input from the **IN** drop-down box in the right-hand corner in the FL Studio Mixer while the **To Disk** track is engaged.

2. While the **To Disk** track is still engaged, send this track to the **Monitor** track **(INS 2)**. This is done by engaging the **To Disk** track and then clicking on the area above **FX** on the **Monitor** track. The small circular button will appear as shown in *Fig 6.27* on the **Monitor** column.

3. Now engage the **Monitor** track.

4. While the **Monitor** track is engaged, use one of your send channels on the FL Studio Mixer to send a reverb effect to the **Monitor** track. (This was reviewed earlier in this chapter and is called *Using send tracks in the mixer*.) You will have to add a reverb effect on the send track, but be mindful of what track is engaged. To actually send the reverb to the **Monitor** track, the **Monitor** track will have to be engaged; you can use the send knob on the reverb send mixer track.

5. You can also add compression or any other effect to the actual **Monitor** track. This is done by engaging the **Monitor** track and selecting an effect slot plugin (1 to 8 in the vertical effect list).

6. Your input will be recorded dry, yet you will hear the input routed through the **Monitor** channel, which contains any effect you want and any send effect you desire (usually reverb).

See also

- The *Using send tracks in the mixer* recipe
- The *Recording external audio* recipe
- The *Sending a channel to a mixer slot* recipe in *Chapter 3, Working with the Step Sequencer and Channels*

7
Sampling Using Edison

In this chapter, we will cover:

- ▶ Finding a sample
- ▶ Obtaining a seamless loop
- ▶ Embedding your tempo information
- ▶ Importing your new saved sample
- ▶ Time-stretching your sample in your project
- ▶ Fine-tuning your sample

Introduction

Edison is an extraordinary WAV editor within the FL Studio program. It is a scratch pad of sorts where you can record or manipulate audio in different ways. You will also be able to drag audio files directly from your desktop into Edison. As far as sampling goes, the parameters you manipulate in Edison give you the ability to sample any song that inspires you. This can be from any time period. Moreover, it encapsulates acapella, instrumentals, and standard songs with music and lyrics. You can also sample any sound or effect from other WAV or MP3 sources. When you want to use a certain loop or musical measure from a song that inspires you, you must take specific steps within Edison to make sure your settings are optimal for use in FL Studio. The creative possibilities for sampling are boundless. You can create your own spin and develop remixes. There are also legal issues in selling your song after sampling, but we will review entertainment law, publishing, composing rights, and copyrights in the *Appendix*.

Finding a sample

You can find samples and get inspired at any point in your life. This means you may have songs that connected with you during your childhood, bands you saw in concert, orchestras you attended, YouTube videos you enjoy, or the most popular method in electronic, rap, and pop music: digging through vinyl records. Vinyl records and turntables can be recorded in the same manner as a microphone used while recording vocals. The only difference is that you will be using a line-level signal while recording vinyl records into FL Studio. It signifies that audio output for condenser microphones will generally use XLR cables and record players or turntables will use RCA, one quarter inch, and/or SPDIF outputs. You will simply select your vinyl record audio input in the same manner that you choose your input for vocals, guitar, or keyboards.

Getting ready

To get started with sampling in Edison, you will want to open up a new audio editor. The FL Studio hint bar will notify you that your mouse is hovering on **Open (new) audio editor**, which is the symbol with the scissors in the following screenshot:

Fig 7.1

How to do it...

Now let's begin sampling with Edison by carrying out the following steps:

1. Open up Edison by clicking on the scissors symbol, as mentioned earlier.
2. Drag-and-drop an MP3 or WAV file from your desktop into Edison, as shown in the following screenshot:

Fig 7.2

3. In order to arrange and resize your FL Studio main window, you may click on the maximize/restore button, as shown in *Fig 7.3*. In this manner, you can resize the entire FL Studio program in order to drag-and-drop your MP3 or WAV file.

Fig 7.3

4. An alternate method to the drag-and-drop method is to simply click on the disk/file icon on Edison and select **Load sample...**, as shown in *Fig 7.4*. This will enable you to browse anywhere on your computer to select the audio file that you want to listen to and edit in Edison.

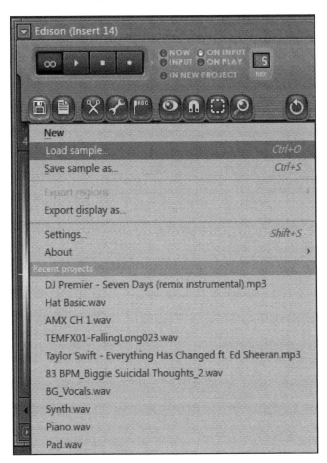

Fig 7.4

5. Once your sample is loaded in either method, you will see the audio waveform of your file in a graphical display, as shown in the following screenshot:

Fig 7.5

6. Click-and-drag inside the waveform in order to highlight an area you want to sample or preview. Your selection will show in red and you can simply click on the left- or right-hand side of your red selection to resize.

 Resize Edison by hovering your mouse to the leftmost, rightmost, top, or bottom area until your cursor changes into an arrow. Use the **Detached** mode (upper-left-hand corner triangle drop-down box) to drag Edison to a separate computer monitor / screen.

7. Select an area of your file that you want to capture (sample). Generally, you can highlight a short area that has a quick percussion hit / FX or a measure, beat, bar, or loop of music. When working with a loop, select the infinity symbol on the top-left and your selection will loop back around, allowing you to trim the beginning or end of it. In the following screenshot, we have selected a loop:

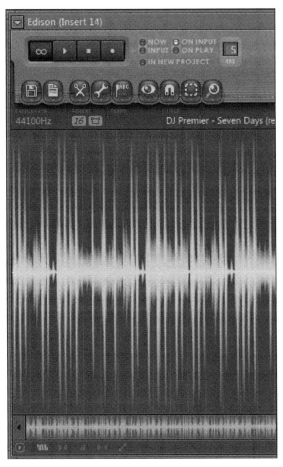

Fig 7.6

8. While your Edison window is engaged, press the Space bar to play back your sample and adjust the start and end times with your mouse.

Fig 7.7

9. In order to use a sample that you have selected in Edison in your actual FL Studio project, simply click on the **Drag / copy sample / selection** button and drag your sample into the step sequencer. The **Drag / copy sample / selection** button is the second icon from the far right in *Fig 7.7*. We discussed the various ways to drop audio into the step sequencer in the *Working with rhythm and percussion* recipe in *Chapter 4, Building Your Song*. Keep an eye on the FL Studio hint bar when you hover your mouse in order to make sure you are using the proper function.

You may also use the **Save sample as...** feature by clicking on the disk icon inside the Edison window. This allows you to organize and archive your sample outside FL Studio.

How it works...

Basically, we are importing an audio sample into Edison, selecting the part we want to use, and dragging it into the step sequencer. Once you have your audio sample inside the step sequencer, you can utilize it in the same manner you use any channel in the step sequencer.

Make sure you resize the Edison window in order to optimize your workflow and make things easier to see. You can hover your mouse on any part of the Edison window until your cursor changes to a resize arrow. You can do this on any corner of the Edison window in addition to the top or bottom. Another crucial tool when working with Edison is the S key on your QWERTY keyboard. Clicking this will change your audio view into a spectrum instead of a waveform, and it will help you find a loop. We will review getting a seamless loop in the next recipe.

A crucial tool when working with any type of audio file in Edison is the use of the *Page Up* and *Page Down* keys on your QWERTY keyboard. *Page Up* will zoom in on your sample and help you find the exact location you want to start or stop your highlighted selection. *Page Down* will zoom out so you can get an overview of what your entire audio file looks like and where your current selection actually is in relation to the whole sample. The zoom-in function can get extremely close (up to the milliseconds of your sample), and this is sometimes needed to perform audio surgery and get the best possible selection we can. Take care while choosing the proper selection because you will be using the sample in your music project.

Press *Ctrl + Shift* and click/drag to the left or right at the bottom of Edison in order to zoom in and out. Press *Crl + Alt* and click/drag up and down to zoom in and out. This is similar to using the scroll bar in the playlist, as reviewed in *Chapter 5, Using the Playlist*. With Edison, you use the **Zoom/ Scroll** bar near the bottom of the window.

There's more...

You may also use the **Detached** function—the exact function used on the FL Studio Mixer. This will allow you to detach Edison and drag it to another screen or computer monitor. Clicking on the small triangle on the upper-left-hand corner in Edison drops down a menu with the **Detached** functionality. Clicking on that will help you separate and isolate Edison so the entire graphical window is easier to work with. Also, be aware of where Edison actually exists on our FL Studio mixer. Sometimes, it will pop up on one of our FL Studio Mixer chain slots in the FL Studio Mixer. Edison is actually a Fruity effect and can be added to any FX slot (1 to 8 vertically) in the FL Studio Mixer.

You may also right-click on where your audio file is displayed on Edison. This will bring up a variety of parameters used to manipulate and tweak your audio. Additionally, be sure to experiment with all of the icons in the previous screenshot. Edison is a very powerful audio editor and it can definitely enhance the sound of your FL Studio project.

You can also edit any type of sample in your browser within Edison in order to tweak it to your needs. Basically, Edison can be used as an audio editor and audio sampler, as well as an audio recording system.

Send to playlist as audio clip / to channel is a newer function that enables you to send your highlighted selection directly to the FL Studio playlist. It also creates a channel in the step sequencer. This is the last icon to the right in *Fig 7.7*. You may also use **Save icon**, which we saw previously in the *How to do it...* section, in order to use the **Save sample as...** feature and save your highlighted selection wherever you desire on your computer. This can sometimes be an external hard drive or a dedicated folder and may help with organization. If you do not use this method, your dragged sample (once dragged or moved into the step sequencer) will be saved automatically in the `Sliced beats` folder on the FL Studio Browser.

See also

- ▶ The *Obtaining a seamless loop* recipe
- ▶ The *Sending a channel to a mixer slot* recipe in *Chapter 3, Working with Step Sequencer and Channels*
- ▶ The *Working with rhythm and percussion* recipe in *Chapter 4, Building Your Song*
- ▶ The *Recording external audio – keyboards, vocals, guitar, and devices* recipe in *Chapter 6, Using the FL Studio Mixer and Recording Audio*

Obtaining a seamless loop

Obtaining a seamless loop in Edison means making your loop sync in time and on beat. This is usually done in 4/4 time, but you can also find loops in 3/4 time or any variation of time you need. We will be adjusting the start and end points of the loop and making sure everything flows in musical beats and bars. If you have too much empty space at the beginning or end of your highlighted loop selection, your sample simply won't be practical to use in your musical project because the timing will be off. Your looped sample must be seamless – you are extracting the musical idea and this must be in perfect sync with respect to time or as close as possible.

Depending on your source genre, it may sometimes be a tad difficult to get a seamless loop because the song in question is not actually played in perfect time. This is usually acoustic or rock genres because some bands don't actually play with a "click track", which is a guiding tempo used during recording. Some bands don't use a click track on purpose, because it can add a more human element to their entire recording. Nevertheless, when working with Edison and trying to find a seamless loop, no matter what the source, you can usually come very close to finding a useable loop because you generally will only be extracting certain sections of your source material.

The source material doesn't always have to be long, as long as it can translate. You can also fine-tune and stretch your sample once it becomes a channel in the step sequencer, and we will review this in the final two recipes of this chapter. It may be a tad easier to find your seamless loop when working with electronic, rap, pop, and hip hop genres because they are inherently created using a strict digital tempo.

Getting ready

In order to find a seamless loop in Edison, you will want to have Edison open and a WAV or MP3 file loaded into the editor. You can load samples by using the disk icon and browsing on your computer or by dragging-and-dropping a sample from your desktop directly into Edison, as discussed in the previous recipe.

How to do it...

Let's have a look at the steps required to obtain a seamless loop.

1. Click on the loop symbol at the upper-left-hand corner of Edison. It will turn yellow when engaged, as shown in the following screenshot:

Fig 7.8

2. Click on the **Disable autoscrolling** button near the upper-right-hand corner of the Edison interface. When disabled, it will have a slash mark through it, as shown in the following screenshot:

Fig 7.9

3. Use your left and right scroll feature located at the bottom of Edison, as shown in *Fig 7.10*. When you hover your mouse over the left- or right-hand corner of the scroll bar at the bottom, notice that you can zoom in and out. You may also scroll left or right by clicking and dragging on the middle of the scroll bar.

[Press *Ctrl + Shift* and click/drag left and right on the **Zoom/Scroll** bar at the bottom as well as *Ctrl + Alt* and click/drag up and down in order to zoom in and out.]

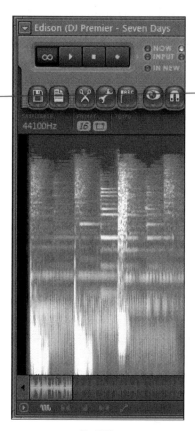

Fig 7.10

The following screenshot shows the exact location of the scroll bar area:

Fig 7.11

4. Hit the S button on your QWERTY keyboard in order to change the view from a waveform to a spectrum and vice versa.

5. Adjust the start and end points of your highlighted sample by clicking on them within Edison.

6. Press the Space bar to start and stop your sample.

7. Zoom in by pressing *Page Up* and zoom out by pressing *Page Down*. You may also need to adjust your scroll bar when doing this in order to see the exact location of your edits.

8. If you notice any pops and clicks at the start or end points of your loop, right-click on your highlighted area, hover your mouse on **Tools**, and select **Declick in** (beginning/ start point of your highlighted section) or **Declick out** (end point of your highlighted selection), respectively. This action is shown in the following screenshot:

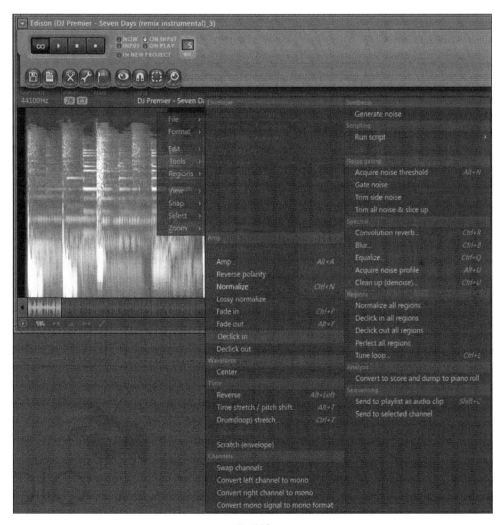

Fig 7.12

9. Once you are satisfied with your loop and highlighted section, hold down *Ctrl* and press the *Delete* key. This is the **Trim** tool and can also be found by right-clicking on your audio in Edison, selecting **Edit**, and then selecting **Trim**.

How it works...

We are basically adjusting the highlighted section of the loop we want to sample and capture/extract, and using the various tools in Edison to assist us in this process. Disabling autoscrolling will turn off automatic autoscrolling, and you can then use the scroll bar at the bottom of Edison to adjust the view of your Edison interface. Please remember that you can adjust the whole graphical interface or main window of Edison by hovering your mouse on the corners, top, or bottom of Edison to make your view as user friendly as possible.

Using the S key while adjusting your sample can greatly help you find where your beats and bars are, because the spectrum view shows straight vertical lines where certain musical phenomenon occurs. For example, there will usually be a vertical line on the down beat of your sample. This is usually where the kick drum or cymbal hits can assist you in finding the start point of your loop.

Once your loop is close to perfect in terms of musical time, you can zoom in on your sample (*Page Up*), use the scroll function to get in very close on the properties of your sample, and adjust your start point or end point accordingly. The closer you are zoomed in, the more audio surgery you can perform. You can also get rid of clicks and pops by zooming in very close and adjusting the highlighted portion carefully. Sometimes, the smallest adjustment when you are zoomed in can greatly help the musical feel of your sample.

An easier way of getting rid of unwanted noise, pops, and clicks at the beginning or ending portion of you sample is to use the **Declick in** or **Declick out** functionality. Trimming your sample at the final stage of your process makes your highlighted section the exclusive audio inside of Edison and removes any part of your audio that is not selected.

Once you are happy with your seamless loop, you can save it anywhere on your computer, drag it into the playlist, or drag it into the step sequencer. You can use it as a step on the step sequencer or within the piano roll. Once you have found your loop, your audio will act the same as any other type of audio used in FL Studio. You will still have your channel settings and the ability to send it to the FL Studio mixer for further processing.

There's more...

You may also slice and chop your loop or any audio loaded into Edison. The button with the **+** sign in *Fig 7.13* enables you to add manual slices, and the button to the right of that automatically slices your sample for you. Once you have your slices, you can drag your sliced sample into the **Fruity Slicer** channel by using the **Drag / copy sample / selection** button. This will enable you to play all of your slices with separate keys on a MIDI controller or with the Piano roll because it further separates your sample into individual pieces and parts. You can create a **Fruity Slicer** channel by going to **Channels | Add one | Fruity Slicer**. You can then use **Drag / copy sample / selection icon**, which has been discussed in the previous recipe, and drag it directly onto the **Fruity Slicer** channel on the step sequencer. Working with sliced audio may help you find more creative ways to utilize your samples. The **Fruity Slicer** channel can be sent to a mixer slot, but all of the samples/slices within it will be governed by one mixer slot.

Fig 7.13

See also

- ▸ The *Importing your new saved sample* recipe
- ▸ The *Time-stretching your sample to your project* recipe
- ▸ The *Fine-tuning your sample* recipe
- ▸ The *Exploring Channel settings* recipe in *Chapter 3, Working with Step Sequencer and Channels*
- ▸ The *Working with rhythm and percussion* recipe in *Chapter 4, Building Your Song*

Embedding your tempo information

Embedding the tempo of your seamless loop inside of Edison will enable you to time-stretch your sample to the tempo of your FL Studio project. This can be any type of seamless loop discussed in the previous recipe, or an acapella sample, which means a vocal track without any type of instrumentation. When you embed tempo information into an acapella sample, you can time-stretch it to the tempo of your FL Studio project. We will review time-stretching in the final two recipes of this chapter, but finding your sample tempo is crucial to having creative control of your musical project.

Getting ready

In order to embed your tempo information into your Edison audio, you will want to have completed the previous recipe. Your seamless loop should be selected and trimmed so that the only audio within Edison is the exclusive material you have adjusted.

How to do it...

Let's go through the necessary steps to embed your tempo information.

1. Engage Edison and hit the Space bar to start your sample.

2. While your sample is playing, right-click on your main FL Studio **TEMPO** readout and select **Tap...** as shown in *Fig 7.14*. This will bring up the **Tempo tapper** window.

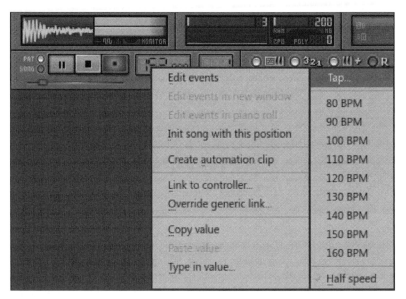

Fig 7.14

3. Hit the *T* key on your QWERTY keyboard in sync with your sample's beat (T stands for tap). Your tempo will change as you do this, but will remain fixed once you find your beat. The following screenshot shows your tempo as **185**:

Fig 7.15

4. Right-click on the small area beneath the **TITLE** readout on Edison. In the following screenshot, you will see we have right-clicked on the text that says **DJ Premier - Seven Days (remix instrumental)**:

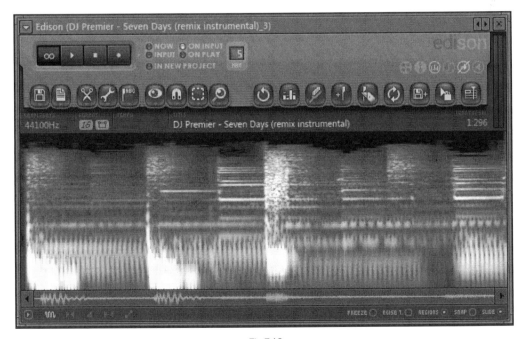

Fig 7.16

5. After right-clicking on the **TITLE** area, the **Sample properties** window will appear as shown in *Fig 7.17*.

6. In the **Tempo** section, enter the information that you previously discovered during the **Tempo tapper** process into the **Tempo (BPM)** field and click on **Accept**, as shown in the following screenshot:

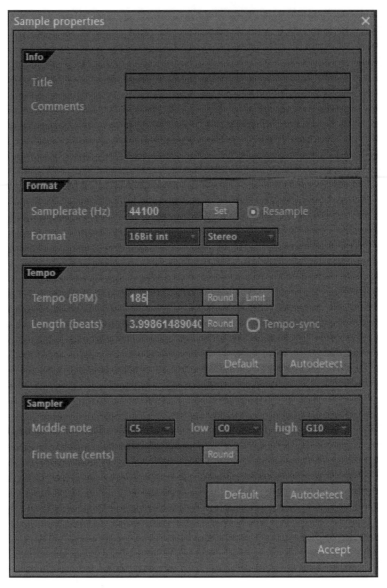

Fig 7.17

7. Once accepted, the values you entered in the **TEMPO** section in the **Sample properties** window will show up inside of Edison beneath the **TEMPO** field. In *Fig 7.18*, our Edison sample now shows **185BPM**. The tempo information is now embedded in your audio sample.

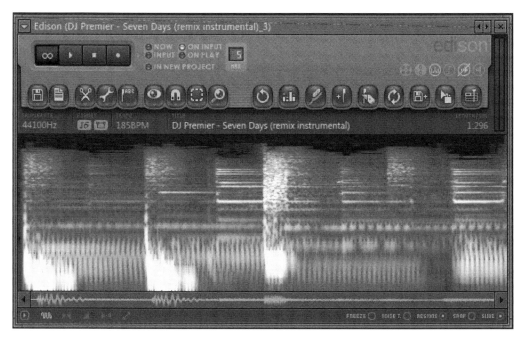

Fig 7.18

8. Click on the disk icon and select **Save sample as...** as shown in *Fig 7.19* if you want to save it anywhere on your computer or external hard drive. You could also use the **Drag / copy sample / selection** button or select **Send to playlist as audio clip / to channel**.

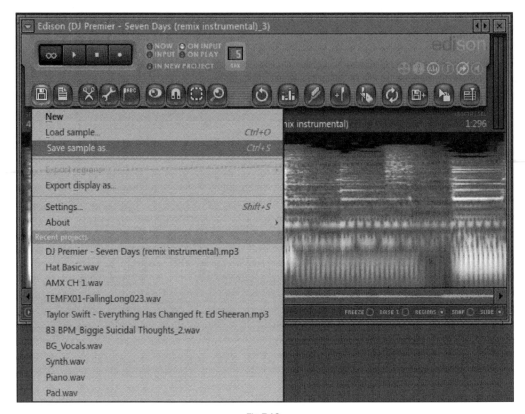

Fig 7.19

How it works...

We are embedding the tempo information of our sample in order to eventually stretch it to your main FL Studio project tempo, which will be reviewed in subsequent recipes. This way, you have more options to work with your sample and the creative possibilities are greater. Once you save your tempo information into the **Sample properties** window, it is embedded. From there, you can either save it or drag it out of Edison into the playlist or step sequencer, respectively. Edison is only a scratch pad / audio editor; you must bring it into the step sequencer or playlist to actually use the audio in your FL Studio project.

There's more...

After opening the **Tempo tapper** window, you can either tap out your tempo by pressing the *T* key on your QWERTY keyboard or use your mouse. To tap with your mouse, simply click in the area that reads **TAP** once the **Tempo tapper** window has opened.

In order to tap out these tempos, you have to get into the groove of your sample. As long as you have rhythm and can keep a beat, you are golden. Sometimes, your sample will already have tempo information embedded within the file. You can double-check the information that is already there by simply performing the **Tempo tapper** method.

As far as file organization is concerned, it may help to save your new samples (with tempo information embedded) in a dedicated folder or external hard drive. This works in the same manner as saving audio recordings, which we discussed in *Chapter 6, Using the FL Studio Mixer and Recording Audio*. Saving and organizing files properly is half the battle when composing music in any type of DAW. If you have a good system in place, it will make your life much easier, especially if you are an engineer or producer working with clients.

See also

- ▸ The *Finding a sample* recipe
- ▸ The *Obtaining a seamless loop* recipe
- ▸ The *Importing your new saved sample* recipe
- ▸ The *Time-stretching your sample on your* recipe

Importing your new saved sample

Importing your new saved sample can be achieved in various ways, much like there are many ways to skin a cat. It basically depends on your own personal workflow and the ways in which you feel most comfortable with the program. When inspiration strikes, you may want to drag files out of Edison and into your step sequencer as quickly as possible. However, at some point, you should make sure your files are retrievable and saved in the proper manner. You may need them as a reference for clearance purposes or even to use them again a second time around.

Getting ready

In order to import your new, saved sample from Edison into your FL Studio project, you will want to have Edison open and your sample edits and parameters saved. It doesn't matter if you have a loop, embedded tempo, or simply a one-shot small section highlighted. The method of importing is the same.

How to do it...

Let's us review the steps required to import your new saved sample.

1. Click on the disk icon inside of Edison and select **Save sample as...**, as shown in the following screenshot:

Fig 7.20

2. Browse/save your file to a location or folder that is best for your workflow.

3. Select **CHANNELS** from the top of the main FL Studio window, hover your mouse on **Add one**, and select a **Sampler** channel, as shown in the following screenshot:

 Select a channel and press *Alt + C* to clone the channel and create a new one directly beneath it. Be mindful that all of the source channel settings will be duplicated except its notes and events.

CHANNELS	VIEW	OPTIONS	TOOLS	H	More...		SimSynth
Add one				►	Browse presets		Slicex
Clone selected			*Alt+C*		Plugin database		SynthMaker
Delete selected...			*Alt+Del*		Plugin picker		Sytrus
Move selected up			*Alt+Up*		Layer		Toxic Biohazard
Move selected down			*Alt+Down*		Audio clip		Wasp
					Automation clip		Wasp XT
Group selected...			*Alt+G*				Wave Traveller
Color selected				►	Sampler		
Zip selected			*Alt+Z*		TS404 bassline synthesizer		
Unzip all			*Alt+U*		Speech synthesizer		
					3x Osc		

Fig 7.21

4. A new **Sampler** channel will be created in the step sequencer as shown in *Fig 7.22*. This is simply a blank channel that says **Sampler**.

You can also use the FL Studio Browser (*F8*) and expand the folder called `Channel presets`. You can then expand the `Sampler` folder and drag the **Default** option into the step sequencer. When using this method, your new blank channel will read **Default**.

Fig 7.22

5. Click on the small folder icon directly under the **SMP** tab within your sampler's **Channel settings**. This will open up another window where you can browse and retrieve your saved sample. Once retrieved, the area to the right of the small folder icon will change to your sample name and the bottom of your channel will show the waveform.

    You may also use FL Studio Browser (*F8*) to scroll through your saved samples as well as drag files over from a separate window into FL Studio. If you are using FL Studio Browser in this manner and you are saving files to an external hard drive or somewhere not inside the FL Studio, make sure your FL Studio Browser extra search folders include the proper locations. This setting can be found by pressing *F10* and clicking on FILE. The following screenshot shows the settings in the **SMP** tab:

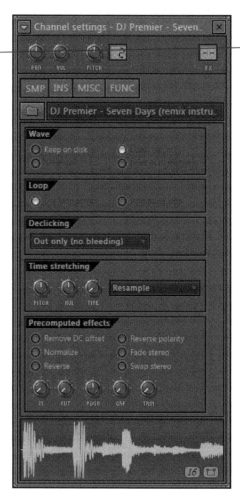

Fig 7.23

6. The name of your channel will automatically change to the sample you have selected, as shown in *Fig 7.24*. It will squeeze as much text as possible into the **CHANNEL** view on the step sequencer. Hover your mouse on the channel and look at the FL Studio hint bar to see the full name of your channel.

Fig 7.24

How it works...

When saving your file to your computer or external hard drive, FL Studio defaults your saved file into the Microsoft WAV file format. You have the ability to change this to a Microsoft-compressed WAV file, WavPack audio file, MP3, or OggVorbis by using the **Save as type** drop-down box before saving. You can also set your folder location as a favorites by using the **+** sign next to the **Favorites** area. If you have an external drive, make sure your drive is connected to your computer, or it will not bring up the drive location.

There's more...

Remember that when working with the step sequencer, you can easily add a new channel by right-clicking on any channel in the step sequencer and then selecting **Insert**. This avoids the need to go to the main **CHANNELS** menu.

You may also save your file to a location inside of the FL Studio Browser. In this manner, when your browser is refreshed, you can choose your files from inside the browser. The computer hierarchy to save your files in the browser is reviewed in *Chapter 2, Using Browser*.

You can also simply use the **Drag / copy sample / selection** or **Send to playlist as audio clip / to channel** button in Edison. Additionally, you can drag your waveform from the bottom of your **Channel settings** into the FL Studio Playlist. There are many options available when working with Edison and it all depends on your personal workflow.

See also

▶ The *Finding a sample* recipe

▶ The *Obtaining a seamless loop* recipe

▶ The *Getting new sounds in the browser* recipe in *Chapter 2, Using Browser*

▶ The *Exploring Channel settings* recipe in *Chapter 3, Working with Step Sequencer and Channels*

Time-stretching your sample to your project

Time-stretching the samples you have used in Edison is arguably the most enjoyable and rewarding process, especially for remixers and mash-up producers. This doesn't necessarily have to be a sample from a commercially released song. You can also be working with percussion, drum, and audio loops of all sorts. Anything that has a detectable rhythm is fair game. The pitch of your sample, the embedded tempo of your sample, and the main project tempo in FL Studio are all related. This recipe will break down what this means.

Getting ready

To time-stretch your sample from Edison to your FL Studio project tempo, you *must* have your tempo embedded in your sample. Once this is done, you simply need to have your sample exist in a channel on the step sequencer. This is extremely vital to working with your sample and getting the best out of your project. If your tempo is not embedded in your sample, these steps will not work.

How to do it...

Let's study the steps required to time-stretch our sample to our FL Studio project.

1. Get an audio sample from Edison into a channel in the step sequencer with your tempo information embedded.

2. Go to the **SMP** tab in **Channel settings**, right-click on **TIME**, and select **Autodetect** as shown in the following screenshot:

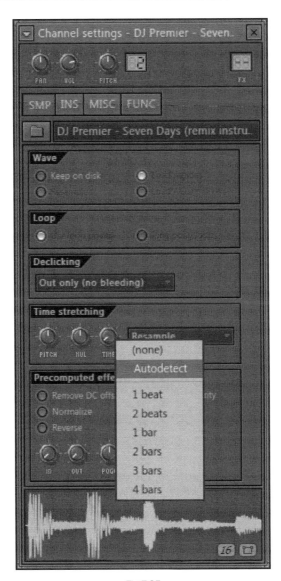

Fig 7.25

3. The **Tempo detection - DJ Premier - Seven Days (remix instrumental)** window will appear. Click on the option that says 185 (embedded). This is basically telling you that there is a tempo embedded in the file. In this example, we want the 185 tempo because this is the work we previously did in the Edison **Sample properties**! The following screenshot shows the 185 (embedded) option in the tempo detection window:

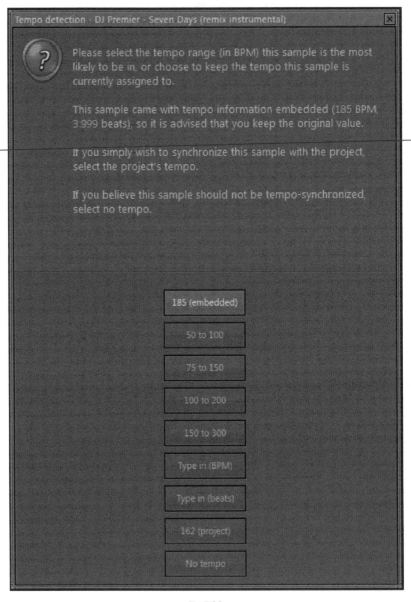

Fig 7.26

4. Test out your sample by clicking on the first step on your given channel in the step sequencer. In the current situation, our tempo of 185 (embedded, in our sample) is stretching to the FL Studio project tempo of 144! The following screenshot shows the step sequencer with the new tempo settings:

Fig 7.27

5. Select **Pro default** from the drop-down menu next to **TIME** in order to keep the same pitch of your original Edison sample when your main FL Studio Tempo is adjusted. This is shown in the following screenshot:

Fig 7.28

How it works...

When you adjust your FL Studio project tempo as shown in *Fig 7.26*, your sample will stretch accordingly, but the pitch will change. This is because your drop-down menu next to **TIME** is still defaulted to **Resample**. The lower your project tempo, the lower in pitch your sample will become, but it will still stretch as much as it can. When working with a loop, you will notice the pitch of your sample (both the harmony and the percussion) will get very low when adjusting to a slow tempo. When you raise the tempo higher, your sample pitch will increase accordingly and simultaneously get faster.

Fig 7.28 shows different rules because we have changed our stretching method to **Pro default**. This means that our sample will keep the same pitch irrespective of our main project tempo. If we adjust the main project tempo very slow, our sample will be very slow, but it will maintain the same pitch as that of the original sample. If we make our tempo fast, our sample will get faster, yet still maintain the same pitch as the source audio sample from Edison.

There are different reasons for using both of the methods mentioned earlier. Sometimes, you want to keep the same pitch no matter what your project tempo is (using the **Pro default** method). At other times, you want to have a chopped and screwed type of effect, and that can be managed by keeping your stretching method as **Resample**.

When using this method or working with any type of audio samples in FL Studio, you may also drag your sample from the bottom of the **SMP** channel settings folder (where the waveform appears) directly into the FL Studio Playlist. This will create a second instance of the sample as an audio clip. You can then use the knobs in the **Time stretching** section and get super handy visual feedback by looking at how your waveform changes as you adjust the knobs. You may also press and hold *Alt* while moving samples in the playlist to toggle the grid on and off.

See also

- ▸ The *Finding a sample* recipe
- ▸ The *Obtaining a seamless loop* recipe
- ▸ The *Exploring Channel settings* recipe in *Chapter 3, Working with Step Sequencer and Channels*
- ▸ The *Sending a channel to a mixer slot* recipe in *Chapter 3, Working with Step Sequencer and Channels*
- ▸ The *Adding effects and your effect chain* recipe *Chapter 6, Using the FL Studio Mixer and Recording Audio*

Fine-tuning your sample

Sometimes, it can be difficult to get a loop in perfect tempo, so do your best in Edison but remember that you have another weapon in your FL Studio arsenal—the **MUL** button. The hint bar reads that the **MUL** button is the **Time Stretch (multiplicator)** functionality. This can make your loop time stretch very finely in order to move it ever so slightly in time, forwards or backwards. This recipe does not relate to the pitch or tune, but shifts the timing in fine increments.

Getting ready

You will want to have a sample completed in Edison (looped, embedded tempo, and saved, as discussed in the earlier recipes) and open in an FL Studio channel in the step sequencer. You should also be using the **Time stretching** button, where you right-click and select **Autodetect**. We will be working with the **SMP** tab within **Channel settings** and adjusting the knob that reads **MUL**.

> **Prerequisites**
>
> You must right-click on the **TIME** knob and select **Autodetect** in the exact same way as the previous recipe, *Time-stretching your sample to your project*.

How to do it...

Let's review how to shift your sample ever so slightly in time (forwards or backwards).

1. Open an FL Studio channel, hold down *Ctrl*, and click-and-drag with your mouse to the left or the right with the **MUL** knob, as shown in the following screenshot:

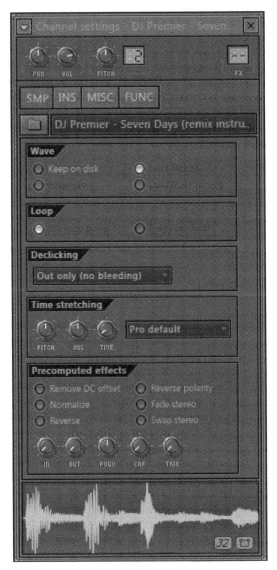

Fig 7.29

2. While dragging, look at the FL Studio hint bar (have a look at *Fig 7.30*). **99.72%** means it has been clicked-and-dragged (while pressing *Ctrl*) to the left.

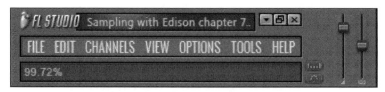

Fig 7.30

How it works...

After you get as close to a seamless loop as possible and set your time stretch to autodetect a sample (by setting **Autodetect**), the **MUL** knob adjusts ever so slightly in either direction. You may hold down *Ctrl* for even finer increments. Sometimes, only a slight adjustment either way can greatly impact the timing of your samples. You may also press the *Ctrl* key on most knobs in FL Studio for extremely small adjustments. If you want to adjust in chunks of time, you don't need to hold down *Ctrl*. You can simply click-and-drag the **MUL** knob.

There's more...

You must have patience to salvage your sample with the **MUL** knob when getting a seamless loop proves to be difficult. This involves testing different settings with the **MUL** knob. You can also use an EQ technique called a **low pass filter** on your sample to find the bassline. You want to get as seamless a loop as humanly possible. The **MUL** knob is a great helper in order to pinpoint the exact groove of your hard work in Edison.

Also use the **POGO** knob located on the **SMP** tab within the **Precomputed effects** section. This helps adjust any silences in the beginning of the sample, in cases where it wasn't chopped correctly from the beginning. This usually helps when working with sampled percussion.

See also

- ▶ The *Finding a sample* recipe
- ▶ The *Obtaining a seamless loop* recipe
- ▶ The *Sending a channel to a mixer slot* recipe in *Chapter 3, Working with Step Sequencer and Channels*
- ▶ The *Exploring Channel settings* recipe in *Chapter 3, Working with Step Sequencer and Channels*
- ▶ The *Perfecting equalization* recipe in *Chapter 6, Using the FL Studio Mixer and Recording Audio*

8
Exporting and Rendering Your Project

In this chapter, we will cover:

▸ Exporting an MP3 or WAV file

▸ Exporting your audio stems

▸ Highlighting your song in the playlist

▸ Rendering files

▸ Exporting and reimporting a WAV file

Introduction

Exporting your music project means that it will be rendered down to one single audio file where you can play it back on many types of music players and systems. MP3 files are highly compressed and usually chosen for online streaming. WAV files are of a higher quality and are used before burning your song onto a CD or when you send your audio file(s) to a sound engineer.

Exporting an MP3 or WAV file

Exporting your finished song as an MP3 or WAV file is the final step to hearing your song play back in your car, entertainment systems, phone, tablet, any music media device, or even hearing it while it streams online.

Getting ready

In order to export your song as an MP3 or WAV file, you will want to have some type of data in your FL Studio Playlist.

How to do it...

1. Highlight the data in your FL Studio playlist by pressing *Ctrl + A*. This will select all of the patterns and data in your playlist, as shown in the following screenshot:

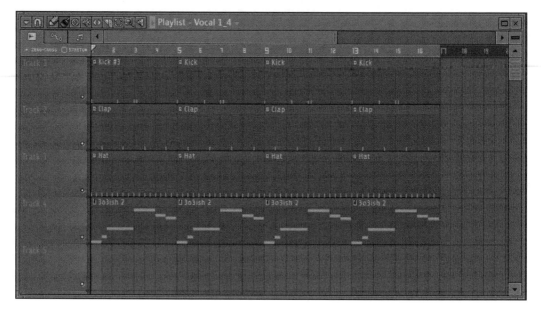

Fig 8.1

2. Select **FILE** from the main FL Studio window, hover your mouse on **Export**, and select **MP3 file...**, as shown in the following screenshot:

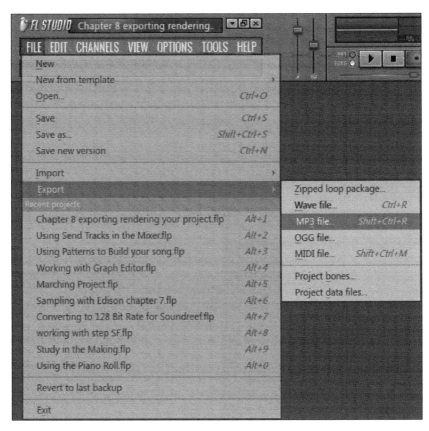

Fig 8.2

3. It will then bring up the **Save As** box, where you can name your file and specify the exact place you want it to appear on your computer. You will then click on **Save**.

4. The rendering box will then appear as shown in the following screenshot. Click on **Start** to start rendering.

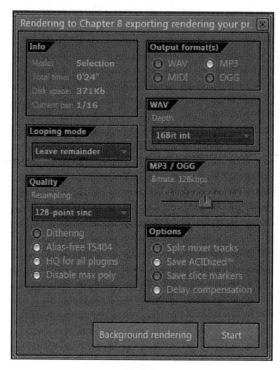

Fig 8.3

5. You will then see the progress of your rendering process. This can take anywhere from a couple of seconds to a couple of minutes, depending on the data inside of your FL Studio project. When it reaches 100 percent, the render box will disappear and you can find your audio file in the location you saved it to earlier.

6. You can now play your song through your computer because it is an MP3 file. The following screenshot shows the generated music file icon:

Fig 8.4

How it works...

As seen in the previous process, exporting your file to an MP3 turns your FL Studio project into a file you can actually play back outside of FL Studio. Try to get your project to sound as good as possible inside FL Studio, but know in the back of your mind that it may sound better or different once exported. Sometimes, it may actually sound worse when the depth is lost due to working with loads of plugins and filters. Remember to see your **MP3 / OGG** setting in the **Output format(s)** section on your rendering dialog box. You should use the slider to specify what bitrate will be exported. Generally, you should be using **128kbps**, **192kbps**, or **320kbps**. Keep an eye on the **Info** section of your rendering box because your disk space will increase as you increase the bitrate.

Going with 128 kbps will result in a lower quality MP3 file that can sound decent when playing back. If you have numerous virtual instruments on your project, 128 kbps may sometimes not render all of your instruments properly and may induce pops and clicks on your actual rendered file. 192 kbps is the safest bet for all types of music projects, and will result in good quality no matter where you play your rendered file. 320 kbps is the highest MP3 setting and quality available in FL Studio. You may be able to hear a difference between 192 kbps and 320 kbps, so it's all up to your ears and comfort level.

In order to export a single rendered WAV file, you may simply click on **Wave file...** in the screen depicted in *Fig 8.2*. The current **Sample rate (Hz)** setting used in conjunction with the WAV file export can be found in your **AUDIO** settings, as shown in the following screenshot:

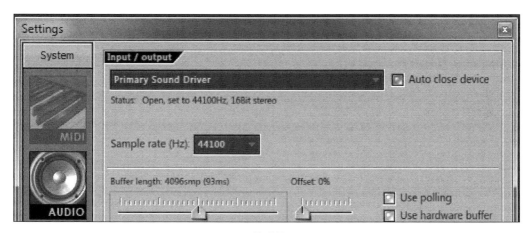

Fig 8.5

The optimal setting is to keep your sample rate at 44,100, which is 44.1 kHz, and render as a 16-bit WAV file in the **Depth** area of your render box. This is equal to the CD audio format and is the standard method. You can also specify 24-bit if you are sending your project to an engineer during the mastering process or if you want to continue working on your projects in other types of audio editors and DAWs. When working in a professional production environment, 16-bit WAV files are the standard.

There's more...

FL Studio does not actually burn audio files to CDs. You will need third-party burning software such as Roxio, iTunes, or Windows Media Player and a CD-R format CD. You may also save MP3 files or WAV files to an external hard drive, USB thumb drive, or a CD-RW (for burning and playing back, you must use a CD-R format). This will back up your files so you can have a physical back up or transfer them to other computers. Additionally, you can attach MP3 files in an e-mail. If your e-mail cannot handle the size of the files, you can use a service such as the one available at www.wetransfer.com in order to send your files, or cloud sharing options such as Dropbox and Google Drive. You must remember that to actually hear your song in a car or entertainment system, you will be using a CD-R.

Also, be conscious of the current sound card device on your computer and in FL Studio. If the file is not playing after you save it to your desktop or any other location, you may need to close FL Studio first.

See also

> ▸ The *Exporting your audio stems* recipe
> ▸ The *Knowing your sound cards or audio interfaces* recipe in *Chapter 1, Configuring FL Studio*
> ▸ The *Using patterns to build your song* recipe in *Chapter 5, Using the Playlist*
> ▸ The *Understanding master tracks and loud wars* recipe in *Chapter 6, Using the FL Studio Mixer and Recording Audio*

Exporting your audio stems

Exporting your audio stems allows you to render your individual mixer tracks (FX/insert slots) as individual stems. The audio stems will track out as 16-bit WAV files and will span as long as your selection in the FL Studio playlist.

Getting ready

In order to export your mixer tracks as individual pieces, you will need to have your given channels sent to mixer/INS slots in the FL Studio Mixer. This was discussed in the Sending a channel to a mixer slot *Chapter 3, Working with Step Sequencer and Channels*, and Using patterns to build your song *Chapter 5, Using the Playlist*.

How to do it...

1. Send your channels to the mixer slots in the FL Studio Mixer and paste your patterns into the playlist. An example of the patterns we are working with can be seen in the following screenshot:

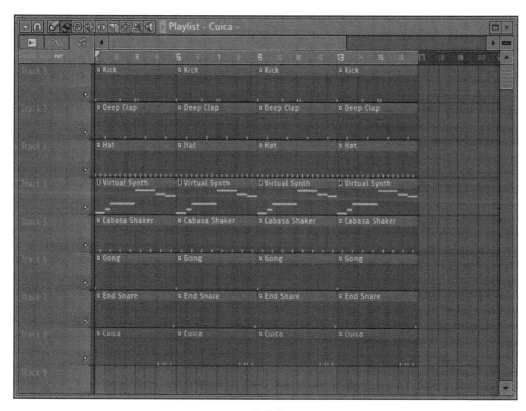

Fig 8.6

2. Right-click on the small green light located on the master track in FL Studio Mixer, which will mute all tracks except for the master. Then click on all the mixer tracks you want included in the export. The small green circle is the **Mute / solo** button.

Fig 8.7

3. From the topmost main window in FL Studio, go to **FILE | Export | Wave file...**.

4. You will now have the opportunity to save your stems to a folder or new folder you create, as well as name the root for each stem. In the following screenshot, we are saving our stems to a folder titled `Audio stem Export Cookbook` and our root name is `Recipe Man`:

Fig 8.8

5.   Click on **Split mixer tracks** in the rendering box and then on **Start** to render your wave stems. Notice that when you hover your mouse on **Split mixer tracks**, the FL Studio hint bar reads **Batch export mixer tracks into separate wave files**. The following screenshot shows the rendering progress:

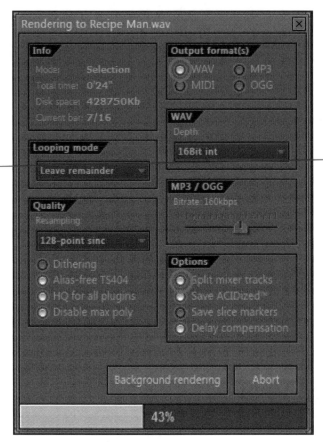

Fig 8.9

6.   Your audio stems will now be located in the folder you previously specified and will automatically generate an underscore and mixer track name (taken directly from your mixer slot names) for each file. Your root name will stay intact on every single file.

7.   When you preview each track and play it on your computer, you will find each track spans the length of your selection in the playlist.

How it works...

Note that we have highlighted our selection by pressing *Ctrl + A* while on the FL Studio playlist, as shown in *Fig 8.6*. On the screen depicted in *Fig 8.7*, we are double-checking our mixer slots and making sure all of our channels from the step sequencer are sent to a mixer slot. We have also renamed eight of these mixer slots. **INS 1** is **Kick**, **INS 2** is **Deep Clap**, **INS 3** is **Hi Hat**, **INS 4** is **Virtual Synth**, **INS 5** is **Cabasa Shaker**, **INS 6** is **Gong**, **INS 7** is **End Snare**, and **INS 8** is **Cuica**. The track names seen in *Fig 8.6* in FL Studio Playlist have no bearing on any of this. You can, of course, rename the track names that are located on the playlist on the screen depicted in *Fig 8.6*, but it will only be for your own organizational purposes. When we export mixer tracks, they are correlated with channels sent to an FX / mixer / INS slot in the mixer slot and the length of time associated with each one.

Clicking on the **Split mixer tracks** button in the rendering box tells FL Studio that you will be exporting each mixer track in the FL Studio Mixer as separate files (all of the ones with a green light on the **Mute / solo** button). You can then take your stems to an engineer, save them on a USB or thumb drive, store on a CD, use them in remixes, share in collaborations, and so on.

If you forget to specify the exact mixer tracks you want in the export, your export will have all 99 mixer slots rendered. If necessary, you can delete the ones you don't want. Sometimes, your selected slot (the lone track to the right of your send tracks) will be exported with your stems. This is due to the fact that it still had a green light engaged on the **Mute / solo** button. If you don't want to include it, click on the green light to deselect it.

There's more...

You can send more than one channel to the same mixer slot; just know that when you render your audio stems in this fashion, both channels will be rendered into one stem. This technique is very useful for a musician who would rather layer, mix, and compress their kicks/percussion before handing out a final mix of stems to a mastering engineer.

It is also up to your own workflow and creative end vision if you want to include any effects on the mixer effect chains. If you leave everything completely dry, with no effects whatsoever, it gives your engineer the opportunity to make your mix outstanding. Other times, you might want to include some effects because you like your mix a certain way. The engineer's job is to then polish, complement, and enhance your sound. Generally, you will want to leave headroom for your mastering engineer so he or she can significantly increase your song's volume (if you are joining loud wars!).

Exporting stems can help with backing up your audio files in case your computer goes bad or your hard drive corrupts. Try to back up everything three times. Better safe than sorry!

See also

- ▸ The *Exporting an MP3 or WAV file* recipe
- ▸ The *Rendering files* recipe
- ▸ The *Sending a channel to a mixer slot* in *Chapter 3, Working with the Step Sequencer and Channels*
- ▸ The *Using patterns to build a song* recipe in *Chapter 5, Using the Playlist*
- ▸ The *Adding effects and your effect chain* recipe in *Chapter 6, Using the FL Studio Mixer and Recording Audio*

Highlighting your song in the playlist

Highlighting your song in the FL Studio Playlist allows you to render down and export your musical production.

Getting ready

To highlight your song (the highlighted section will turn red), open the FL Studio Playlist by hitting *F5*. You should have patterns and musical data that populate the playlist, unless you are actually recording an external audio such as vocals, violin, guitar, or turntables. Highlighting your song can serve two very different purposes: getting ready to export, or getting ready to record a specific chunk of time for vocals or instruments.

How to do it...

1. Click inside of the playlist and hold *Ctrl + A* and you will see a window as shown in *Fig 8.10*. It will turn red in the selected area. You also want to have your snap settings set to **Cell**, as shown in the following screenshot:

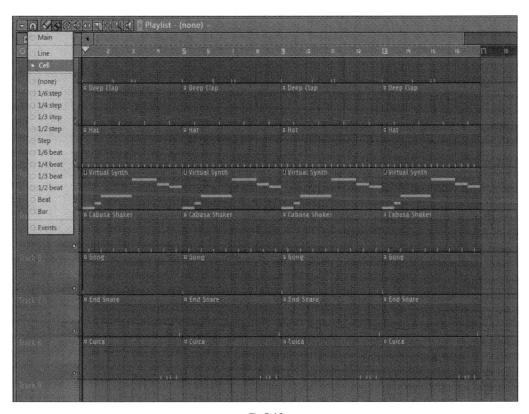

Fig 8.10

2. Go through the same steps as discussed in the *Exporting an MP3 or WAV file* recipe of this chapter. Have a look at the **Looping Mode** drop-down box, shown in the following screenshot:

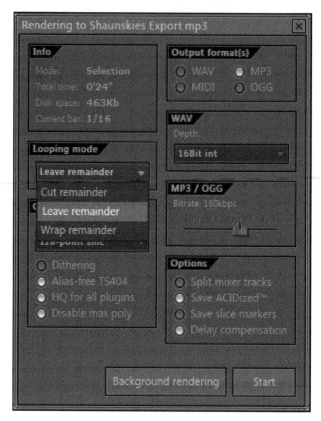

Fig 8.11

3. The following screenshot shows what the looping mode section signifies:

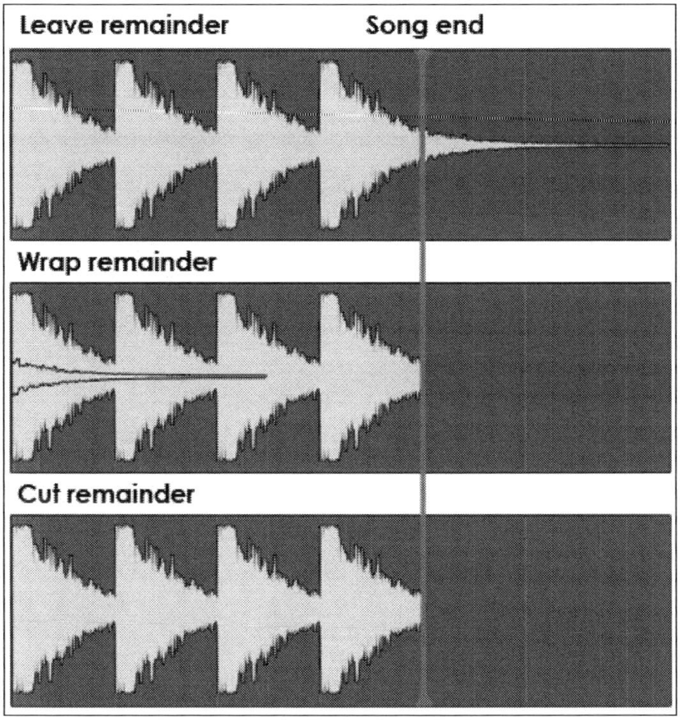

Fig 8.12 – Picture courtesy FL Studio help file

4. Name your music file, specify your file location, and click on the **Start** box on your rendering dialog box.

How it works...

The **Leave remainder** portion is the default setting that allows your reverb or instruments to tail off past the final bar or cell in the playlist. **Wrap remainder** wraps any decaying sound at the very end of the song onto the beginning. **Wrap remainder** is good for loops with effects. **Cut remainder** cuts your song off at the final cell, bar, beat, column, or measure.

In *Fig 8.10*, the track ends directly before bar 17, hence it is 16 bars. Remember that you can use the FL Studio Playlist to cut your audio samples, data, and patterns. In fact, many people like to produce, slice, and edit their playlist audio as opposed to their step sequencer data.

You may do this by selecting **Slice tool** at the top of the **Playlist** window, having a proper snap setting, and slicing down, as shown in *Fig 8.13*. The blue slice is directly correlated with your **Snap to grid** setting and will form a perfect vertical line on the columns inside of your playlist, which are the columns of your **Snap to grid** setting and how close or far you choose to zoom. The columns in the following screenshot are your beats per bars:

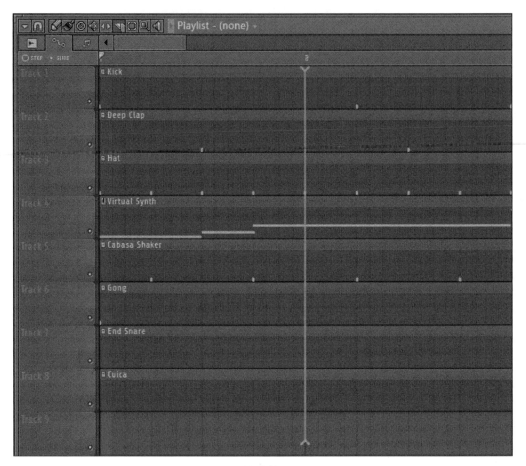

Fig 8.13

Once you let go of the blue slice line, it will slice the audio or pattern data in your playlist. You can then use the **Paint** or **Draw** tool next to each little button on a pattern. In *Fig 8.14*, we clicked on the dot next to the **Cuica** pattern. When slicing audio files, selecting Make unique will make a new channel in the step sequencer. When slicing patterns and selecting **Make unique**, it will make a new pattern.

This is also a great way to slice and delete things you do not want included in your song, as well as copy and paste patterns you want to repeat. It is for this reason that many people enjoy using the **Slice** tool in their productions—as a method to come up with creative ideas and experiments. As far as inserting silence, many radio-ready songs insert a quick silence at certain parts/beats/bars of the song. This acts like an effect that cuts out all audio, and adds emphasis to your vocal or groove.

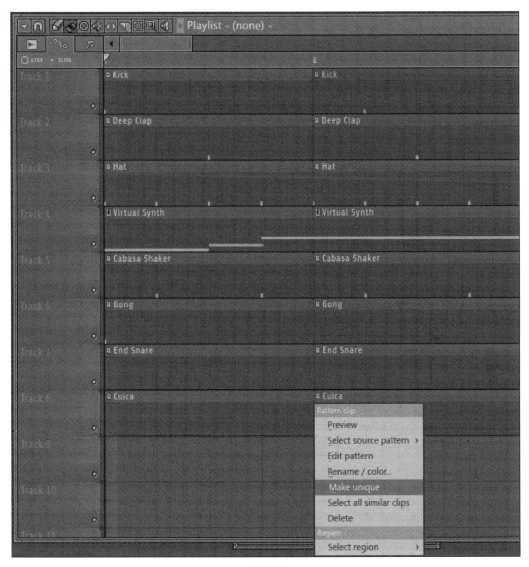

Fig 8.14

There's more...

There are other ways to highlight your song in the playlist and they are listed as follows:

- ▸ You can also zoom in and select different **Snap to grid** settings. When you experiment with the snap settings, as shown in *Fig 8.10*, you will find the smaller the setting, the more the columns in the playlist cells get narrow, and you are then able to zoom in and select small durations of time.

- ▸ You can also highlight the sections you will be recording vocals onto. This is an invaluable tool that helps in selecting your recording length for an intro, verse, chorus, bridge, or outro.

See also

- ▸ The *Rendering files* recipe
- ▸ The *Exporting and re-importing a WAVE file* recipe
- ▸ The *Introducing the step sequencer* recipe in *Chapter 3, Working with Step Sequencer and Channels*
- ▸ The *Using patterns to build your song* recipe in *Chapter 5, Using the Playlist*
- ▸ The *Adding effects and your effect chain* recipe in *Chapter 6, Using the FL Studio Mixer and Recording Audio*

Rendering files

Besides exporting your song to be played as an audio file in any type of media device or streaming it online, there are export options that allow you to back up your project work. The export files that help back up your project are `Project bones`, `Project data files`, and `Zipped loop package`.

Getting ready

To get started with exporting your project bones, you will simply need to have a music project started or completed in FL Studio.

How to do it...

1. Browse to the **FILE** menu, hover your mouse over **Export**, and select **Project bones...**.

2. The **Export project bones** window will then appear, where you can specify the location you want to save your project bones to. You can also create a new folder (using **Make New Folder**) on the **Project bones** window, as shown in *Fig 8.15*. Click on **OK** once you have your location.

Fig 8.15

3. Your folder will then incorporate all of your project bones. In *Fig 8.16*, we have created a folder called `Export the Horse`, which is located on our desktop. FL Studio automatically gives your project bones the same name as your FL Studio project. In this example, the `Project bones` folder is called `Chapter 8 exporting rendering your project` (inside of the `Export the Horse` folder), as shown in the following screenshot:

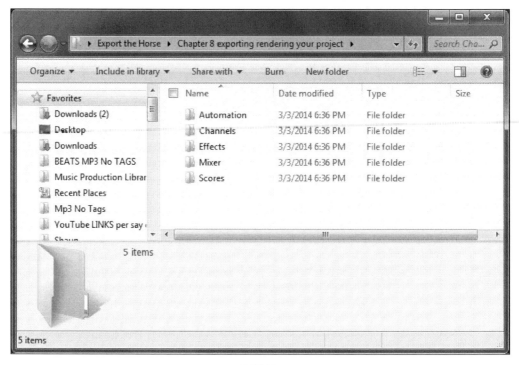

Fig 8.16

4. FL Studio will also automatically create a folder in the browser if you have saved your project bones on your desktop. This works similarly to your patches folder for FL Studio, but this method opens up your desktop folders in the FL Studio Browser, as shown in the following screenshot:

Fig 8.17

5. In the preceding screenshot, we opened up the Desktop folder directly from the FL Studio Browser, and we can see that our Export the Horse folder includes the exact same data and settings as seen in *Fig 8.16*.

How it works...

Exporting your project bones exports all of your **Automation clips**, **Channels**, **Effects**, **Mixer** settings, and **Scores** in one consolidated folder. This is handy for merging your components from one project into another. You can drag these directly into existing projects from your `Desktop` folder. You can also load the mixer track states, as reviewed in *Chapter 6, Using the FL Studio Mixer and Recording Audio*.

There's more...

After hovering your mouse on **Export**, you also have an option to export **Project data files....** This option will export all your samples inside of the step sequencer as well as your TS404 shapes, **SimSynth/DrumSynth** presets, and other plugin data used in your current project. This is handy for a backup or to use in other projects.

There is an option to export as a zipped loop package. This will create a ZIP file whose contents include your `.flp` (FL Studio project file) and the audio files used in your channels. This can be thought of as a consolidation of your `.flp` file and your project data files.

There are also options on the **FILE** menu to **Import** or **Export** a MIDI file. You also have the option to import or export files in MIDI format on every Piano roll in FL Studio. Importing MIDI data will automatically populate your channel with note data. Once your MIDI data is inside the Piano roll, you can change the sound or edit the note data to anything you want! This is a great way to learn a tremendous deal on how popular songs are structured. You can also use MIDI files for remixing or karaoke. A great source for MIDI files is `www.mididb.com`. Remember, MIDI is not audio; it is the location, length, and velocity of your notes. Exporting MIDI will allow you to have a backup of your Piano roll score data, collaborate with other musicians, or use it in live shows.

See also

- The Exporting your audio stems recipe
- The *Getting new sounds in the Browser* recipe in *Chapter 2, Using Browser*
- The *Introducing the step sequencer* recipe in *Chapter 3, Working with Step Sequencer and Channels*
- The *Using the Piano roll* recipe in *Chapter 4, Building Your Song*
- The *Getting the best out of your mixer* recipe in *Chapter 6, Using the FL Studio Mixer and Recording Audio*

Exporting and reimporting a WAV file

Rendering your completed music project before mastering into a WAV file allows you to render down all of the various elements of your song into one consolidated file. This will free up the processing load placed on your computer, especially if your project includes many virtual effects in your various effect chains. This is basically the same thing explored in the *Exporting an MP3 or a WAV file recipe*, but in this case, we are exporting an extremely high quality WAV file directly before the final stage of mastering. If we do not want to do it this way, we can use the master track on our FL Studio Mixer in our existing project, but only if your computer can keep up with the processing load.

Getting ready

In order to get ready to use a WAV file to master, your entire music project should be complete.

How to do it...

1. Highlight your song in the FL Studio playlist as shown on the screen depicted in *Fig 8.18*. You may do this by pushing *Ctrl + A*. Your song should then be highlighted in red.

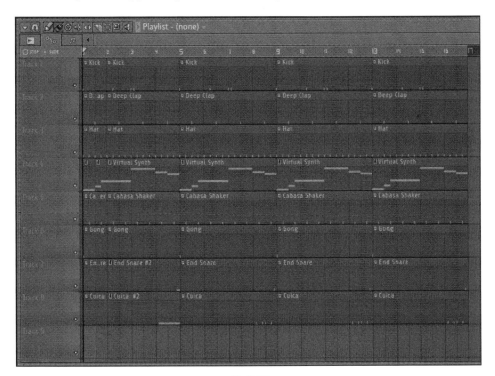

Fig 8.18

2. Select **FILE** from the main FL Studio window, hover your mouse over **Export**, and select **Wave file...,** as shown in the following screenshot:

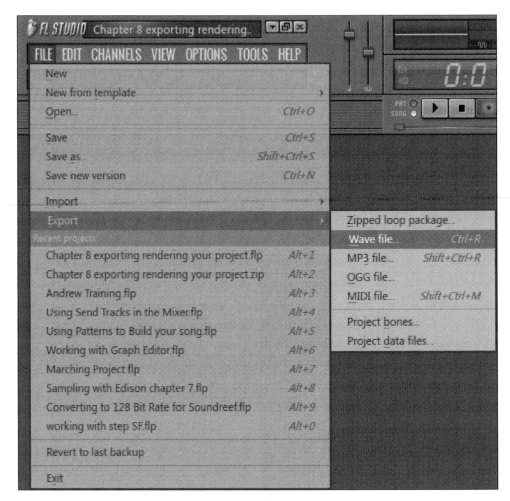

Fig 8.19

3. You will then be able to name your export and pick a location on your computer.

4. Next, select **24bit int**, as shown in *Fig 8.20*, and click on **Start**. In this example, we have named our song `Clapmatic`. This will render your project.

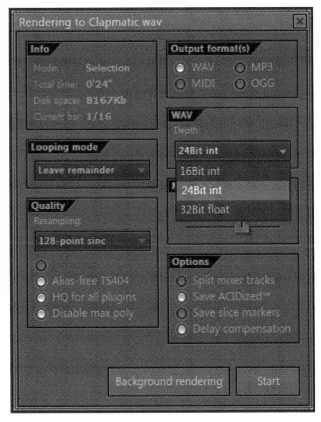

Fig 8.20

5. Start a brand new empty FL Studio project as shown in *Fig 8.21*. Select **FILE** and then **New**.

Fig 8.21

6. Click on the **Maximize / restore** button, which is directly next to the **Minimize** button at the top of the main window of FL Studio. Resize your FL Studio window in order to drag your WAV file into the FL Studio playlist. The following screenshot shows the resizing options:

Fig 8.22

7. Drag your rendered WAV file directly into the FL Studio Playlist. You could also drag it from the FL Studio Browser.

8. Your audio file will now populate the playlist as shown in *Fig 8.23*. Go to the **SONG** mode in FL Studio, drag your file all the way to the left (in order to set an immediate start time), select your original **TEMPO**, and master your project using the master track effect chain in the FL Studio Mixer.

Fig 8.23

How it works...

Usually, if you do not export your file before mastering, all of your plugins and data are running at the same time, and taking up various mixer slots in the FL Studio Mixer. However, in this manner, there will only be one mixer track running—the master track that is playing your WAV file! Also, the WAV file was exported at 24-bit, making it super high quality before the mastering stage! If you want your playlist to line up with the tempo of your exported project (the same project you are working with now), just set your FL Studio main tempo to the exact number as your rendered project. In this way, you can use the **Slice** tool to further edit your song if necessary. You will want to review the *Chapter 6, Using the FL Studio Mixer and Recording Audio* effect chain recipe and make your master track sound remarkable. You may use the limiters and compressors within FL Studio, as well as third-party sources such as Waves and iZotope. When you are done, you can then export the file as an MP3 or 16-bit WAV file. Remember, a 16-bit WAV file with a 44100 Hz sample rate is the standard setting for audio CDs. The MP3 format is useable for Internet streaming.

You may also use this method for resampling. If you are working with 10 virtual synths that are sucking your PC's processor dry, export them as WAV files and reload them. Be sure to delete or mute the original virtual channels as you now have rendered down wave files. However, you should also save your project as a new version so you don't completely lose any MIDI data from your virtual channels.

There's more...

Remember, your file is now its own channel in the step sequencer! You can look at your channel setting and possibly use the **Normalize** or **Reverse** functions. Remember to save your current project so you keep everything organized. You can also import or drag your WAV file directly into Edison for further processing.

There are no rules to working with this exported file. Sometimes, you will want to practice these exact steps before recording vocals. In this way, you can record vocals on a rendered WAV file without worrying about too much load placed upon your computer. You can even continue to work on your song or add in new elements for remixing.

See also

> ▸ The *Comparing patterns and audio* recipe in *Chapter 5, Using the Playlist*

> ▸ The *Using markers and snap* recipe in *Chapter 5, Using the Playlist*

> ▸ The *Viewing the playlist* recipe in *Chapter 5, Using the Playlist*

> ▸ The *Adding effects and your effect chain* recipe in *Chapter 6, Using the FL Studio Mixer and Recording Audio*

> ▸ The *Understanding master tracks and loud wars* recipe in *Chapter 6, Using the FL Studio Mixer and Recording Audio*

Humanizing Your Song

9

In this chapter, we will cover:

- ▸ Humanizing with the OFS knob
- ▸ Humanizing with the Graph editor
- ▸ Humanizing with the Piano roll
- ▸ Humanizing with the Playlist

Introduction

Humanizing your song means you can change the small intricacies of any sound. When working with digital music, everything is very robotic and stiff. This is by far the true nature of music and for those that play instruments in live settings, there are small nuances where the members of a band may get slightly out of sync but then hit their groove and enjoy the magic that happens. When using the step sequencer in FL Studio, it makes the steps perfectly timed and machine like. This is exactly what is needed when composing. However, once all of your pieces come together, you may find it to be a tad unemotional and mechanical. Sometimes this may be desired, and other times you may want to tweak the groove of some of the parts. FL Studio makes this very easy to do. Humanizing your song means introducing more feeling into your composition and making things less computerized. Yes, it's ironic that we are trying to make a computer program less computer-like. Nevertheless, it's a crucial tool that will separate a good song from a great song. You may use all of the following recipes on any type of sound, including vocals, percussion, audio, and virtual instruments.

Humanizing with the OFS knob

When humanizing your percussion, it may help to use the **OFS** knob within the **Channel settings** window.

Getting ready

In order to start humanizing your song using the **OFS** knob, you will want to have data within a channel on your step sequencer. When you click on a channel in the step sequencer, the **Channel settings** window will open up.

How to do it...

Let's take a look at how to humanize your song using the step sequencer and **FUNC** tab within the **Channel settings** window through the following steps:

1. Right-click on your hi hat or shaker type of sound and select **Fill each 4 steps** as per *Fig 9.1*.

 You don't necessarily have to use the **Fill each 4 steps** function. This simply makes automatic entries on your step sequencer and may save you time.

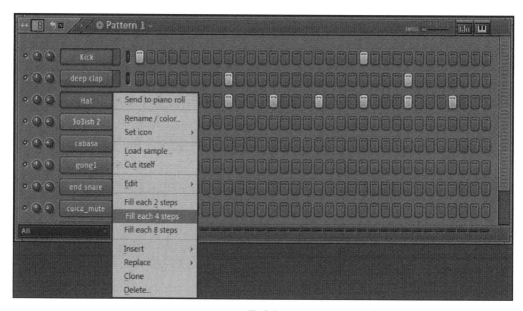

Fig 9.1

2. Click on the **Hat** channel (making sure the small green slit is engaged) to open up **Channel settings** and click on the **FUNC** tab as per the following screenshot:

Fig 9.2

3. Click-and-drag the **OFS** knob (fine time shift) to the right as per the following screenshot:

Fig 9.3

4. You will find that the timing of your sound will be extremely off when the **OFS** button is turned farthest to the right. You will want to turn the knob slowly, starting from the farthest left, while holding *Ctrl* for incremental control. Observe the following screenshot for the position of the **OFS** button, which will usually work to humanize your percussion sound:

Fig 9.4

How it works...

When you click-and-drag the **OFS** button to the right, you will notice that the timing of your sound will shift to the right and be totally off beat. This helps you understand the function of the **OFS** button. After realizing that turning it all the way to the right makes things totally off beat, we will slowly turn it to the right while holding down the *Ctrl* key. How far you turn this knob is up to your personal taste and the vibe you are going for. It all depends on the existing sounds in your project and the mood you want to establish.

There's more...

Adding a human feel is also directly correlated to adjusting the velocity/volume. When working with a hi hat or any type of percussion, you can adjust the volume of the individual steps. You can do this using the **Piano roll** or **Graph editor** menu as reviewed in *Chapter 3, Working with the Step Sequencer and Channels*. For a more global change on all of the channels within a pattern, review the swing slider, which was also reviewed in *Chapter 3, Working with the Step Sequencer and Channels*. You can also add a touch of reverb sometimes, as discussed in *Chapter 6, Using send tracks in the mixer*, or any type of effect on the FL Studio Mixer in your mixer chain.

See also

▶ The *Working with Graph editor* recipe in *Chapter 3, Working with Step Sequencer and Channels*

▶ The *Using the Piano roll* recipe in *Chapter 4, Building Your Song*

▶ The *Using send tracks in the mixer* recipe in *Chapter 6, Using the FL Studio Mixer and Recording Audio*

▶ The *Adding effects and your effects chain* recipe in *Chapter 6, Using the FL Studio Mixer and Recording Audio*

▶ The *Fine tuning your sample* recipe in *Chapter 7, Sampling Using Edison*

Humanizing with the Graph editor

Humanizing your song with **Graph editor** allows you to control every individual step on a channel in the step sequencer. This differs from the **OFS** knob, which is the global setting for your steps, and shifts all of them simultaneously. Depending on your final vision, both methods have their place in the music production.

Getting ready

To get started with using **Graph editor**, you will simply want to have step data on a channel within the step sequencer.

How to do it...

In this example, we will be working with the **Hat** channel again. Let's take a look at how to humanize your song using **Graph editor** on the step sequencer with the following steps:

1. Once you have a channel selected (the small green slit is engaged), click on the **Graph editor** button in the upper right-hand corner of the step sequencer. This is directly to the left of the **Keyboard editor** button as per the following screenshot:

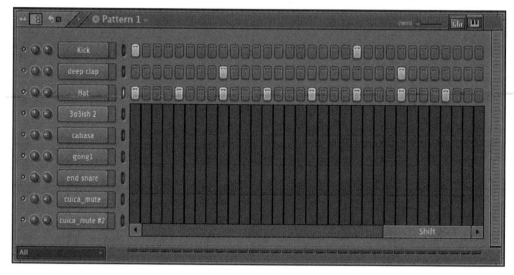

Fig 9.5

2. Click on the bottom scroll bar that appears after you click on the **Graph editor** button. From left to right, it will read as **Pan, Velocity, Release, Mod X, Mod Y, Fine pitch**, and **Shift**. Click-and-drag the scroll bar to the extreme right to reach the **Shift** parameter as per the previous screenshot.

3. Click-and-drag each column to form blue, vertical lines. The lines will affect the steps directly above each column as per *Fig 9.6*. The color will change from blue to green the higher you make the column.

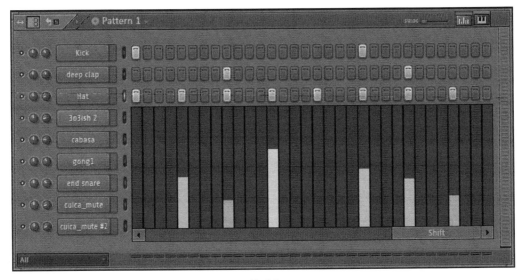

Fig 9.6

How it works...

The greater the height of the blue/green line, the more in time your step will shift to the right. If you experiment with this process, you will be able to hear the changes in your sound and steps. You may right-click or hold *Alt* + left-click in order to delete the column data.

There's more...

Be sure to use the **Velocity** function within the **Graph editor** window (use the scroll bar that pops up when you click on the **Graph editor** button and then scroll to **Velocity**). Adding a human feel is directly related to changing the time and volume (velocity) of your sound. The **Velocity** function will show in pink columns.

If you hold down *Shift* while right-clicking-and-dragging on any parameter in **Graph editor**, it will enable you to add incremental columns up or down. FL Studio refers to this as ramps. If you hold down *Ctrl* while adjusting a column, it will make uniform adjustments to all of the columns simultaneously.

See also

▶ The *Exploring Channel settings* recipe in *Chapter 3, Working with Step Sequencer and Channels*

▶ The *Working with Graph editor* recipe in *Chapter 3, Working with Step Sequencer and Channels*

▶ The *Sending a channel to mixer a slot* recipe in *Chapter 3, Working with Step Sequencer and Channels*

▶ The *Using the Keyboard editor* recipe in *Chapter 3, Working with Step Sequencer and Channels*

Humanizing with the Piano roll

Humanizing with **Piano roll** allows you to shift your notes ever so slightly to the right. This entails using a **Snap to grid** setting (none) within the **Piano roll** window. When you have opened up the **Piano roll** window and are working with a sound, this method can help make a particular groove fit with your entire music production.

Getting ready

To start humanizing your sound using **Piano roll**, you will want to have a particular channel use **Piano roll**. You can do this by right-clicking on a channel and selecting **Piano roll**.

How to do it...

Humanize your notes inside of the **Piano roll** window using the following steps:

1. Click on the **Snap to grid** setting (it resembles a magnet) inside of **Piano roll** and select **(none)** as per *Fig 9.7*. This will allow you to slide your notes independent of the grid.

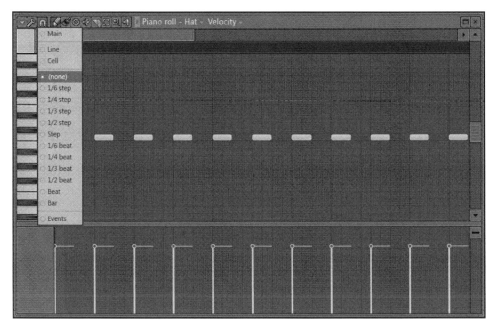

Fig 9.7

2. Click-and-drag a note you want to slide to the right or left. *Fig 9.8* shows the first four notes that have been dragged to the right. Note that they are not directly on a grid line like the remaining notes.

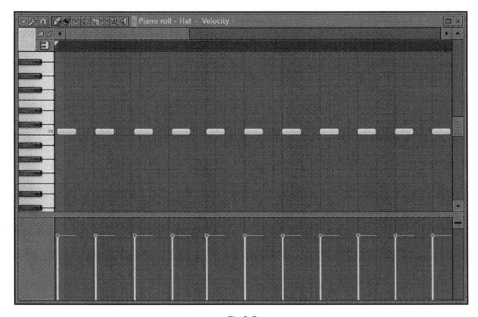

Fig 9.8

How it works...

Changing your **Snap to grid** setting inside of the **Piano roll** to **(none)** allows you to slide your notes that are unrelated to the grid setting. This can help with percussion and virtual instruments of all sorts. In fact, anything inside of the **Piano roll** window is fair game.

 Press *Alt* + drag a note to momentarily separate the note from the grid.

Sometimes, a sound's starting point can be a little bit delayed even though you have it set directly on the grid. This means that your actual sample does not start immediately on time. To remedy this, you can drag or slide your sound component to the left in **Piano roll** or open up Edison to delete the space at the very beginning of your sample. In a music file, we will work with small fragments of time, and in some cases, we will have to edit the waveform in Edison. Other times, a slight delay is desired if it adds to the groove of the song. This depends on your given music project and the direction and feeling you want it to embody.

There's more...

Be sure to use the bottom portion of **Piano roll** where you can adjust the **Velocity** value and other individual parameters. Sometimes, you may want to adjust the **Velocity** value before shifting notes. This was reviewed in the final recipe of *Chapter 4*, *Building Your Song* and relates to the **Note properties** drop-down box. You can also double-click on any note inside **Piano roll** to change the parameters. For the global adjustment of notes, hold *Ctrl* and click-and-drag around a group of notes. You can then double-click and affect a global selection of **Note properties**.

See also

- ▸ The *Working with rhythm and percussion* recipe in *Chapter 4*, *Building Your Song*
- ▸ The *Adding virtual instruments* recipe in *Chapter 4*, *Building Your Song*
- ▸ The *Using the Piano roll* recipe in *Chapter 4*, *Building Your Song*

Humanizing with Playlist

Humanizing your song with **Playlist** works similarly to **Piano roll** because you will be working with the snap and zoom settings. Since **Playlist** allows you to work with audio files, its greatest ability may be that it can adjust the settings of the files. You can, of course, adjust your patterns on the playlist in the same manner, but moving your audio samples or slices is most helpful. As usual, it will come down to your individual workflow. We will be sliding our audio or musical parts forwards or backwards ever so slightly.

Getting ready

To start humanizing your parts in **Playlist**, you simply need to press *F5* or select the playlist icon.

How to do it...

Humanize your parts inside **Playlist** using the following steps:

1. Zoom in and resize the playlist window in order to work with the audio file. We are working with the audio file titled **Audio VOX** as per the following screenshot:

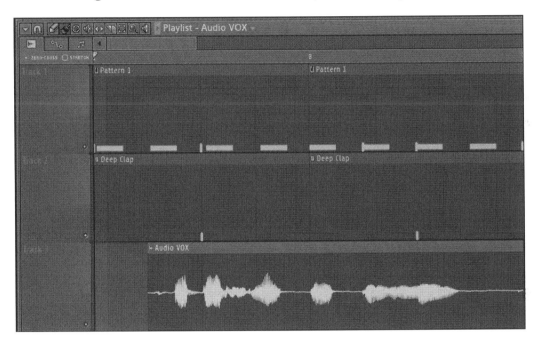

Fig 9.9

2. Select **(none)**—the button that looks like a magnet—from the **Snap to grid** setting as per the following screenshot:

Fig 9.10

3. Use the **Draw** or **Paint** tool and slide your audio to either the left or right, as shown in the following screenshot:

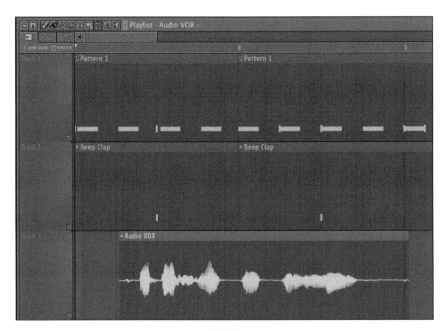

Fig 9.11

How it works...

When we select **(none)** in the **Snap to grid** setting, it enables us to be free of the beats and bars grid on the playlist. Make sure you zoom in as close as possible because your minute sliding action will only correlate to very small durations of time. This was reviewed in *Chapter 5, Using the Playlist*, so please make sure you take a look at it.

> To enable zooming, use *Ctrl + Shift* and click-and-drag to the left and right using the scroll bar in **Playlist**. Also use *Ctrl + Alt* and click-and-drag up and down using the scroll bar in **Playlist**.

You can test how certain parts sound when they are moved ever so slightly to the left or right, which is forwards or backwards in musical time. Sometimes, an effect or percussion sound you have in your song might need to be more in sync with your groove and less robotic. Alternatively, it may simply begin too quick or too late in time. Using this feature in **Playlist** allows you to fix these types of situations. It ignores the rigid nature of the cells/beats/bars that are actually needed and valued in the music-making process, but only to a point. Remember to put your snap setting back to **Cell** or whatever setting you need it to be after making changes using the **(none)** setting.

> Press *Alt* + click-and-drag on a pattern or sample to momentarily separate its snap setting from the grid.

There's more...

All four recipes in this chapter can be used on any type of sound in your project. This means that they can be used on all percussion, vocals, audio, and virtual instruments. To give your project a truly human feel, you can choose to record external audio into it. When you actually use your voice (sound effects or vocals), hands (for clapping), other physical percussion, a guitar, or a keyboard, the recorded part will clearly have human nuances because you are a human! Nobody is perfect, and no human recording can be perfectly timed. It is this fact that makes live music very enjoyable to musicians and their audience. You will also feel more connected to and proud of your music project if you record some of your own parts with a microphone or another instrument.

As with anything, a good balance of your DAW, a good recording level, and your human talent will provide the best results. For example, creating your initial rhythm with wave samples inside the step sequencer is extremely quick and intuitive. You might then want to physically play in an analog keyboard as audio.

See also

▸ The *Exploring Channel settings* recipe in *Chapter 3, Working with Step Sequencer and Channels*

▸ The *Working with Graph editor* recipe in *Chapter 3, Working with Step Sequencer and Channels*

▸ The *Using the Piano roll* recipe in *Chapter 4, Building Your Song*

▸ The *Viewing the Playlist* recipe in *Chapter 5, Using the Playlist*

▸ The *Recording external audio* recipe in *Chapter 6, Using the FL Studio Mixer and Recording Audio*

10
Recording Automation

In this chapter, we will cover:

- ▶ Using automation for virtual instruments and effects
- ▶ Creating automation clips

Introduction

Automation is a tactic used by all professional engineers and music producers. Almost every knob and slider in FL Studio allows you to automate music. You can automate filters, effects, virtual instruments, channel settings, volume, and panning. The movements you record (recording your automation movements) are referred to as automation curves. The automation movements you record will be represented by a correlated readout in the FL Studio Playlist. You can record these automation curves with your mouse, a MIDI controller, or by manipulating shapes and lines on the FL Studio Playlist. Drawing or painting in points, lines, curves and shapes affects your mix as soon as you implant your drawing; it doesn't need to be recorded as a performance. These are referred to as automation clips. The shapes and lines will correlate with certain parameters. You can also see the parameters you are affecting within the FL Studio browser. You may also right-click on a volume or panning knob next to every channel in the step sequencer and click on the **Edit** events for pattern automation.

Recording automation is truly the icing on the cake; the suspenseful high pass and low pass filters are crucial tools for dance and electronic music of all types. It allows you to manipulate your sounds inside your spatial field, and can make your track more human and distinct. It is loved by many users because it allows you to use physical controls. Again, we will mention MIDI controllers. Today, MIDI controllers designed to control automation include turntables, touchpads, knobs, sliders, and buttons. The mixer slots and sliders you work with in FL Studio can all be mapped to a MIDI controller. It allows you to feel more connected to the mix because you can manipulate and play with parameters on the fly instead of drawing them statically. You may also map multiple knobs or controls by using the **Multilink to controllers** function discussed the *Working with MIDI controllers and MIDI pads* recipe in *Chapter 4, Building Your Song*. All of the steps mentioned here can be performed with a mouse or a MIDI controller's physical knobs, buttons, and sliders. Automation can also serve as an on/off button, totally silencing or disabling a control, then turning it back on like a light switch.

Using automation for virtual instruments and effects

The basic knobs, sliders, buttons, and parameters equipped for automation include the step sequencer's panning and volume, all channel settings, and the FL Studio Mixer. We will illustrate a fundamental example on the **Channel panning** knob, which can be found directly next to each channel.

Getting ready

The steps that need to be performed to record automation are similar to the steps used before recording audio. However, in this case, we will be recording mouse movements as we click-and-drag a knob. If we wanted to use a physical MIDI control like a knob or slider, we can right-click on the function to be automated, select **Link to controller**, and then move the knob or fader you want to assign. This was reviewed in the *Working with MIDI controllers and MIDI pads* recipe in *Chapter 4, Building Your Song*. However, some third-party VST plugins don't allow that exact method, but there is a workaround. In cases where your plugin does not show any options after right-clicking on a parameter you wish to assign to a physical control, you can do the following:

1. Click on your **Plugin options** drop-down box (the upper-left-hand corner triangle of your plugin window).

2. Select the **Browse parameter** option and then right-click on the parameter you want to automate, which will be populated in the **Browser** window.

3. You will then be able to select **Link to controller**. You can also click on plugin knobs and the pertinent parameter will be automatically focused on the **Browser** window.

Moreover, you may also simply click-and-drag a parameter you want to assign by going to the FL Studio **TOOLS** main menu, hovering on **Last tweaked**, and selecting **Link to controller...**.

How to do it...

Let's commence recording automation with the **Channel panning** knob using the following steps:

1. Highlight a section on the playlist. We have selected four measures as shown in the following screenshot:

Fig 10.1

2. Click on the record button on the transport controls on the main FL Studio window and then select **Automation & Score**, as shown the following screenshot:

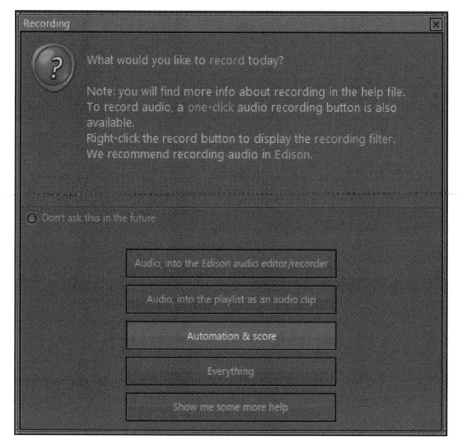

Fig 10.2

3. Press the Space bar to begin recording. During your song's playback, adjust the **Channel panning** knob by clicking-and-dragging. In Fig *10.3*, note that the **Time** panel at the top of the window is a little bit past bar 4 (**4:10:014**). At that particular moment in time, we have the panning knob pulled to the right. In this example, when the automation recording started, we began at the far left and then slowly moved the knob all the way to the right for a sweeping type of effect—from the left, up to the center position, and finally turning to the right. Remember, this example is a four-measure recording example. Have a look at the following screenshot:

Fig 10.3

4. Our recording will end based on our selection in the playlist. You may now look at the playlist to see the automation curve you made with your mouse on the **Channel panning** knob, as shown in the following screenshot. You can see that the graphical representation shows the gradual turn from left to right we did with our mouse. When you play your song back, the **Channel panning** knob next to the **wolf-howl1** channel will be moving from the left to right like a ghost! This is playing back the exact movements we made during our automation performance.

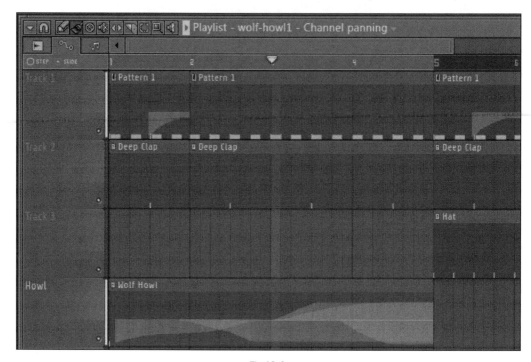

Fig 10.4

5. Double-clicking on the **Wolf Howl** automation clip on the playlist will bring up the **Event Editor** menu. You may also click on the small box next to **Wolf Howl** and select **Edit pattern** to bring up the **Event Editor** menu. The **Event Editor** menu will enable you to edit your automation movement as per the following screenshot:

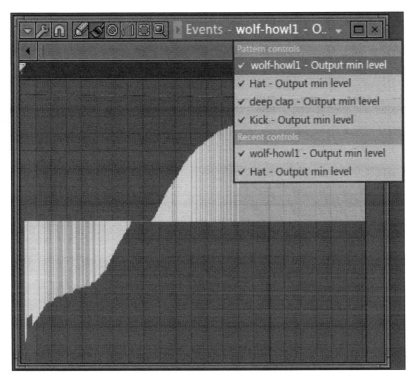

Fig 10.5

6.   While **Event Editor** is open, we may also use the options in the drop-down menu as per the preceding screenshot and choose different automation pattern controls.

How it works...

In this example, we clicked-and-dragged our performance parameters with our mouse. You could very well have used a physical knob on a MIDI controller. It all depends on your individual preference. These parameters can also be mapped to a MIDI controller for greater control and for live performances. Be sure to review the **Multilink to controllers** function in the *Working with MIDI controllers and MIDI pads* recipe in *Chapter 4, Building Your Song*.

Also, we don't necessarily have to highlight a section in the playlist. We can simply record the automation and then turn any knob we want while the song is playing. While doing this, you can tweak multiple knobs during automation recording and all of the song's information will be saved and played back. The opportunity for creativity is boundless.

The same exact principles hold true with the knobs and parameters on virtual instruments and virtual effects. In a typical scenario, we would have recorded our harmony of the instrument on the Piano roll, though you could simultaneously use automation and note performance. The automation ability adds icing to the cake. We can tweak as many knobs as we want on any type of plugin. The same holds true for all effect plugins in the FL Studio Mixer effect chain. In the screen depicted in the following screenshot, we could use our mouse or MIDI controller knob/slider on the **VCF**, **TUNE**, and **VOLUME** controls in the lower-left-hand side of the **TAL U-NO-60** virtual instrument plugin. As mentioned earlier, some third-party plugins require you to select **Browse parameters** (the dropdown on the upper-left-hand corner) and then right-click on a parameter in **Browser**. This is true for the **TAL U-NO-60** plugin, as shown in the following screenshot:

Fig 10.6

See also

- The *Building your digital audio workstation* recipe in *Chapter 1, Configuring FL Studio*
- The *Working with Browser* recipe in *Chapter 2, Using Browser*
- The *Working with MIDI controllers and MIDI pads* recipe in *Chapter 4, Building Your Song*
- The *Viewing the playlist* recipe in *Chapter 5, Using the Playlist*
- The *Adding effects and your effect chain* recipe in *Chapter 6, Using the FL Studio Mixer and Recording Audio*

Creating an automation clip

Automation clips are a great way of controlling synthesizer parameters (your software virtual plugin). For example, the pulsation virtual synth has elements such as chorus knobs, delay, distortion, filters, envelopes, LFOs, pulses, and so on.

Specifying shapes, curves, tensions, and drawings of automation clips enables powerful audio manipulation. We are able to have various automation clips, which are like directions for your plugin parameters. Generally, a 0 percent value is the minimum value of the clip and 100 percent is the maximum.

The previous recipe showed how to use automation with a knob or a physical MIDI device. This recipe is based on drawing inside automation clips and on your **Snap to grid** setting in the playlist. Automation clips help you specify precise values of parameters. Automation clips are also a way to automate the tempo of your project.

Getting ready

You may have any virtual instrument or effect open. We will be working with the software synthesizer pulsation in this example.

How to do it...

Let's take a look at the various ways to instruct FL Studio to create automation clips, using the following steps:

1. By default, the automation clip spans the entire project. Select and highlight a specific length in the playlist if you only want a range. Right-click on a parameter you want to use automation on and select **Create automation clip**.

 This method will work for native plugins (plugins that are manufactured/made by FL Studio). For third-party plugins, you may simply tweak the knob you want to create a clip for, go to the main **Tools** menu in FL Studio, hover your mouse on **Last tweaked**, and select **Create automation clip**. You may also use the triangle drop-down box on the left-hand corner of third-party plugins. You will then select **Browse parameters** and FL Studio will automatically open **Browser**. Click on any knob in your given plugin and FL Studio will lend a helping hand by highlighting the correct browser parameter. You can then right-click on it and select **Create automation clip**.

2. Your clip(s) will now exist on the playlist and as a new channel on the step sequencer, as shown in the following screenshot:

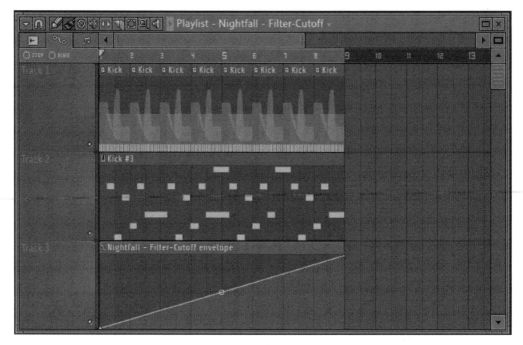

Fig 10.7

You can move the automation clips forward or backward in the playlist and they can automate other patterns during any part of your song. You may also copy and paste them anywhere in the playlist.

3. In the screen depicted in the preceding screenshot, we selected eight measures, and then automation clip titled **Nightfall – Filter-Cutoff envelope** appeared. The default automation shape is a straight diagonal line, as shown in *Fig 10.7*, with two automation points on the either end and a tension knob in the middle. The point to the far-left bottom corner represents 0 percent. The top-right corner represents 100 percent, and is controlling the filter **CUTOFF** section of the pulsation parameter knob, as shown in the following screenshot:

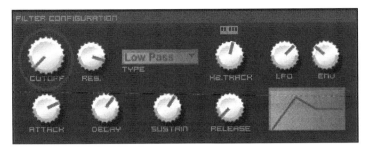

Fig 10.8

Increase or shorten the length of your automation clip by hovering your mouse over its headers to the rightmost side until your mouse becomes a horizontal arrow.

In default mode, right-clicking on the automation line makes a new point and a regular click lets you drag points. Click-and-drag up and down on the middle tension knob to adjust the curve or shape of your line.

4. Right-click on a rightmost point to bring up default options for the shape of your waveform. Also, you can right-click on a point to delete it.

Bring up a default shape like a pulse or wave sign, turning the tension (up and down) knob into a frequency adjuster.

5. When dealing with a single curve, right-clicking on the tension knob returns it to its default position. The single curve is where the tension can adjust the shape and ramping up or down of the automation value.

Look at the upper-left hand corner of your playlist in *Fig 10.7* that reads **STEP** and **SLIDE**. Click on the button to the left of the music note, which is the **Focus: automation clips** function on the FL Studio Playlist. With the **STEP** button enabled, you can now click-and-drag points on your automation line. In step mode, right-clicking and dragging the points will delete them. Turning off step and selecting slide will allow you to drag (slide) a point and all points to the right of it. Both the step and slide functions are locked to the **Snap to grid** setting, so you can hold down *Alt* and click-and-drag to create automation curves irrespective of the grid.

6. Double-click on the automation clip in the playlist to bring up its **Channel settings**, as shown in the following screenshot:

Fig 10.9

7. The **MIN** and **MAX** values in the **Channel settings** shown in the preceding screenshot are the values inside of the automation clip from bottom to top (defaults from 0 percent minimum to 100 percent maximum). If you find a specific range you want to focus on while tweaking a knob, you can specify the range with the **MIN** and **MAX** values. For example, you can set **MAX** to 50 percent instead of the default 100 percent, making your automation clip governed by and locked to that range. This way, you can find where the automation curve sounds best and focus around that so your movements or drawings have more effect and more control.

 The volume and panning knobs next to the automation clip channel in the step sequencer no longer function as volume and panning; they are now the minimum and maximum value ranges of your clip.

8. Engage the **LFO** orange box in the **Channel settings** window to oscillate your given automation parameter. LFOs are generally used to modulate the value of a parameter repeatedly. Make sure you look at the playlist and your automation clip as you adjust your LFO values; it is very cool to visually see what happens to your waveform as you adjust the LFO knobs.

Engaging the LFO switch does not get rid of the main automation you previously drew in the automation clip, even though the original drawing will be invisible. It will be combined and multiplied with the LFO parameters when the **Multiply** switch is turned on. This means the LFO will provide amplitude modulation for the original automation. When the **Multiply** switch is turned off, the original automation and LFO parameters will be added together. Note that you can right-click on any of the LFO parameters and create an automation clip!

9. In order to have a separate parameter or knob move in the exact same manner as your original automation curve, right-click on any parameter you desire and select **Link to controller**. This brings up the **Remote control settings** window. Open the drop-down box under the **Internal controller** section and select your original clip parameter; then click on **Accept**. These actions are shown in the following screenshot:

Fig 10.10

The **Automation clips** drop-down list will be populated in chronological order of when you made them an instance in FL Studio. Use the **Mapping formula triangle** drop-down to bring up default curves and options; in this manner, you can adjust the linked parameter to something slightly different. You can see the shape of any default curve selected in the graphical display next to **Input**. You may also type in equations in the **Input** text field. Engage **Smoothing** (left-hand side corner in the screen depicted in the preceding screenshot) when your automation has really sharp movements that may be clipping or approaching clipping.

How it works...

Using automation clips is an extremely powerful tool because it enables you to precisely specify the parameters you want to affect and to what degree. Your creativity can definitely be taken to the next level when harnessing the power of automation clips. Using the **LFO** section in the **Automation clips** under **Channel settings** is also very powerful, and an example of how an LFO can potentially look is shown in the following screenshot:

Fig 10.11

Generally, the most common uses for LFOs include the quiver and pulse types of effects. With regard to general automation clips, any parameter you believe will add a craftiness and creative angle to your mix can be automated. Other parameters can mimic the exact motion of your clips, as reviewed with the **Link to controller** function.

There's more...

Sometimes, a third-party plugin will not show all the adjustable parameters on its plugin graphical interface. In these cases, use the **Browse parameters** function and scroll all the way down past the main parameter listing. You will then find the **MIDI CC** parameters, which include sustain, expression pedals, modulation wheel, and a plethora of other options. You can then right-click on a parameter to create an automation clip. For example, a sustain pedal can help in cases where you are using a piano sound on a virtual instrument.

Click on any area at the top of the FL Studio Playlist to specify clip sources you want to paste into the playlist. You can also right-click on the top of the playlist header to bring up **PROJECT PICKER**.

See also

- ▸ The *Exploring Channel settings* recipe in *Chapter 3, Working with Step Sequencer and Channels*
- ▸ The *Working with MIDI controllers and MIDI pads* recipe in *Chapter 4, Building Your Song*
- ▸ The *Viewing the Playlist* recipe in *Chapter 5, Using the Playlist*
- ▸ The *Adding effects and your effect chain* recipe in *Chapter 6, Using the FL Studio Mixer and Recording Audio*

11
Rewiring Reason to FL Studio

In this chapter, we will cover:

▸ Understanding the host and the slave

▸ Creating MIDI out channels

▸ Sending Reason modules into FL Studio Mixer

Introduction

Reason is a DAW made by Propellerheads and can be found at www.propellerheads.se. Reason costs $399.00 and comes with 10 software instruments. Reason Essentials includes six software instruments and costs $99.99. A prerequisite for rewiring is to have purchased Reason and have it installed on your computer.

Reason's greatest advantage is that it includes remarkable high-quality software synthesizers and drum samplers. However, the interface for creating and building your song with FL Studio is a bit faster, more intuitive, and has a more capable Piano roll. Consequently, rewiring Reason means that you can simply hijack the software synths and samplers in Reason, but continue to use FL Studio as a sequencer and mixer. We are basically telling Reason that we don't care about their program; we are, however, very impressed with their virtual instruments. The purpose of rewiring is to still use FL Studio's step sequencer, Piano roll, and ease of composing.

 Rewire/rewiring is a term introduced by Propellerheads in order for various DAWS to be linked together. Generally, you will find the terms host and slave when talking about rewiring. In this example, FL Studio is the host and Reason is the slave. This means that the tempo of Reason is slaved and locked to the tempo in FL Studio, allowing you to hijack Reason's instruments with ease.

FL Studio will be the host and Reason will be the slave. This means that FL Studio will be the hub of your music production; you are simply able to incorporate Reason's sounds into an FL Studio channel and mixer slot like any other sound you work with. There are a couple of things you need to set up, which we will review in this chapter. After you set it up, you can save it as a template in both FL Studio and Reason. In that manner, you can be up and running quickly when you want to utilize Reason's sounds in your FL Studio music production.

Understanding the host and the slave

There are specific steps we need to follow in order to make sure FL Studio and Reason are rewired properly.

Getting ready

You must have Reason installed on your computer before rewiring into FL Studio.

How to do it...

Let us review how to rewire Reason into FL Studio using the following steps:

1. From the main FL Studio window, go to **CHANNELS | Add one | ReWired**. This will create your **ReWire** channel. The channel will show as **Reason** as shown in the following screenshot and, when you click on the channel, the **PLUGIN** tab will show the **ReWire** interface.

2. Click on the dropdown named **CLIENT** and select **Reason**. You will want to enable the button that reads **Multi Outputs**; when selected, it will turn orange as shown in the following screenshot:

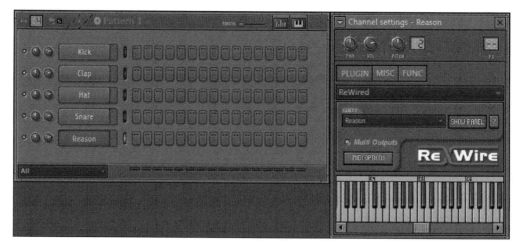

Fig 11.1

3. Click on **SHOW PANEL** to automatically launch your Reason software. The top of your Reason hardware device should read **ReWire Slave Mode**, as shown in the following screenshot. It will generally take two to three seconds to actually launch Reason after clicking on **SHOW PANEL**.

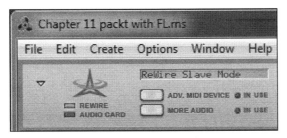

Fig 11.2

4. Click on the **MIDI OPTIONS** button on the **ReWire PLUGIN** interface shown in *Fig 11.1*. This will open up the **MIDI Settings** window, which is shown in the following screenshot. Click on **Add/Change** and it will then automatically map your given port number to FL Studio. This will match up with your **MIDI out** channels, which will be reviewed in the subsequent recipe.

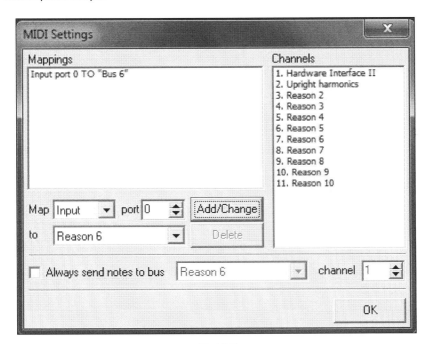

Fig 11.3

How it works...

Using this method will enable you to have FL Studio as the host and Reason as the slave. You may want to save both projects under the same name, and possibly mention ReWire in the filenames in order to stay organized and be able to recall your projects later. Adding the **ReWired** channel in FL Studio is the way to set up your slave. If you have other DAWs that are able to launch as a slave, they will be displayed in the **CLIENT** drop-down box on the screen depicted in *Fig 11.1*. For example, Albeton Live can be a slave to FL Studio.

There's more...

Sometimes, the **SHOW PANEL** button may not be working properly. If that is the case, you may keep your FL Studio project open, minimize it, and launch Reason manually. As long as your Reason software says **ReWire Slave Mode** at the top of Reason's rack, you know you are good to go. If you run into problems with Reason launching, try restarting your computer.

Both the ReWire host and Reason must run on the equivalent operating systems (32-bit or 64-bit). If FL Studio is running on your 64-bit computer, then Reason must be consistent with that.

See also

▶ The *Exploring Channel settings* recipe in *Chapter 3, Working with Step Sequencer and Channels*

▶ The *Adding virtual instruments* recipe in *Chapter 4, Building Your Song*

▶ The *Working with MIDI controllers and MIDI pads* recipe in *Chapter 4, Building Your Song*

Creating MIDI out channels

Creating MIDI out channels in FL Studio is how you actually connect your Reason sound modules to an FL Studio channel. You can then use the FL Studio Piano roll to trigger your Reason sound like any other channel you have used in FL Studio. Using a MIDI controller is also fair game.

Getting ready

To begin adding MIDI channels in FL Studio and connecting them with Reason virtual instruments / modules / synthesizers, we need to have completed the first recipe of this chapter. We also want to have Reason modules loaded within the Reason project.

How to do it...

Let's examine the steps needed to create an instance of Reason's sounds inside the FL Studio step sequencer:

1. From the FL Studio main window, go to **CHANNELS | Add one | MIDI Out**. This will create a MIDI out channel in the FL Studio step sequencer.

2. Load up a sound module in your Reason rack. In this example, we have loaded the NN-XT Advanced Sampler.

3. Take a look at your **MIDI OPTIONS** button (within the **PLUGIN** tab on your **ReWired** main channel from the first recipe of this chapter), which will bring up the **MIDI Settings** window as shown in the following screenshot:

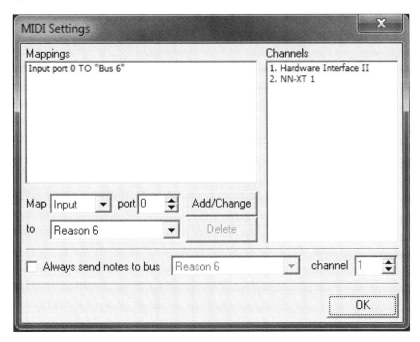

Fig 11.4

4. In the **Channels** list shown in the preceding screenshot, we can see that **NN-XT 1** is the second channel. Also note that the **port** number is **0**. We will correspond this exact information to the **MIDI out** channel.

5. Open up the **MIDI out** channel, hover your mouse over the **Channels** area, and click-and-drag it until you reach the **CHANNEL 2**, as shown in the *Fig 11.5*.

This will now control the **NN-XT 1** channel because our FL Studio **MIDI out** channel is engaged on **CHANNEL 2**, and our Reason **MIDI Settings** menu (from the **MIDI OPTIONS** button) shows that the **NN-XT 1** is the second channel. They are congruent, as shown in the following screenshot:

Fig 11.5

How it works...

Once you have followed the steps outlined in this recipe, you can use the **NN-XT** sound module in the FL Studio **MIDI out** channel! You can use the step sequencer steps to enter data or send your sound to the Piano roll like any other virtual instrument in FL Studio. It may be wise to rename your **MIDI out** channel to the name of your sound patch in any given Reason synthesizer/virtual instrument. To do this, right-click on your **MIDI out** channel and rename it.

 Pressing *Shift* and clicking on a channel will also allow you to rename it.

You can even set an icon as a visual reminder. In Reason, you can even rename your sound module by clicking directly on the module name and typing in a new name. This will then show up in the **MIDI OPTIONS/MIDI Settings** list on your main **ReWired** channel, instead of just naming the Reason module.

If you want to add more Reason sounds, simply add them to your Reason rack. You can verify the exact Reason channel number in the **MIDI OPTIONS/MIDI Settings** list. Then you may simply add another FL Studio **MIDI out** channel and select the corresponding channel number. In order to avoid doing this over and over, you may set up a template in FL Studio and a template in Reason!

There's more...

The ports must always be coordinated on the same channel. It defaults to port 0 in the Reason **MIDI Settings** and **PORT 0** on an FL Studio **MIDI out** channel, so you should be good to go. If you need to change this port, make sure you change it in both areas.

See also

- ▶ The *Working with MIDI controllers and MIDI pads* recipe in *Chapter 4, Building Your Song*
- ▶ The *Using the Piano roll* recipe in *Chapter 4, Building Your Song*
- ▶ The *Exporting an MP3 or WAV file* recipe in *Chapter 8, Exporting and Rendering your Project*

Sending Reason sounds to the FL Studio Mixer

Once you have established your Reason sounds to play on an FL Studio channel as per the previous recipe, the inevitable question that comes up is, "Can I put these Reason sounds on the FL Studio Mixer?" The answer is yes, and is another reason why using Reason ReWired is super creative. However, you will not be using an FX slot in the normal way we send channels to the FL Studio Mixer (there is no option on an FL Studio **MIDI out** channel to send it to an FX slot). We will have to connect our Reason sound modules to the Reason hardware device; they will then show up on the FL Studio Mixer slots where we can further process the sound!

Getting ready

We do not need to do anything special in Reason besides having its hardware device showing. This is not a problem because the Reason hardware device cannot be deleted and will always be showing at the top of the Reason rack. You must have your sound modules in Reason connected to FL Studio **MIDI out** channels as per the previous recipe.

How to do it...

In our example, we will again be working with the Reason NN-XT Advanced Sampler. Let's see how to send the audio output of your Reason sound modules into the FL Studio Mixer using the following steps:

1. Open your Reason software and then press *Tab* to turn your Reason rack around.

2. Click-and-drag the left audio output of your Reason sound module into output **3** on your Reason hardware device. Alternatively, you can also right-click on the left audio output of the NN-XT module, hover over **Hardware Interface II**, and select **Output 3**, as shown in the following screenshot:

Fig 11.6

3. Your NN-XT sound module will now be sent to mixer slot 1 on the FL Studio Mixer, as shown in the following screenshot:

Fig 11.7

How it works...

You never want to send any Reason output to output 1 or output 2 on the Reason hardware interface/device. Outputs 1 and 2 on the Reason hardware device are dedicated as the automatic main stereo output for **HARDWARE DEVICE** so that FL Studio is accessible.

In the previous example, with the NN-XT, sending it to output 3 on the Reason hardware device will, in turn, make it show up on FL Studio insert slot 1. We can clearly see this in the preceding screenshot. We have also renamed our **MIDI out** channel to read **NN-XT Piano** and the **Insert** mixer slot to read **NN-XT Grand Piano**.

The process needs to be repeated if you want to include additional Reason instruments to the FL Studio Mixer. If you send a Reason sound module to output 4, it will show up as track 2 of FL Studio Mixer; if you send a Reason sound module to output 5, it will show up as track 3 of FL Studio Mixer; and so on.

It will always be two slots behind with regard to **HARDWARE DEVICE** and the FL Studio insert slots. Once you have your Reason modules sent to the **HARDWARE DEVICE** outputs, you can save both Reason and FL Studio as a template.

There's more...

Please be mindful of the volume of your Reason sound module, the volume of the **MIDI out** channel in the step sequencer, and the volume on your FL Studio Mixer. They are all related. The level of your Reason instruments may look like a lower value on the peak meter display on each mixer slot compared to regular sounds in FL Studio. The best advice is to use your ears. You may also want to start with a suitable drum sequence using wave samples from your FL Studio Browser in order to make sure your Reason instruments will be mixed at a suitable level. Using a reference CD of a high-quality music production sample always works.

Using send tracks on Reason instruments in the FL Studio Mixer is a great tool. Sending a little bit of reverb or delay produces awesome results. If you are familiar with utilizing Reason as a standalone DAW, you can still add effects inside Reason or use a mixer inside Reason before sending it through HARDWARE DEVICE.

See also

▶ The *Using send tracks in the mixer* recipe in *Chapter 6, Using the FL Studio Mixer and Recording Audio*

▶ The *Adding effects and your effect chain* recipe in *Chapter 6, Using the FL Studio Mixer and Recording Audio*

▶ The *Getting the best out of your mixer* recipe in *Chapter 6, Using the FL Studio Mixer and Recording Audio*

▶ The *Humanizing with the OFS knob* recipe in *Chapter 9, Humanizing Your Song*

▶ The *Creating automation clips* recipe in *Chapter 10, Recording Automation*

Your Rights as a Composer and Copyrights

Any musical piece (for example, a song) you make in FL Studio comprises the following: the master recording and the song (the song can be considered the music). If you understand that, you can understand the entire songwriting industry. Your musical production (song) in FL Studio is made up of the master recording (sometimes referred to as masters) as well as the *music* in the *song*. The music/song is owned by you alone if you made the harmonies that embody the song. Otherwise, it can be split 50-50 with a lyricist because, inside a song, the music is 50 percent and the lyrics are 50 percent. If there is more than one lyricist that created original lyrics for the song, that portion may be split by two lyricists. In that scenario, the music is 50 percent and the lyrics would be divided into 25 percent each. That would represent an even split; there are many cases where it may not be exactly even. It is purely based on business and negotiations.

[There are many situations that arise with regard to who created what and what stake they have. The best thing to do is to communicate, agree, and document how the song rights are allocated.]

The music is the notes or the sequencing of the Piano roll in FL Studio, and may or may not include lyrics. The master recording is the entire production transcribed onto a physical medium.

If you sell music to a film production company, they will be buying the master recording as well as the music. The master recording is the master use license and music is the synchronization license. The synchronization, meaning the music inside the song that is synched with visual images, is also your clout as a songwriter and part of your publishing income.

The music within a song is also the entity that can be used to create cover versions (those who choose to make and distribute covers must pay a fee to the original songwriter).

If you single-handedly create your own original song in a fixed, tangible form, you are instantaneously the copyright owner, composer, and publisher of your work. This is an amazing thing that the US government recognizes. To be safe, you will also want to officially copyright your music productions with the US government so they have it on record. In the US, you may use the website `www.copyright.gov` and enter into their online eCO portal, which allows you to register, pay, and upload songs directly online. A cool thing about copyrighting a batch of songs is that there is only one payment needed for a group of songs. Knowing this, it may be wise to get as much material as you can together in order to copyright it all at once. If you want to use paper forms, you can use the form SR for sound recordings and mail in the works you want to copyright along with your payment and physical CD.

A copyright means that you have exclusive rights to use and distribute your work for a limited amount of time in order to make money. If anyone infringes on those rights, you can take them to court. This is your song, your idea (transcribed onto a physical medium or device like a CD), and your intellectual property.

When registering, the US government will want to know the type of work (usually sound recording and music), application title, title, copyright claimant, date of creation, date of publication, nation of first publication, and authorship on application. The authorship allows you to specify if you are the creator of the sound recording, performance, production, music, and lyrics. You can always resubmit a copyright claim when new people in your network seize different parts of the song.

Music publishing, publishers, and performance rights societies

In today's day and age, there have never been more opportunities for a songwriter or music publisher. Songs are published by companies of various shapes and sizes, and they are as close as a Google search. On Google, conduct a search for music production libraries or something similar. Each library generally has its own niche. There are varying degrees of quality and licensing terms. Of course, there are humongous music publishers such as Universal Music Publishing.

A music publisher's job is to get music into all media. There are in an incredible number of places thanks to the Internet and digital age; you may get music into streaming online content, apps, and any audio-visual medium. You may also try to exploit the music (exploiting is a super nice term in music publishing because you find a home for the music) in films, TV, trailers, promos, commercials, radio, video games, and all the new media or those that will be available any time in the future.

Exploiting, in music publishing terms, is a positive term and not a negative one. Exploiting your music in media is good because it means it is coupled together with another medium, which is usually advertising and audio visuals. You can think of exploiting as finding a place for your music. Finding a place for your music isn't just good—it's awesome! As a music publisher, you earn an upfront fee when you license the music into media. Sometimes, a songwriter signed to a publishing agreement receives a portion of the upfront fee.

If this is a TV series or film that later makes it to broadcast television, you earn additional royalties directly from a separate entity in the music industry: **performing rights society** (**PRS**). This is paid out as a 50-50 split between the publishing owner and the songwriter. This is known as the publisher's share and the writer's share. When played in public places, it is known as a performance royalty. The broadcasting companies know who to pay because they will read *cue sheets*, a very important term in the performing rights industry. This also means you must register your music at a PRS. You will need to specify the ownership rights of both the publishing share and the writer's share. If the TV series has lots of reruns on broadcast TV, guess what? You get royalties every time it is played. If the TV series gets distributed to a different country and plays it on their station, you earn royalties, which are called foreign performing royalties.

The purpose of PRS is to collect money from public places such as radio, television, live venues, satellite radio, and elevator music. These types of companies are paying for the right to play songs in public. A PRS then directly pays 50 percent to the songwriter and 50 percent to the publisher. If a songwriter has a percentage of the publishing rights, they would collect that money directly from the publisher, after the publisher receives it from their PRS.

There are varying terms in music licensing, so you will want to hire a good entertainment attorney. You will want someone who has experience in your niche, not a slick-talking salesman who has cash but no real experience.

So, as a songwriter, the world is wide open. You can start your own publishing business or try to sign a publishing deal with a music library. If you have your own publishing business, you can then be the judge of the type of music you want to include in your catalog and what type of composers you will sign, if any, to agreements in order to exploit your whole catalog.

When peddling songs in any type of song transaction, there is usually a question of a non-exclusive track / agreement versus an exclusive song agreement. When you sell an exclusive track, the music cannot be sold again to a third party. This is also known as a buyout deal. An exclusive agreement is coveted much more in the industry. At high levels, a large company will want to have sole rights of a particular piece of music. This is so they can have the proper branding and control the distribution. Therefore, a publisher will sometimes want to have exclusive rights over your music in order to make it more desirable to ad agencies and other media. Sometimes, there is a fee paid to a songwriter from a music publisher in order to gain rights on an exclusive track. There are then back-end royalties, in varying amounts, depending on the agreement a songwriter signs with a publisher.

As a songwriter, you have to decide whether you want to keep your songs non-exclusive. This means you can have them in various libraries around the world. However, what if the company who wanted an exclusive track has many networks and connections in the industry? It is up to the songwriter how he or she wants to handle their music catalog. Sometimes, it is best to let music publishers do their job. You can always write new songs.

As a songwriter, you want to be honest and generally have original works. This means they don't infringe upon or include any music from a third-party source. Original works are works that serious companies will want to have, otherwise a lawsuit may ensue. If you do happen to sample something, it will usually have to be cleared or agreed upon by the master recording and songwriter of the song. Otherwise, you could be knee deep in legal battles.

As a songwriter, you may also earn revenue from mechanical fees. This is when a record company wants to use your song on a record. There is a 50-50 split between the publisher and the writer and various circumstances, legal verbiage, and rights. The mechanical rights means a record company wants to sell and distribute the song. If your song is part of an album that is distributed, a record company has to pay you for every copy sold. It is governed by a legal term called a Compulsory Mechanical License rate, which is handled by the US government yet again!

Key terms in publishing agreements – master recording and song

As mentioned earlier, it is crucial to understand that the master recording is the main upfront licensing fee. The master means the final product transcribed onto a physical medium (a songwriter can also have part of this, depending on the agreement). The song is made up of two parts: the music and the lyrics.

You will need to know how much percentage is gross or net from the sales of the masters, the compositions (the music), synchronization fees, mechanical license fees, and your performing rights slice of the pie. You should usually be getting 100 percent of your writer's share, which is 50 percent of ASCAP fees for public performances (the other 50 percent goes to the publisher).

Sometimes, you will hear of a **work-for-hire agreement**. Bear in mind, this means that the publisher is signing a songwriter to a work-for-hire agreement. This entails that the person doing the hiring is now the sole creator of the music and now owns the copyright and publishing. You may still have your rights to your writer's share (from PRS) and other shares as a songwriter of the music, but the work-for-hire owner makes you sign over the copyright. Understand this concept fully and weigh up the pros and cons.

Term and territory are two other key terms in a publishing agreement, besides exclusive or non-exclusive. You always want to consult a lawyer or entertainment attorney to view legal agreements. We have reviewed the key terms and concepts when you are a composer or songwriter, so we will quickly touch on the same concepts when you are an artist on a record.

Quick artist blurb

There is another end of the spectrum if you are actually an artist on a record. In this case, you would receive record royalties for every copy sold, including digital downloads. You will also have the opportunity to collect SoundExchange performing royalties. Finally, as an artist, you earn a fee when a record label licenses your master recording. Remember how the master recording is the actual final music production that is transcribed onto a physical medium like a CD? If you are an artist on that record, you are obviously included on the master recording!

What are ASCAP and PRS?

Performing societies do you a favor (and also take their cut for administering the whole process) by collecting all music fees from public places. This includes venues, concerts, restaurants, radio stations, nightclubs, television stations, and large outfits of the same. Licensees (owners of all these public places that play music) pay the **peforming rights organizations** (**PROs**) a blanket license fee, which is based on what genre of music is being performed and how great an audience reach it has. The PROs then distribute or pay out royalties to publishers and songwriters throughout the year, depending on public airplay and broadcasting.

The prominence and length of your song is a tremendous factor in the amount you will be paid if your song ever makes it to broadcast TV. If you can get an intro song on a popular TV show on broadcast TV, you will see royalties for years to come! You will still receive money if your song is only played for a couple seconds in the middle of the show, but if you can get it on the intro or outro, you will be golden.

 ASCAP, BMI, and SESAC are the three main players, and Soundreef has established a music rights management system in Europe.

Things to consider when signing a publishing deal

How can you get your songs exploited? You can start your own publishing business and make your own connections, but that obviously takes hard work. Nevertheless, it can be done.

Do you want to sell your tracks as exclusive or non-exclusive? Non-exclusive allows you to peddle them in many different places basically forever, but an exclusive cannot be sold to anyone else again. An exclusive track is usually wanted by reputable and major companies.

What is the term and does it renew itself? Can you look at your publisher's books and conduct an audit? When can you do this? Does the publisher have a good track record and can you talk to other composers signed there?

Places to make a living with audio or music

There are a tremendous number of outlets and tangents in order to make money in the music industry. There are more tangents than you would believe at first.

You can be a synthesizer sound designer and engineer who actually makes the patches in a keyboard. The same type of job can be for new plugins and virtual instruments that are coded by sound designers. Any retail item that sells in stores has a history of sound, and you can work for these companies or create your own brand of products. These include guitars, amplifiers, keyboards, headphones, speakers, guitar FX pedals, DJ equipment, virtual effects and instruments, and any type of APP. Sometimes, a sound designer ends up starting his or her own line of equipment because they have seen it and connected with it at the ground level.

If you want to be a music engineer, this involves more inside-the-studio work and working with many types of artists. In this role, you will be mixing live rock bands or recording tracks with rap, R&B, or reggae artists. Your job is to get the best sounding mix. You need to be able to work well with many types of personalities. Although not technically producing (it can be that too), music engineers get paid to mix or master songs. The figures can easily get into the thousands if you are a reputable engineer that delivers a crisp sound. If you are interested in reading music and playing an instrument, you can join an orchestra in many places of the world. You can also be a concert pianist or conductor. You may work in the department of forensic audio, as you see on many legal TV series. You may be a consultant who designs the best sounding rooms for recording.

When you enjoy sharing your knowledge with others, you can become a teacher in elementary school, high school, or college, as a professor. There are also many new audio schools where you can become an instructor. You can also be a music tutor of some type of niche.

If you are curious about the inner workings of human ears, you can become an audiologist. Though not actually making music, you are helping people to use their ears or install hearing aids for those who need it, allowing them to hear all the sounds in the world. Of course, you can become an artist and make it big and become famous in a variety of ways. You can harness the power of the Internet to build your own brand and then create a buzz with a major label. As far as being a composer goes, we have already reviewed the lucrative nature of songwriting and publishing.

You can also be an in-house music composer at a variety of places. Large advertising agencies usually have an in-house composer or sound designer/engineer instead of using production music. There are many different types of DJs, including but not limited to those who perform at weddings, clubs, bars, private parties, karaoke, bar mitzvahs and bat mitzvahs, cruises, and amusement parks. Many DJs take the leap into the production world, where they end up being producers and composers.

A producer doesn't necessarily make the music, but he or she is the main manager of the final master recording. He or she can be the one working side by side with the recording engineer and guiding the song in the right direction. Nowadays, we do refer to major talents as producers, for example, Dr. Dre and Timbaland.

Recording studios hire recording engineers, studio musicians (who specialize in playing a certain instrument, for example, flute, piano, or guitar; providing background vocals; and so on), and mixing and mastering engineers. Composing for major films, for example, what Hans Zimmer does, is absolutely amazing. In this case, you will be scoring the music to specific scenes in a film. You can earn a lucrative living this way, especially if the film makes it to broadcast TV.

Any one, regardless of age, gender, or nationality, can make it as a composer. As long as you can create songs that enhance audio-visual messages, you will have a place in the music industry. Usually, you will want to write songs about lost love, found love, happiness, sadness, and anything that needs to match a brand, promotion, or mood.

Rights for new media, YouTube ads, streaming music, and satellite broadcasts

YouTube now has an algorithm that can detect the song uploaded in videos. If it finds it matches third-party content, the original content publisher earns revenue from the advertisements at the beginning of the video.

With regard to streaming, there are many companies that now pay out a small fee to artists or composers from live streaming. If you have a hit song, it can obviously add up to substantial earnings. Digital satellite radio broadcasters and streaming music may also be paying SoundExchange, who will then pay your artist royalty, as discussed previously. C.D. Baby has many programs that distribute your work and collect on your behalf. If you are a record label, publisher, artist, or composer, you can license your songs to be used in apps. The same goes for ad agencies that produce video promos for large companies such as Apple or Toyota. Many companies have more video promos online than they do on TV commercials. Many movie trailers are now streamed online, so being a composer for them can be lucrative.

If you have a YouTube channel with original music of any sort, or you are a teacher of how-to videos, you can earn your own revenue through Google Advertising. Streaming media is currently evolving quicker than the courts and legal system can handle it. The music industry is jumping forward with new changes at a rapid rate.

Index

W

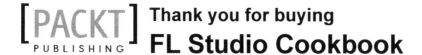

About Packt Publishing

Packt, pronounced 'packed', published its first book "*Mastering phpMyAdmin for Effective MySQL Management*" in April 2004 and subsequently continued to specialize in publishing highly focused books on specific technologies and solutions.

Our books and publications share the experiences of your fellow IT professionals in adapting and customizing today's systems, applications, and frameworks. Our solution based books give you the knowledge and power to customize the software and technologies you're using to get the job done. Packt books are more specific and less general than the IT books you have seen in the past. Our unique business model allows us to bring you more focused information, giving you more of what you need to know, and less of what you don't.

Packt is a modern, yet unique publishing company, which focuses on producing quality, cutting-edge books for communities of developers, administrators, and newbies alike. For more information, please visit our website: www.packtpub.com.

Writing for Packt

We welcome all inquiries from people who are interested in authoring. Book proposals should be sent to author@packtpub.com. If your book idea is still at an early stage and you would like to discuss it first before writing a formal book proposal, contact us; one of our commissioning editors will get in touch with you.

We're not just looking for published authors; if you have strong technical skills but no writing experience, our experienced editors can help you develop a writing career, or simply get some additional reward for your expertise.

Getting started with Audacity 1.3

Getting started with Audacity 1.3

ISBN: 978-1-84719-764-1   Paperback:220 pages

Create your own podcasts, edit music, and more with this open source audio editor

1. Teaches basic techniques for using Audacity to record and edit audio tracks - like podcasts and interviews.

2. Combines learning to use software program with the simple theories behind digital audio and common audio terms.

3. Provides advanced editing techniques and tips for using Audacity beyond a first project.

4. Uses a task based, step-by-step approach to guide newcomers into the world of audio editing.

Mahara 1.4 Cookbook

Mahara 1.4 Cookbook

ISBN: 978-1-84951-506-1   Paperback: 308 pages

Over 50 recipes for using Mahara for training, personal, or educational purposes

1. Discover the flexibility of the Mahara system for portfolio use and web page development.

2. Filled with tips and techniques for varied uses of features including HTML blocks, Journals, and Collections.

3. Learn how to leverage the social networking components and groups features to build collaborative communities.

Please check **www.PacktPub.com** for information on our titles

Moodle 1.9 Multimedia

ISBN: 978-1-84719-590-6   Paperback:272 pages

Create and share multimedia learning materials in your
Moodle courses

1. Ideas and best practices for teachers and
   trainers on using multimedia effectively in
   Moodle.

2. Ample screenshots and clear explanations to
   facilitate learning.

3. Covers working with TeacherTube, embedding
   interactive Flash games, podcasting, and more.

4. Create instructional materials and design
   students' activities around multimedia.

Ext JS 4 Web Application
Development Cookbook

ISBN: 978-1-84951-686-0   Paperback: 488 pages

Over 110 easy-to-follow recipes backed up with real-life
examples, walking you through basic Ext JS features to
advanced application design using Sencha's Ext JS

1. Learn how to build Rich Internet Applications
   with the latest version of the Ext JS framework
   in a cookbook style.

2. From creating forms to theming your interface,
   you will learn the building blocks for developing
   the perfect web application.

3. Easy-to-follow recipes step through practical and
   detailed examples which are all fully backed up
   with code, illustrations, and tips.

Please check **www.PacktPub.com** for information on our titles

Made in the USA
Middletown, DE
01 September 2017